Unplanned development

Tracking change in South-East Asia

JONATHAN RIGG

Zed Books

LONDON | NEW YORK

Unplanned Development: Tracking Change in South-East Asia was first published in 2012 by Zed Books Ltd, 7 Cynthia Street, London N1 9JF, UK and Room 400, 175 Fifth Avenue, New York, NY 10010, USA

www.zedbooks.co.uk

Set in OurType Arnhem and Monotype Futura by Ewan Smith, London
Index: ed.emery@thefreeuniversity.net
Cover design: www.thisistransmission.com
Printed and bound by CPI Group (UK) Ltd, Croydon, CRO 4YY

FSC
www.fsc.org
MIX
Paper from responsible sources
FSC® C013604

Distributed in the USA exclusively by Palgrave Macmillan, a division of St Martin's Press, LLC, 175 Fifth Avenue, New York, NY 10010, USA

A catalogue record for this book is available from the British Library
Library of Congress Cataloging in Publication Data available

ISBN 978 1 84813 989 3 hb
ISBN 978 1 84813 988 6 pb

Contents

Tables, figures, illustrations, boxes

Tables

Figures

Illustrations

Boxes

Abbreviations and glossary

ADB   Asian Development Bank
Asean   Association of Southeast Asian Nations
Bapak Pembangunan   The 'Father of Development', the title given to Indonesia's former President Suharto (Indonesia)
BAPPENAS   Badan Perencanaan Pembangunan Nasional (National Planning Agency) (Indonesia)
BEDB   Brunei Economic Development Board
BKKBN   National Family Planning Coordinating Board, established in 1970 (Indonesia)
CBNRM   Community Based Natural Resource Management
CFA   Catfish Farmers of America
CGD   Commission on Growth and Development
CPT   Communist Party of Thailand
doi moi reform, renovation (Vietnam)
EAM   the *East Asian Miracle* report of the World Bank (1993)
EDB   Economic Development Board (Singapore)
EGAT   Electricity Generating Authority of Thailand
EPU   Economic Planning Unit (Malaysia)
FDI   foreign direct investment
ho khau household registration (Vietnam), equivalent to China's *hukou* system
HPAEs   High Performing Asian Economies, a World Bank-coined term for the eight rapidly growing economies of East and South-East Asia
hypergamy marrying up, into a higher class or caste
IFLS   Indonesian Family Life Survey
IGP   inter-generational poor
IGT   inter-generational transmission of poverty
IMF   International Monetary Fund
IRRI   International Rice Research Institute
IWRM   Integrated Water Resources Management
kaanpattana development (Thailand)
kampung village (Malaysia)
Kinh   majority, traditionally lowland, 'Viet' population of Vietnam
krismon the monetary or financial crisis in Indonesia, 1997–99

MARD	Ministry of Agriculture and Rural Development (Vietnam)
MITI	Ministry of International Trade and Industry (Japan)
MoNRE	Ministry of Natural Resources and Environment (Vietnam)
NEDA	National Economic and Development Authority (Philippines)
NEDB	National Economic Development Board (Thailand)
NEB	National Economic Board (Thailand)
NEP	New Economic Policy (Malaysia)
NESDB	National Economic and Social Development Board (Thailand)
NFFP	National Family Planning Programme, established in 1970 (Thailand)
NGO	non-governmental organization
NIC	newly industrializing country, namely Hong Kong, Singapore, South Korea and Taiwan
NIE	newly industrializing economy, namely Hong Kong, Singapore, South Korea and Taiwan
PAP	People's Action Party (Singapore)
pembangunan	development (Indonesia)
PSID	Panel Study of Income Dynamics (USA)
PWC	Post-Washington Consensus
RBO	River Basin Organization
RBPMB	River Basin Planning Management Board
samai pattana	development era (Thailand)
sethakit phor piang	sufficiency economy (Thailand)
TDRI	Thai Development Research Institute (Thailand)
total fertility rate	the number of children a woman would bear at the prevailing fertility rates of all ages for a given year
TVA	Tennessee Valley Authority
UNDP	United Nations Development Programme

Acknowledgements

This book emerges from over three decades of research in South-East Asia, including extended periods in 'the field' in the Lao PDR, Thailand and Vietnam, and to a lesser extent in Indonesia and Malaysia, as well as Sri Lanka. Much of this has been connected with an assortment of research grants that have enabled me to work with scholars from Australia, Canada, Denmark, Italy, the UK and the USA and, most significantly, from the countries of the region itself – the Lao PDR, the Philippines, Singapore, Thailand and Vietnam. Many of the ideas and much of the empirical scaffold contained in this book come from these stimulating collaborations.

In the UK, I have been thankful for and invigorated by the intellectual inspiration of Kate Gough, Terry King, Emma Mawdsley, Craig Jeffrey, Mike Parnwell, Rachel Harrison, Anthony Bebbington, Dave Little, Cecilia Tacoli, Janet Townsend, Gina Porter, Geoff Wilson, Deborah Bryceson, Raymond Bryant, Ann Booth, Becky Elmhirst, Rob Potter, Katherine Brickell, David Simon and David Booth (who kindly read the final chapter, which draws on his governance work). Beyond the UK, I have been assisted and inspired by Niels Fold, Jytte Agergaard, Irene Nørlund, Magnus Jirström, David Henley, Randi Jerndal, Pietro Masina and Michel Bruneau in Europe; by Nancy Lee Peluso, Terry McGee, Phil Dearden, Rodolphe de Koninck, Michael Leaf (who provided trenchant comments on Chapter 2), Phil Kelly, Melissa Marschke, Sarah Turner, Steve Déry, Steffanie Scott, Tania Murray Li, Jean Michaud and Peter Vandergeest in North America; and by Rob Cramb, Andrew Walker, Phil Hirsch, Lisa Law, George Curry, Tubtim Tubtim, Matthew Tonts, Brian Shaw, Holly High and Mark Beeson (who provided feedback on Chapter 3) in Australia.

Turning to South-East Asia, my thanks go to a number of scholars and researchers with whom I have been fortunate to work and to have contact: Wong Tai-Chee, Chusak Wittayapak, Goh Kim Chuan, Shirley Hsiao-Li Sun, Pujo Semedi, Carl

Grundy-Warr, Stan Tan, Adam Fforde, May Tan Mullins, Myo Thant, Mark Ritchie, Gavin Jones (who kindly read Chapter 6), Bounthong Bouahom, Linkham Douangsavanh, Buapun Promphakping, Wathana Wongsekiarttirat, Sakunee Nattapoolwat, Suriya Veeravongs, Lalida Veeravongs, Piyawadee Rohitarachoon, Pham Van Cu, Luong Thi Thu Huong, Nguyen Tuan Anh, Dinh Thi Dieu, Doracie Zoleta-Nantes, P. Hewage, Annuska Derks and Chaminda Kumara. There are others whom, I am sure, I have mistakenly overlooked in this list and for which I apologize in advance. My thanks go equally to them.

I owe, if anything, an even greater debt to my research students over the years, who have enabled me to be connected to the field even while I have been stranded in Durham, challenging my views and assumptions along the way. Their ideas also permeate this book. Most of these students have worked in South-East Asia, including Helen Clover, Siriluck Sirisup, Albert Salamanca (with whom I have worked since), Guillaume Lestrelin, Hamzah Muzaini, Jitsuda Limkriengkrai, Roy Huijsmans, Adeline Tengku Hamzah, Javier Gonzalez-Soria, Georgina Jordan and Wasana La-orngplew. But equally I have gained enormously from my students working in other regions of the world. These are: Undala Alam, Abdullatif Al-Shaikh, Fergus Lyon, Mike Alderson, Marloes van Amerom, Ann Le Mare, Katie Oven, Lata Narayanaswamy, Clare Collingwood, Catherine Button, Kate Cochrane, Manush McConway and Nayeem Ansari.

A significant portion of the book was written while I was a Gledden Senior Visiting Fellow at the University of Western Australia in Perth, and I am grateful to Susan Takao, Brian Shaw and Matthew Tonts for their welcome and support at UWA. In addition, towards the end of the fellowship, Alan Chan and K. K. Luke at Nanyang Technological University (NTU) made funds available for me to organize a 'resilience' workshop in Singapore, which shaped some of the ideas presented in Chapter 5.

Undergraduate students rarely get much acknowledgement in books such as this one, but I can sincerely say that teaching our students at Durham University is not only a challenge but also (usually) a singular delight. Taking undergraduates on field courses to South-East Asia, and putting them into villages to live with local families in Thailand, has, in particular, reassured me that the world is not worn flat, and that the spirit of adventure and intellectual ambition lives on.

In the Geography Department at Durham, I am fortunate to have had access to expert cartographers, and Chris Orton and Michelle Allan skilfully produced the figures and diagrams included in the book. At Zed Books I am grateful to Tamsine O'Riordan, who commissioned the book, to Jakob Horstmann who took on the role of encouraging its completion, and to Ewan Smith who skilfully and patiently guided it from manuscript to final copy. They all cajoled me along the way, but only gently.

Most of the scholars and former students listed above are not just individuals from whom I have gained and gleaned much in academic terms – although that is certainly the case; most of them I can also count as my friends. It is this that I cherish most.

Jonathan Rigg
Durham University, Durham, UK

Preface

The bulk of this book was written in 2011, and no recent year better illustrates the perils of prediction and the follies of forecasting: revolutionary upheavals in the Middle East and North Africa; Japan's earthquake, tsunami and nuclear disaster; the crisis in the Eurozone; and the devastating earthquakes in Christchurch, New Zealand. Perhaps more than any year since 1968, 2011 was a year of economic turning points, historical breaks, environmental catastrophes and political watersheds.

In part this book is about such breaks and turning points which at the time seem so very momentous but which, often in a matter of months, become normalized as none too surprising, even expected. Before long we will be retrospectively reassuring ourselves that yes, of course, the Middle East and North Africa were powder kegs waiting to ignite, just as the Soviet Union is now characterized as an unwieldy empire bound to fragment under the weight of its multiple frailties and failures. But the book is not just about the vicissitudes of history. It is also about the vagaries of everyday life: the ways that lives can be turned upside down at a stroke. These may be connected with wider-level historical events – such as those thousands who were uprooted by the Fukushima Daiichi nuclear disaster of March 2011. But more often they are low-visibility and highly personal: a car accident, a failed business, or the costs of a funeral or a wedding. The themes of complexity and contingency, and the surprising knock-on effects of events, thread their way through the discussion. Finally, the book is about human actions and behaviours which so often lead scholars to play explanatory catch-up and policy-makers to wring their hands.

This book is, therefore, about the inadequacies of models, the deficiencies of grand theories, the ineffectiveness of planning, and the limits of government and statecraft. Its origins lie in my experiences of fieldwork in Asia, the personal histories that have been recounted to me, and my inability to second-guess how countries will perform and what individuals will accomplish.

The book is also distinctly modest in its claims. It does not deliver an overarching vision, a grand theory or a policy recipe for development. Instead it seeks to make the case for an approach to understanding and interpreting development that is inductive in attitude, empirically informed, historically sensitive and geographically grounded.

For Janie

1 | The hidden geometries of development

Economic theorists, more than other social scientists, have long been disposed to arrive at general propositions and then postulate them as valid for every time, place, and culture. There is a tendency in contemporary economic theory to follow this path to the extreme. (Myrdal 1968: 16)

Economists (and other experts) seem to have very little useful to say about why some countries grow and others do not. Basket cases, such as Bangladesh or Cambodia, turn into small miracles. Poster children, such as Côte D'Ivoire, fall into the 'bottom billion'. In retrospect, it is always possible to construct a rationale for what happened in each place. But the truth is, we are largely incapable of predicting where growth will happen, and we don't understand very well why things fire up. (Banerjee and Duflo 2011: 267)

Introduction: outlining the hidden geometries of development

Why is it that economic crises – not to mention economic miracles – come out of the blue? Why does the Prince of Serendip seem to reign supreme in the ways of women and men? Why do humans so often act in ways that do not accord with the rules of *Homo economicus*? Why does history's arrow follow a trajectory different from the one that geometry might suggest? Why do the most carefully constructed plans go awry? Why do the empirics of change rub uncomfortably up against theory? Why do accepted orthodoxies fail to resonate in any convincing manner with country experiences? It is these questions which this book aims to illuminate – and does so with reference to the South-East Asian region.

In shedding light on these questions, the book covers a good deal of disciplinary ground. I am interested in the trajectories of history; the failures and successes of governments; the art and science of plans and planning; the assumptions of academics and policy-makers; the behaviour of individuals and the functioning of households and families; the norms of society and the rules of economy; and the role of culture. At the heart of the book, and at the most general level, is a twin puzzle. Why is it that things so rarely turn out the way we expect? And why are our explanations for the patterns of the world so often partial, incomplete and far from universal in their application? Looking across the development experience of Asia over the last half-century, it is tempting to see a pattern of change and a set of developmental paths that can be 'explained' by reference to unifying conceptual models and frameworks. This desire to impose explanatory order is, this book will suggest, problematic on a number of grounds, and not least because the experiences that reveal themselves are more different than they are alike.

Making the claim, however, that 'context matters', though undoubtedly true, does not greatly help in bringing greater traction to understanding *why* the experience of development demands explanatory frameworks that open up and normalize heterodoxy. This book aims to elaborate on just this question, and does so by focusing on four axes of contingency. These comprise, first, the *country conditions* that comprise the development milieu within which change is embedded. Development does not occur in a governance vacuum; it is not a technocratic and managerial exercise that can be unproblematically implemented and exported from one country to another. The failure of so many expert missions arises because of a tendency to adopt a cookie-cutter approach to the 'problems' identified, expecting that countries will somehow conform to generalized models (see p. 183). Secondly, development always needs to be seen as partially governed by the prevailing (time-sensitive) national and international *historical contexts* that exist at any given time, and our understanding needs to be attuned to such historical conditions and historical moments. These two axes provide the high-level explanatory script that should caution against reductionist interpretations. At a finer level, and thirdly, development is often strongly influenced by idiosyncratic local sets of *personal circumstances* that shape the choices, decisions and development experiences of communities, households and individuals. Finally, and fourthly, we also need to be attuned to the *human character(istics)* of the people whose choices we are seeking to understand. There are sufficient examples of people acting counter-intuitively to warn against attempts to second-guess behaviours. The nature of these axes and the ways in which they operate to shape the development present and development futures are returned to and developed in the final chapter.

As we seek to weave an explanatory fabric to make sense of the world, the point that the black boxes labelled 'unknown', 'unexpected' and 'unintended' are larger than expected may be regarded as frustrating. Personally, however, I find it ultimately satisfying and liberating that people do not act according to the script of economics, the designs of governments, the assumptions of multilateral organizations, or the conceptual frames and theoretical models of academics, accreted over decades of dedicated study.

The breadth of subject matter in this book has meant that the supporting literature also crosses a broad swathe of the social sciences, encompassing geography, anthropology, history, area studies, sociology and cultural studies, economics, development studies and development economics, and political economy. Also included here is reference to a good deal of applied and policy-related literature. My own interests are in the development challenges of South-East Asia, and so I have chosen to situate much of the argument in that region. I would like to imagine, however, that the themes I introduce have relevance beyond South-East Asia and therefore that the book will be of value and interest to scholars and practitioners working in and on other places.

The title of the book – *Unplanned Development* – directs attention to the unplanned, unseen and unexpected and, therefore, to the gaps between planning designs and planning experiences, between what is seen and measured and what ultimately proves to be important, and between expectations and outcomes. These things are not usually 'hidden' in the literal sense. They are overlooked because of the way that the world (society, economy) is framed; because people act in ways that do not accord with the script of development or the rules of governance; because states either cannot or will not implement their own policies; and because the passage of history is hard to second-guess.[1]

From the big picture to the minutiae

Across the board, from the grand, overarching explanations of Asia's growth to the micro-level explanations for the progress of an individual village or a particular household, it seems that we lack the wherewithal to make convincing interpretations of why things are as they are and, therefore, to map out likely trajectories of future change. Looking across fifty years of growth and stagnation across the world, Rodrik concludes:

... reality has been unkind to our [development economists'] expectations. If Latin America were booming today and China and India were stagnating, we would have an easier time fitting the world to our policy framework. Instead, we are straining to explain why unorthodox, two-track, gradualist reform paths have done so much better than sure-fire adoption of the standard package. (Rodrik 2007: 55)

It has become usual for scholars of South-East Asian development to reflect that shortly after the end of the Second World War the countries of the region which appeared to be best placed to modernize were Burma (Myanmar) and the Philippines. As it has turned out, their development experiences have – to date – been among the most disappointing in the region. From the performance of countries to the progress of households, a similar theme emerges. In Caroline Moser's compelling *Ordinary Families, Extraordinary Lives*, which charts the progress of families in the urban slum of Indio Guayas on the outskirts of Guayaquil, Ecuador, between 1978 and 2004, she observes that only a longitudinal study, rather than a time-bound one, can bring explanatory clarity to the fact that 'while men were ... considered "hopeless shits" (*pendejos*), overall it was still considered better to have any man than no man at all' (Moser 2009: 180). When poverty is aggregated and generalized, when livelihoods are decontextualized, and when experiences are detemporalized, we lose the ability to explain what is happening and why. This has a further important implication: governments (thank goodness) do not have the ability to control and shape economy and society in anywhere close to a deterministic manner. There is a good deal of hubris when it comes to state planning initiatives. The state is 'all fingers and no thumbs'.[2]

A core reason for this state of affairs is that lives are messy and social science is not in a position to arrive at simple explanations for processes and patterns that are, at core, not fully coherent or knowable. 'Events and processes', John Law writes in his book *After Method: Mess in social science research*, 'are not simply complex in the sense that they are technically difficult to grasp. Rather, they are also complex because they *necessarily exceed our capacity to know them*' (2004: 6, emphasis in original). The development industry is particularly prone to an auditing culture and enthused by templates, recipes and models because it seems so important to arrive at clear policy prescriptions. Governments and policy-makers do not find it helpful to be told, 'it's complicated'. This book questions how we undertake this process of distillation and reduction, whether the resulting models provide an accurate and therefore truthful insight into the 'realities' they seek to explain, and whether the prescriptions that are then extracted are useful in policy terms.

The limits to agency and government This book emerges from the twin empirical puzzles outlined above and these, in turn, arise from my personal experiences in the field. In most years over the last three decades I have engaged in fieldwork, whether with farmers in rural settlements in Laos or Thailand, among migrants in urban Vietnam, or with factory workers and tea estate employees in Sri Lanka. More often than not, what people do defies my attempts at neat explanation; and when it comes to accounting for change, I find myself playing explanatory catch-up. Each time I return to the field I find that my ideas have to be recalibrated and my understanding reassessed. Why this might be the case is another question that threads its way through the book.

Personally and temperamentally, I am enamoured of the power of individual agency. I cherish the notion that the mostly poor and generally powerless people I have interviewed over the years have more of a hold over their lives than their depiction as marginalized and socially excluded, and beholden to rich classes and powerful states, permits. I am not, however, too much of a romantic not to appreciate that there are limits to agency, and I recognize that 'power's matrices' (Li 2007: 288) to a degree capture and shape what people are able to do. But, and this is a second theme in the book, power's matrices are not as hard and fast as the term 'structure' implies. They are less scaffolds of control than networks of possibility. States may, as the later chapters will illustrate, try to 'plan' development interventions, control fertility, guide migration and stage-manage land-use decisions, but these often have less purchase than the rhetoric of planning and intervention implies.

In light of this, while the structure/agency binary is valuable as a didactic device, it fails adequately to capture the ways in which causal processes are tied up with structural factors that lie outside a locality, social processes are embedded internally, behavioural traits are individualized, and historical trends are lumpy rather than smooth. Taken together, these serve to create the complex causal relationships which this book tries to elucidate and which make development processes and experiences particularly difficult to 'know' and therefore to explain.[3]

Beyond the problem of agency, a third theme that this book addresses is the contrast between people's respect for the state and their belief in its power (see Jeffrey 2010), reflected in the way in which state officials continue – generally speaking – to be admired and esteemed, and the liminal but equally widespread recognition that government and the agents of government rarely deliver. The same is true of development professionals, who often seem to have all the answers. Jeffrey Sachs in *The End of Poverty* writes that 'Our generation can choose to end ... extreme poverty by the year 2025' (2005: 1) and then proceeds to 'show the way toward the path of peace and prosperity, based on a detailed understanding of how the world economy has gotten to where it is today, and how our generation can mobilize our capacities in the coming twenty years to eliminate the extreme poverty that remains' (ibid.: 3–4). This book counsels against such simplifying tendencies and universal answers.

Although the book seeks to challenge mainstream views of development and its interpretation and achievement, this is not, inherently, a radical book. The politics of development makes an entrance, but this is largely with a lower-case 'p'. If there is an ideological tenor it might be termed critical localism. By this I mean that while the local most certainly does not provide an adequate or sufficient answer to the challenges of development, taking a local perspective does provide an insight into why state-led initiatives so often fail, or succeed but in unexpected ways.

The structure of the book and the argument

The book contains five core chapters which set out the case for the arguments rehearsed above. In summary they focus on the following themes:

- Plans and planning
- States and markets
- Histories and turning points
- Events and processes
- Behaviours and outcomes.

Each chapter provides a different but complementary insight into the hidden geometries of South-East Asian development but, taken together, they contribute to the wider case. This wider case is more than the claim that 'context matters' (which is certainly an element in the argument).

The following chapter, Chapter 2, looks at the science, art and experience of comprehensive development planning. The failures and disappointments of planning have been remarked on since the 1970s and yet the act of planning continues to be a central feature of development in almost all poor countries. This, in itself, is something of a puzzle. Every five years or so, governments feel the need to set out, often to a remarkable degree of detail, what they seek to achieve, and how. These plans are characteristically out of step with what governments are *able* to do in terms of their capacities and capabilities, what domestic political realities *permit* them to do and, moreover, what ensuing events *allow* them to achieve. The result is either that plans fail or that they never even get to the point where they might succeed or fail. The failure of planning, however, should not be extrapolated to imply a failure of development. Putting aside the cautionary caveats, the experience of the South-East Asian region is one of developmental success. Planning failure, in other words, has been accompanied, in many instances, by considerable development achievements.

This discussion of planning leads to a wider discussion, in Chapter 3, of the respective – or 'proper' – roles of states and markets. This discussion is juxtaposed around four events and/or areas of debate: the Asian economic 'miracle', the Asian financial 'crisis', the existence and role of developmental states, and the place of industrial planning in industrial change. The overriding lesson here is, rather unsatisfactorily, that there is no neat lesson or single silver bullet that might deliver development. If a lesson is to be drawn from the region it is that the development experience of South-East Asia emphasizes the importance of heterodoxy and eclecticism in terms of policy, and sensitivity to the opportunities afforded by history. It is certainly important to learn from history and from other countries' experiences, but not to be dictated to by them.

The theme of history is examined in greater detail in Chapter 4, with a focus on historical directionalities. In part this chapter sets out to look at how history unfolds, and whether it does so in neat and predictable ways or, alternatively, whether history is characteristically 'lumpy'. This question is approached both at the high level – and in particular by looking at the impact of the Plaza Accord of 1985 on South-East Asia's development path and prospects – and in small ways. The latter are elucidated through an analysis of the role of everyday technologies and low-visibility processes from the shrimp-tail pump in transforming farming in the Mekong Delta to boom crops, especially in the uplands of Vietnam. These micro-revolutions provide a link between the wider structural and historical trajectories that characterize South-East Asian development, and their impacts and effects on communities, households and individuals.

Chapter 5 takes this concern for the interplay between national development and personal progress farther, moving the discussion and the argument from higher-level and broader-scale processes to consider how these processes imprint themselves in terms of individual structures of living, and how, in turn, individual actions contribute, cumulatively, to the bigger story recounted in Chapters 2, 3 and 4. The discussion seeks to illuminate the disjunctures and inconsistencies between the aggregate and the particular, asking the question: what do aggregate stories omit, distort or gloss over? This is pursued through an analysis of poverty dynamics, leading to an exploration of the power of ordinary events to determine outcomes and a consideration, using panel and longitudinal studies, of the inter-generational transmission of poverty and prosperity. The poor are not only extremely varied, notwithstanding the tendency to treat them as a group with shared characteristics, but so too are the processes that lead the non-poor to become poor, and vice versa. The chapter shows that the devil really is in the detail, and that even though the aggregate story may sometimes seem fairly clear and self-evident in the lessons that it provides us, the picture from the local perspective and the individual standpoint is far more mixed and contingent.

The final substantive chapter in the book, Chapter 6, examines South-East Asia's demographic transformation over the last half-century. In 1960, few scholars expected fertility to markedly decline in the region, and yet that is what happened – and it did so remarkably quickly in a number of very different places, including Muslim-majority Indonesia, Theravada Buddhist Thailand and communist Vietnam. The experience of countries like Indonesia, Thailand and Vietnam challenges the sequencing imputed in the demographic transition model, and has motivated demographers to rethink their assumptions about the causalities involved in the process. The chapter is not just, however, about South-East Asia's surprising fertility revolution, important though it is. The causes and effects of the smaller families that have become the norm in the region are numerous: late marriage, singlehood, changing gender relations, reworked household structures and livelihood footprints, and growing mobility. The responses of the populations of South-East Asia to government policies and invectives as well as to economic incentives have been characteristically surprising, and occasionally apparently perverse or counter-intuitive. It is for these reasons that, even now, scholars and policy-makers do not know where the demographic trends and associated processes set out in the chapter will lead, and whether therefore the past provides a useful guide to the future.

What do the arguments pursued and the material explored in earlier chapters mean for our understanding of the causes, character and consequences of development in the South-East Asian region? And what does this mean, in turn, for policy? While this book has not been written with policy issues and ramifications to the forefront, these are considered in the final chapter, Chapter 7.

From South-East Asia to the global South: the case against orthodoxies and rule books

The bulk of the detailed discussion in the book draws on the experience of the South-East Asian region. This is mainly for the straightforward reason that much of my field experience has been in South-East Asia. It is the region I know best and therefore also the region where I am best placed to 'test' theoretical positions, conceptual framings, descriptive generalizations and policy prescriptions against my experiences, and the 'facts' as I see and have experienced them. However, the message of the book is not limited to South-East Asia; the arguments here are viewed as equally pertinent to conditions and experiences in other regions of the global South and, indeed, to the richer world. The 'lessons', as outlined in more detail in the final chapter and illuminated by the chapters that lie between, are that empirics are important, that we should entertain a good portion of modesty regarding our ability to look into the future, that inductive reasoning is critical if we are to begin to understand processes of social and economic transformation, and that theoretical positions should be tested and retested against experience. These are not just lessons for South-East Asia.

Returning to the four axes of contingency rehearsed above, we can speculate on how they operate in the context of South-East Asia. The role of the *conditions* of development means that economic progress in the countries of the region has been achieved on different terms. Looking for commonalities in experience tends to obscure the differences that exist; and these differences may be *more* important in illuminating the causes of change. The *historical contexts* of development that accompanied growth in Singapore in the 1960s, Malaysia in the 1970s, Thailand in the 1980s and Vietnam in the 1990s direct our attention to, for example, the regional and global conditions that have shaped flows of foreign direct investment. This, though, does not tell us a great deal about how individuals and families have engaged with the outcomes of such foreign investment. To shed light on this question, we need to seek to understand individual, *personal circumstances*. Beneath the aggregate picture of declining poverty, for example, is a surprising degree of turbulence often linked to untoward or serendipitous events. Finally, we need to challenge the tendency towards excising from our explanatory models the *character* of the people and societies which are the subjects of development.

This is a book that in tone and content is set against the charting of conventional wisdoms, one-size-fits-all orthodoxies, standardized recipes, canonical models or binding rule books. The chapters that follow seek to set out why this is the case.

2 | From development plans to development planning

> ... planning becomes the intellectual matrix of the entire moderniza-
> tion ideology. (Myrdal 1968: 711)

> There is a certain security that individuals attain from knowing that
> someone is in charge, and has matters under control. ... The control
> mentality is based on two fallacies: it overestimates the powers of
> direct control and it underestimates the powers of indirect control.
> (Stiglitz 1989: 33, 34)

Introduction

We all plan: holidays, dinner parties, birthdays, next week's meals,
even books like this one ... Usually discrete events, and preferably in
the not-too-distant future. We are aware that the more complicated
and long-term plans become, the more contingent they are. Planning
a career, for example, quickly becomes an exercise in wishful thinking,
prey to all sorts of unforeseen events and serendipitous moments. And
yet while we all intuitively know that planning is almost inevitably held
hostage to events, a key feature of the way in which the developing world
has been 'managed' is through development plans and the associated
technologies of planning. In itself, this is noteworthy: few rich countries
place development plans centre stage. Yet there is something about
the post-colonial, developing world – along with the socialist world –
which has attracted the science and art of planning, and has done so
in abundance and for well over half a century.

There is a mystery at the heart of development planning which also
lies at the core of this chapter. As will become clear as the chapter
unfolds, planning 'dilemmas' have multiplied as each development decade has passed. Notwithstanding these multiplying doubts, however,
and the fine-tuning of development planning in response, planning
not infrequently continues to occupy a central position in the way that
developing countries govern, manage, shape and direct development.
This chapter explores the history, practice, experience and persistence
of development planning: the emergence of development planning at
a certain point in world history; the way it took a particular shape;
the multiple reasons why development planning has failed to live up

11

to expectations; and, finally, the puzzle of development planning's continuing influence. The chapter will expand upon the illustrative experiences of planning in Thailand, city planning in Vietnam, river basin planning and management in the Mekong, and participatory planning in Indonesia. The case of industrial planning in East Asia, often held up as the finest example of successful planning, is considered in the next chapter, Chapter 3.

The desire to direct development is strong among governments and many development economists. This ranges from grand, comprehensive national development plans spanning five- or ten-year horizons; to regional development or river basin plans; to the micro-management of crop types and chemical input use. In a sense, this is only human: as the 'problems' of the developing world have been set out in ever-growing detail by scholars, journalists and NGO activists and laid bare in government statistics, so the urgent desire to 'do something' has grown. There is also a strong imperative among governments to maintain the appearance of control, to make people and places legible for planning, to assign contexts and condition as somehow 'problematic', to render these problems technical, and to reimagine the world in a plan-rational guise (Li 2007: 7–12; Scott 1998).

This leaves open, however, the question of the scope of the state to plan on the one hand, and populations to be subjected and subjugated to planning on the other. And not just to plan in an abstract sense, but to deliver on those plans. With a handful of exceptions – and an important question is whether we should treat them as exceptions or as exemplars – the lessons of the last half-century or so are not encouraging. The experience has been one of failure or disappointment. Plans have very rarely delivered, and when they have there is the abiding sense that this has been more by accident than by design. Among non-communist countries, India has probably directed more human and financial resources at planning than any other. In 1990, not long before the country's economic liberalization from mid-1991, Byrd observed that '... the problems and shortcomings of Indian economic development over the past four decades can be viewed at least in part as manifestations of the failure of planning as formulated, organized, and implemented in India' (1990: 714).

The science (and art) of plans and planning
Making plans

The basic principle in the ideology of economic planning is that the state shall take an active, indeed the decisive, role in the economy: by its own acts of investment and enterprise, and by its various controls – inducements and restrictions – over the private sector, the state shall initiate, spur and steer economic development. These public policy measures shall be rationally coordinated, and the coordination be made explicit in an over-all plan for a specific number of years ahead. (Myrdal 1968: 709)

Economic planning may be described as the conscious effort of a central organization to influence, direct, and, in some cases, even control changes in the principal economic variables of a certain country or region over the course of time in accordance with a predetermined set of objectives. The essence of economic planning is summed up in these notions of *influence, direction, and control*. (Todaro 1971: 1, emphasis in original)

Plans are concerned with the shaping of the future; Sagasti defines planning as 'anticipatory decision making' (1988: 431). They are anticipatory to the degree that they set out desirable objectives – which tend to be mostly economic but may also be social, environmental and/ or (though rarely) political – and a set of guiding policies and interventions to meet these objectives. Plans are informed by development planning models, and because these models are models of the economy it is not altogether surprising that it is the economics of development which has tended to hold centre stage (Stiglitz 1998a: 5). Development plans, therefore, can be said to embody three key characteristics. They are: (i) *interventionist*; (ii) *rationalist*; and (iii) *economistic*. Perhaps the most important underpinning justification and explanation for the planning agenda is that states *should* intervene in planning, directing and managing the economy. In that sense plans are also normative, and are so in two senses: there is the assumption that government *should* plan and, moreover, *should* plan in a certain way. As regards the latter, this was originally mainly because of the presumed need to correct for market failures, as explored in greater detail later in this chapter, and to mobilize scarce resources.

Plans and planning during the planning era: 1950–80 Planning emerged in the late 1940s, coinciding with decolonization and the first concerted efforts to 'develop' the poor world. In the expanding eastern bloc of the Soviet Union and its satellites, planning was tied up with the ideals of socialism and communism. This was *socialist planning*, *central planning* or *command planning*. At the same time, but in a different context, planning was also being pursued in the newly independent countries

13

TABLE 2.1 Three development eras and development planning paradigms

Planning era (1950s–70s)	Adjustment era (1980s–90s)	Post-Washington Consensus era (2000s–)
Pervasive market failures	Pervasive government failures	Joint public–private–civil society failures
Government-led development	Market-led development	Country-led development through partnerships
Centrally driven, detailed blueprints	Short-term adjustments	Long-term vision, social transformation, adaptive learning process
Investment-led development	Incentive-led development, with investments and institutions following	Investment, incentives, and institutions considered jointly
Resource allocation by administrative fiat Dominance of planners and engineers	Dominance of economists and financial experts	Multidisciplinary approach
Resource gap filled by donors	Resource envelope determined by donors	Country-driven aid coordination based on comparative advantages
Donor-placed foreign experts	Donor-imposed policies	Donor-provided advisory assistance to empower stakeholders with options
Marginal role for monitoring and evaluation	Donor-driven monitoring of policy implementation	Participatory monitoring and evaluation to enhance learning and adaptation

Note: The periodization of the three periods is only indicative

Source: Hanna and Agarwala (2000: 10) (with minor adjustments)

of the formerly colonial, and almost entirely poor, world. This was *development, guidance* or *indicative planning* in mixed economies (see Table 2.1). The reason why development planning became popular at this particular historical moment was not only because of the conjuncture of decolonization and the impact of US president Harry S. Truman's inaugural address on 20 January 1949, in which he promised that the United States would bring its scientific advances and economic resources to bear on improving conditions in 'underdeveloped areas'.[1] There was an intersection of several other political, ideological and technical explanatory factors. It was at this time that the mathematical models needed for comprehensive development planning and the data to populate and inform such models became available for the first time (Chakravarty 1991). In addition, the market failures of the early twentieth century, the example of managed reconstruction in Europe (in the guise of the Marshall Plan), the apparent success of the Soviet economy, and anti-capitalism coupled with new nationalism all also contributed to the emergence of a planning consensus among politicians and many economists.[2]

Finally, there has always been the strong desire among states to make development 'legible', to provide a developmental script – based on the supposed rationality of development technologies and interventions – that could be followed and which could be linked to a set of identified aims and objectives. James Scott's book *Seeing Like a State* (1998) outlines a series of state simplifications, the 'tools of legibility' as he puts it, such as censuses, standardized measures, scientific forestry, cadastral mapping, tax codes, land titling, and standardized surnames. All these sought (and seek) to inform and achieve the centralizing and controlling tendencies of the state; development planning can be seen as yet another attempt at state simplification. Scott, having surveyed state simplifications as varied as Soviet collectivization, the high modernist city and compulsory villagization in Tanzania, concludes: 'We have repeatedly observed the natural and social failures of thin, formulaic simplifications imposed through the agency of state power' (ibid.: 309). In a similar fashion, Tania Murray Li, drawing on Rose (1999), writes of the way in which the apparatus of development in Indonesia 'renders technical' the domain to be governed, and in so doing simplifies, orders and defines that human and non-human domain in a managerial and plan-rational manner (Li 2007; and see Ferguson 1994).

In December 1961, the UN General Assembly adopted Resolution 1708 (XVI): 'Convinced of the urgent need of the less developed countries to establish and implement national, all-inclusive and well-integrated development plans to build up their societies ...' (UN 1963: 114). This led to the establishment of an expert group[3] tasked with preparing a study of planning. In 1963 the United Nations released the group's deliberations in *Planning for Economic Development*, a handbook that cemented planning as the keystone in a new science of development management (ibid.). Emerging from this and other early forays into development planning was a standard approach which became repeated across the global South: the establishment of a planning agency (usually a planning department, sometimes a planning 'board', occasionally with ministry status); the production of national development plans (normally five years in duration); the division of these national plans into sectoral plans (agriculture, industry and so forth); and, often, the parallel production of regional development plans to confront the particular problems of lagging areas.[4] The World Bank was an important and enthusiastic partner in the production of such comprehensive national development plans, and indeed often made their production a precondition for the disbursement of development assistance (Balassa 1990: 561–2).[5] For programme support to be provided, the World Bank expected the programme concerned to be clearly set out in a planning document (Killick 1983: 72).

The enthusiasm for development planning has varied between countries and over time, and the high point of development planning spanned the three decades from the early 1950s to the end of the 1970s. This was the era of planning (Hanna and Agarwala 2000). Siddiqi, in *An Introduction to Economict Planning* (1964), published during the heyday of planning, opens with the resounding statement, 'These are the days of planning' (ibid.: 1). 'Today', he writes, 'nobody believes in laissez-faire and its magic performance' (ibid.: 2); economic planning and state interference are necessary to remove the 'serious defects' from which a laissez-faire economy suffers. For Siddiqi and many other scholars, development practitioners, politicians and officials, the attractions and logic of planning were self-evident and not based on conjecture. Rather more influentially than Siddiqi, Michael Todaro outlined in his book *Development Planning: Models and methods* the logic and desire for planning as follows:

the quest for rapid economic progress has been predicated largely upon the formulation and implementation of comprehensive development plans. Planning has become a vital instrument in the strategy of modernization. Ministries of economic planning in these [less developed] nations are regularly engaged in the process of drawing up such plans in order to set forth in a logical and consistent manner the priorities, goals, and aspirations of their governments. (Todaro 1971: ix)

The fact that development planning became so clearly linked to the poorer world was because of a widespread view in the 1960s that market failures were particularly pronounced in developing countries, owing to structural rigidities that were not present in more developed economies. Models were developed with the intention that these might better guide investment decisions, overcoming the imperfect markets that were assumed to be a feature of such countries, and meeting identified resource scarcities in the process. This, in turn, then justi-fied a role for governments in directing investment, taking control (or command) of key sectors, and planning the economy:

> Implicitly, it was assumed that the government would behave as a bene-volent social guardian, in the Fabian Socialist tradition. Economists would serve in government, calculating shadow prices and formulating planning models. Selfless bureaucrats would then carry out the plans. Coordination and administration of public sector activity was implicitly assumed to be costless. Moreover, as long as technocrats were in any event going to decide upon an investment and production plan, it was a logical next step to believe that the activities so determined should also be carried out in the public sector. (Krueger 1990: 13; and see Lall 1996: 3; Stiglitz 1998b)

While development planning tended to be restricted to the poorer world, planning was not. In the same decades that development plan-ning became de rigueur in the global South, so too did planning in many countries of the North. However, as Myrdal notes (1968: 739), planning in the developed world was not programmatic: it was pragmatic and emerged *after* industrialization and development; in the developing world, planning emerged as a means to achieve industrialization and de-velopment and was – and has tended to remain – highly programmatic.

National development planning in South-East Asia Planning was no less enthusiastically embraced in South-East Asia during the planning era than it was in much of the rest of the developing world (Table 2.2). As Table 2.2 sets out, all the countries of the region have develop-ment planning agencies and all have instituted national development plans. Mostly these date from the 1950s and 1960s and, in almost every case, such plans continue to be produced, with the apparatus

TABLE 2.2 Planning and planning agencies in South-East Asia

Country	Planning agency	Date[1]	First national plan
Brunei Darussalam	Brunei Economic Development Board (BEDB)	c.1952	1st National Development Plan (NDP) 1953–58
Cambodia	Ministry of Planning	1997	First Socio-economic Development Plan (SEDC I) 1996–2000
East Timor (Timor Leste)	Planning Commission	2002	First National Development Plan (NDP) 2002–20
Indonesia	National Development Planning Agency (BAPPENAS, established 1967)	c.1955	First Five-Year Plan (1956–60); followed by Eight-Year Comprehensive Development Plan (1961–68); and Repelita I (1969/70–1973/74)
Lao PDR	Committee for Planning and Investment (originally, in 1976, State Planning Committee)	1976	First National Economic and Social Development Plan 1981–85 (preceded by Three-Year Plan, 1978–80)
Malaysia	Economic Planning Unit (EPU), Prime Minister's Department	c.1965	1st Malaysia Plan (1966–70)
Myanmar (Burma)	Ministry of Planning and Economic Development, created in 1993 following reorganization of former Ministry of Planning and Finance and before the Ministry of National Planning	c.1950	Eight-year Pyidawtha Plan (1952–60); under current planning framework, First Short-term Five-Year Plan (1992/93–1995/96)
Philippines	National Economic and Development Authority (NEDA), established in 1973. Originally the National Planning Division (1955)	1955	Five-Year Economic and Social Development Program (1957–61)
Singapore	Economic Development Board (EDB)	1961	1st Four-Year Plan (1961–64) (also known as the Singapore Development Plan)
Thailand	National Economic and Social Development Board (NESDB)	1959	1st National Economic Development Plan (1961–66)
Vietnam	Ministry of Planning and Investment	1976	2nd Five-Year Plan (1976–80) (the first plan following Reunification but before doimoi or renovation.

Note: 1. Date of establishment

Most recent national plan	Website
9th National Development Plan 2007–12	www.bedb.com.bn/index.php
National Strategic Development Plan (NSDP Update) 2009–13 (replacing NSDP 2006–10), which followed the Second Socio-economic Development Plan (SEDP II) 2001–05	www.mop.gov.kh/. English translation downloadable from site.
First National Development Plan (NDP) 2002–20	www.pm.gov.tp/ndp.htm
Medium-term Development Plan 2010–14 (RPJMN 2010–14); Longer-term Development Plan 2005–25 (RPJPN 2005–25)	bappenas.go.id/
Seventh National Economic and Social Development Plan (NSEDP) 2011–15	Unofficial translation of the draft of the 7th plan and the full sixth plan available from www.undplao.org/official%20docs/2011/Abridged%20version_14_Oct_2010_NSED P%20VII_combined %20_Eng_PDF.pdf and www.unlao.org/Links/Lao%20NSEDP%20 VI%20Draft%20Final.pdf
10th Malaysia Plan or 10MP (2011–15)	www.epu.gov.my/. Current plan downloadable from: www.epu.gov.my/html/themes/epu/html/RMKE10/rmke10_english.html
Fourth Short-term Five-Year Plan (2006/07–2010/11)	www.mnped.gov.mm/
Philippine Development Plan 2011–16	Current plan downloadable from www.neda.gov.ph/PDP/2011-2016/default.asp
A Second Singapore Development Plan (1966–70) was prepared and printed but was never released; no national development plan has been contemplated since	www.edb.gov.sg/edb/sg/en_uk/index.html
11th National Economic and Social Development Plan (2012–16)	www.nesdb.go.th/
2006–10 Five-Year Socio-economic Development Plan, and 2001–10 Ten-Year Development Strategy	www.mpi.gov.vn/portal/page/portal/mpi_en

of planning largely still in place. There is one notable exception to this: Singapore.

Singapore is the only country among the members of the Association of Southeast Asian Nations (Asean) that does not produce national development plans, and has not done so since the release of the First Four-Year Plan (1961–64), also known as the Singapore Development Plan, by the Economic Development Board (EDB). Dr Goh Keng Swee, a key figure in the management of Singapore's economic success, said in an interview:

> Actually when we [the PAP] first won the elections in 1959, we had no plans at all. We produced a formal document called the First Four-Year Plan in 1960, only because the World Bank wanted a plan. We cooked it up during a long weekend. I have very little confidence in economic planning. (Cited in Toh and Low 1988: 23)

In Schein's book (1996) on the culture of the Economic Development Board, there is virtually no mention of the Singapore Development Plan; in contrast, Lee's *Industrialization in Singapore* (1973) allocates an entire chapter to the plan. A Second Singapore Development Plan (1966–70) was prepared, even printed, but never released. Singapore's ejection from the Federation of Malaya in 1965, the UK government's announcement that it would wind down its military bases in the island state in 1966, and Malaysia's decision to end its involvement in the joint currency board made the Second Singapore Development Plan obsolete before it had even been read. With its national planning role defunct, the guiding philosophy of the EDB became 'strategic pragmatism', and the Board began to operate more as a cheerleader and supporter for Singapore Inc. than as a national planning agency in the manner of Thailand's National Economic and Social Development Board (NESDB) or Malaysia's Economic Planning Unit (EPU). Singapore's EDB pursues an economic strategy, to be sure, but does not seek to set out an economic plan; it is a 'one-stop government agency to promote the establishment of new industries in Singapore and accelerate the growth of existing ones' (EDB Annual Report 1961, quoted in Schein 1996: 42).

Comprehensive national development plans, usually with a planning period of five years, may no longer be prescribed in quite the manner that they once were, but they are still produced, as Table 2.2 makes clear. Indeed, for many planners the question is how to adjust and adapt plans and planning methodology to a new climate of devolution, decentralization, privatization and globalization (see Ikram 2011).[6] The Foreword to the Tenth Malaysia Plan (2011–15) states that the plan:

charts the development of the nation for the next five years, anchored on delivering the desired outcomes for all Malaysians. The Tenth Plan sets the stage for a major structural transformation that a high-income economy requires. The Plan contains new policy directions, strategies and programmes that enable the country to emerge as a high income nation. The national development programmes are attuned to the six National Key Results Areas, outlined in the Government Transformation Programme, the National Key Economic Areas of the Economic Transformation Programme and the strategic economic reforms in the New Economic Model. The Plan details strategies towards a more focused role for the Government as a regulator and catalyst while upholding the principles of 1Malaysia: People First, Performance Now to ensure effective delivery of services. (GoM 2010: iii)

Like Malaysia, Vietnam also has a five-year socio-economic development plan, and behind this a ten-year socio-economic development strategy (2001–10).[7] As one of the world's fastest-growing, and therefore best-performing, countries in the Asian region, Vietnam has certainly 'achieved' most of the planning objectives set out in its 2006–10 five-year socio-economic development plan. In a mid-term review of the plan, the Ministry of Planning and Investment lauds these achievements. Buried deep in the report (MoPI 2009: 114), however, is a short section, less than one page long, that is more reflective and which notes four weaknesses in Vietnam's progress. These identified weaknesses raise questions about the assumed link between planned interventions and performance. They are:

- mechanisms, policies and measures have not been appropriate to Vietnam's context and the changing situation in which the country finds itself;
- lack of knowledge regarding the interrelated issues and aspects necessary for guiding national development processes;
- lack of apparatus and personnel as well as the administrative reforms so that the functions and tasks of each ministry can be pursued;
- weak forecasting ability, and lack of accurate, basic information to advise the government so that it can make timely decisions.

As discussed later in this chapter, these areas of weakness can be mapped on to more generic criticisms of planning (see Table 2.3). What these identified weaknesses overlook, however, is the degree to which the mind-set of planners, which stresses order and rationality, is out of step with the working practices of those at lower levels of administration, where 'flexibility and accommodation appear as pre-eminent values' (Douglass 2002: 1.53; and see p. 34). More generally, they reflect a lack of realism in planning. Plans need to be realistic; when plans are implemented poorly it is commonly because they cavalierly overlook the wider development context, much of which relates to behavioural, cultural and institutional factors.

Development planning dilemmas, development planning failures

> Strategies of the past, even when they have been assiduously followed, have not guaranteed success. Furthermore, many of the most success-ful countries have not actually followed the 'recommended' strategies, but have carved out paths of their own. (Stiglitz 1998a: 5)

> Once we think of the economy and society as a complex, living sys-tem, the frequent failures of policy can be readily understood. These systems are inherently extremely difficult to predict and control. This is not merely a point of intellectual interest, but of great practical im-port. Because it implies that much of the control which governments believe they exercise over the economy and society is illusory. (Ormerod 1998: xi)

While planning agencies remain very much part of the develop-ment architecture of the developing world, as Table 2.2 shows, by the 1970s planning was coming under increasing criticism, reflected in Faber and Seers's two-volume study *The Crisis in Planning* (1972). By the end of the decade it was broadly accepted by most scholars and development practitioners that development planning, however 'comprehensive' it may have been and with whatever levels of human and financial commitment, had largely failed (see also Banerjee and Duflo 2011: 235). Across the board, it is hard to find many examples where we can read off development success from the development plans that have been instituted. For Killick, 'medium-term develop-ment planning has in most LDCs *almost entirely failed* ...' (1986: 103, emphasis added; see also Killick 1976), and Boettke's edited volume is simply titled *The Collapse of Development Planning* (1994). As the rest of this chapter will explore, the reasons for this are multiple, overlapping and sustained. They involve the difficulties of accessing sufficient data and/or sufficient accurate data; shortcomings in the capacity of the state to orchestrate development in line with plan-ning objectives; the unsettling effects of 'politics', both high-level and local; and a lack of agreement at national and international levels as to what to prioritize and how best to pursue development. Surprisingly, as the technologies of planning have become ever more sophisticated, with increasingly finely tuned economic models and the statistics to inform them, development planning has become ever more discredited. It seems that rather than making planning *more* effective, as our tools of planning have become more finely honed so the achievement of planning has seemed to recede farther. That said, while development planning may have lost its credibility among most scholars and many practitioners, governments often remain enamoured of many of the tenets of planning, and have been disinclined to reject the exercise (see Killick 1983). The fact that all the countries of the South-East Asian region, with the single exception of Singapore, continue to produce national economic and social development plans is testament to this fact.

A large part of the reason for the discrediting of development planning is because the process entertains five grand and problematic contextual presumptions and five, equally problematic, analytical assumptions (Table 2.3). The former encompass the presumptions of political continuity, economic stability, administrative competence, technical capacity and financial capability. The contextual assumptions that arise from these presumptions include the assumption that the administrative and human resource competencies exist to produce plans and deliver on them; the assumption that the information and data necessary to inform plans are available and trustworthy (i.e. accurate); the assumption that we understand the interrelationships and interdependencies between planning domains sufficiently well to be able to produce satisfactory models; the assumption that we understand the proper role of the market and the state in directing or managing development (which will be addressed in greater detail in the next chapter); and the assumption that adequate funds are available to finance and meet planning aims and objectives. These misplaced assumptions go some considerable way to explaining the key concerns and doubts that have plagued planning from the 1970s.

Almost from the beginning of the planning era, concerns were expressed that plans were excessively rigid and inflexible. They were produced, usually as printed documents, 'released' with some fanfare and then largely set for the remainder of the planning period specified. While there may be claims that plans are 'reviewed' periodically in the light of events, the institutional structure of planning agencies, and the inertia built into the timetable of planning, makes the review process cursory and therefore often little more than a cosmetic

TABLE 2.3 Generic weaknesses in planning systems and assumptions

Contextual presumptions	Analytical assumptions	Critique	Weaknesses in Vietnam's planning machinery
Political continuity	Assumption that identified planning aims and objectives will remain constant and not subject to changing political circumstances or changes of government	Inflexibility	[Disagreements in the Politburo – between 'reformists' and 'conservatives' – concerning the direction and character of economic management]
Economic stability	Assumption that the national and international economies will remain sufficiently stable such that planning assumptions are not overtaken by events	Lacking in economic realism	Mechanisms, policies and measures have not been appropriate to the changing situation in which the country finds itself
Administrative competence	Assumption that the bureaucracy has the ability, means and desire to deliver on stated plan objectives	Over-ambition, lacking feasibility and realism	Lack of apparatus and personnel as well as the administrative reforms so that the functions and tasks of each ministry can be pursued
Technical capacity	Assumption that the skills and personnel exist, or can be sourced from abroad; assumption that the necessary data are available to plan effectively; assumption that the inter-relationships and interdependencies between elements in the planning framework are sufficiently well understood to be able to model	Unrealistic	Weak forecasting ability, and lack of accurate, basic information to advise the government so that it can make timely decisions
Financial capability	Assumption that funds are or will be available to finance planning dreams	Improbable	–

Note: The points in the final column ('Weaknesses in Vietnam's planning machinery') have been extracted from the Ministry of Planning and Investment's mid-term review of the 2006–10 Five-Year Plan, with the exception of the first in square brackets

exercise.[8] Linked to this issue of rigidity is a second criticism: the isolation of planning and planning departments from other areas of government and society. Plans give the appearance of being apolitical, technical documents when, in reality, planning is highly political and politicized.[9] Planning, therefore, often harbours – at its core – a tension at best, a conflict at worst, between planners and politicians. While the partial insulation of planning agencies from the rough-and-tumble of government might be seen as valuable in formulating an 'objective' view of planning needs, the outcome is that plans are often *politically* unrealistic, however technically sophisticated they might be.

A third concern relates to the feasibility of plans. During the planning era of the 1950s and 1960s it was not unusual, particularly with longer-term plans (three-plus years), for objectives to take the form of a set of unrealistic wish lists, based on the best possible set of circumstances. As early as 1958, Albert Hirschman was writing of the 'permanent tendency of present-day governments in underdeveloped countries to undertake overambitious development plans and projects' (Hirschman 1958: 157), with the result that people did not take plans seriously while also raising the possibility of the planning 'nightmare' that 'all prospective difficulties must be solved at once and the elusive goal be seized through one convulsive investment effort, one large scale expropriation, or one "short" term of dictatorial rule' (ibid.: 201). The government of Vietnam, after the Reunification of the country in 1976, judged it possible for the country to become industrialized by the turn of the century, 'after four to five Five Year Plans' (quoted in Fforde and de Vylder 1996: 128). This ambition and the targets that underpinned it, needless to say, proved to be wildly over-optimistic.

A survey of approaches to planning since the 1950s reveals a shift towards more integrated or comprehensive planning in the 1970s, and then back towards programme-based planning during the 1980s. In 1971, to coincide with the inauguration of the Second Development Decade (1970–80), the UN introduced the idea of a 'unified' or 'comprehensive' approach to development planning, partly as a means to address one of the key areas of criticism up until that time, namely the disconnection between different planning fields and society. By the end of the decade it was recognized that comprehensive modelling and planning were next to impossible, leading to a renewed focus on smaller spatial units (regions, sub-regions) or on particular programmes (family planning, rural credit). While such approaches may seem more manageable, avoiding the grand, panoptic claims of comprehensive development planning, they still encounter the challenge of managing complexity, as the discussion of river basin planning later in this chapter will illustrate.

It may be thought that these summary criticisms of planning are largely historical: that they apply to a situation in the developing world which no longer applies. This is not the case. The contextual assumptions that go hand in hand with planning (Table 2.3) remain just as germane today, indeed perhaps more so given the effects of globalization. Looking back over the decades since 1950, there are few countries that have ever been able to meet the presumptions of political continuity, economic stability, administrative competence, technical capacity and financial capability, even over a five-year period. As Stern writes: 'Until now, we have assumed implicitly that the government is well-intentioned, well-informed, and competent. Governments, however, may be craven or manipulated, they may be very badly informed, and they may be incompetent' (Stern 1991: 251).

The technology and politics of planning To bring together this critique of planning, before turning to a more detailed consideration of the experiences of Indonesia, Thailand, Vietnam and the Mekong region, there are three areas around which the dilemma of planning coalesces. To begin with, there are input requirements. Planning requires accurate information – raw data – and a great deal of it, from financial and human resources to geographical data on the distribution of population and income levels. Even for middle-income developing countries such as Thailand and Malaysia, there are serious questions about whether plans are based on robust, trustworthy and accurate data. In a country like Vietnam the issue is even more pertinent. It is widely accepted that statistics on the geographical location of Vietnam's population significantly undercount the urban population of the country because of the way in which burgeoning migration has not been accommodated by changes to the *ho khau* or household registration system (Nguyen et al. 2012). As a result, Vietnam's 'floating' population numbers between twelve and sixteen million, which, if broadly correct, represents between 13 and 18 per cent of the country's population (UNDP 2010: 5). More widely, the World Bank has questioned whether data on urban poverty and living standards in Indonesia, the Philippines and Vietnam accurately delineate the nature of urban living, based as they are on certain assumptions about rural livelihoods (World Bank 2003: ix).

Secondly, in addition to the raw data, planning requires mathematical models of sufficient complexity to analyse these data, assuming that such models capture the complexity and messiness of the real world. The experience, time and again, is that they do not:

> The abysmal record of actual forecasts which econometricians have made using conventionally defined rules appears not to deter them at all ... They are ever hopeful, that, one day, with a bit of refinement of specification here or a bit of new technique there, they will achieve the success that has so far eluded them. (Ormerod 1998: 91)[10]

And finally, planning requires that the capacity and the desire (two very different things) exist for implementation. Planning depends crucially on enforcement – the ability and power to implement the plans that are drawn up. As Jawaharal Nehru, the first chairman of the Indian Planning Commission, is said to have remarked: 'The real question is not planning but implementing [India's] Plan – I fear we are not quite so expert at implementation as [we are] at planning' (quoted in Ikram 2011: 24; and see Byrd 1990). Many poor countries did not have – and do not have – sufficient numbers of appropriately trained professionals to produce and implement plans. Some professional planners have gone so far as to suggest that formulation is far less important than implementation, as a poorly formulated plan well implemented is preferable to a well-formulated plan that is barely implemented at all (see Ikram 2011: 14–15). This, of course, assumes that planning is necessary and desirable.

Implementation, 'actioning' plans in that ugly phrase, is not, however, merely an issue of capacity, although that is certainly important, but also an issue of political will and opportunity. Plans often give the appearance of being technical documents that carefully and dispassionately map out the best route to developing society and economy. It is not unusual for planners to be labelled 'technocrats', and to be housed separately from the rest of the apparatus of government. This isolation, while it may partially insulate planners from political pressures, also dislocates them from the real world of planning. This extends both to the subjects of planning (see Dey 1982)[11] and the governance of planning (Sagasti 1988: 431).[12] Yet the writing of development plans is an intensely political process, and their implementation even more so. Just as the state is subject to all sorts of pressures from various lobbies, which it is often unable to resist, so too are planners. Even when plans are 'optimal', the implementation of such plans rarely accords with their stated aims. For Killick (1976: 161), the failure of development planning is fundamentally rooted in 'the naivety of the implicit model of governmental decision-making incorporated in the

TABLE 2.4 Planning the Lao PDR

Planning domain	Shortcomings
Technologies of planning	Coordination between ministries, sectoral authorities and between central and local authorities is still very weak
	New legislative framework is in the process of being established and is currently incomplete
	Socio-economic information systems suffer from many limitations and are not timely, especially in the case of statistical data
Everyday politics of planning	Lax implementation of instructions and resolutions issued by the party and legislation enacted by the government, which are even disregarded in certain areas
	Substantial number of civil servants and party members are engaged in corrupt practices
	Slow acceptance of new economic concepts ... obstructing the process of realizing the socio-economic development goals
	Slow institutional (re)organization, [and] slow reform of the civil service and public administration
Human and financial resources of planning	Resource mobilization [i.e. funds] has not yielded the required results and efficiency in using funds is low and the use of such funds is inconsistent
	No long-term strategy or appropriate policies to attract and use foreign direct investments
	Guidance and supervision in the civil service and reform of public administration does not ensure high efficiency

Note: These shortcomings are extracted largely verbatim from the Sixth National Socio-economic Plan (2006–10)

planning literature'. For Evans it lies in a 'disjunction between formal structures and the underlying, more informal structures of power and practice [that] renders the formal structures ineffectual' (2004: 34). Both authors are highlighting the way in which formal plans become diluted, ignored, distorted and corrupted as they make the transition from formal plans through to implementation.

The Lao Sixth National Socio-economic Development Plan (2006–10) contains a frank admission of the shortcomings of the planning context in the Lao PDR (2006: 48). We can see these shortcomings – or 'limitations' as they are phrased – falling into three areas that echo the foregoing general discussion. There are shortcomings connected with the technology requirements of planning; with the everyday politics of planning; and with the resource needs of planning (Table 2.4).

From planning to the grass roots, from plan rational to cultural context Much of the discussion thus far has focused on national development plans. However, there comes a point when plans make contact with the 'grass roots' – the point of connection between the desirable objectives set out by planners and politicians, the policies and interventions designed to achieve these objectives, and the people and places they seek to shape, influence and direct. These points of connection with people and places tend not to link directly to national development plans, but to lower-level sectoral and programme plans. As they are more focused, it would be reasonable to expect a greater degree of connection and traction between such sectoral, area or programme plans on the one hand, and outcomes and performance on the other. Once again, however, such a hope is not infrequently misplaced.

Korten (1984: 176), drawing on his long experience of rural development planning in Asia, highlights four deficiencies which, as he puts it, remain 'the rule rather than the exception'. These echo some of the points already explored at the national level, but which he sees reproduced at lower levels. The deficiencies Korten identifies relate to:

1 Centralized bureaucratic organizations that have limited capacity to respond to diverse community defined needs
2 Inadequate investment in capacity-raising
3 Inadequate attention paid to social diversity
4 Insufficient integration of technical and social elements of development interventions.

The science of development planning is an exercise in rationalizing the development process, subjecting it through modelling to the logic of mathematics and the rationality imbued in *Homo economicus*. Plans are said to be 'plan rational', and there is an assumption that the objects of planning – the planned population – will respond and act in a rational manner. This issue – of whether human behaviour can be modelled – is addressed in greater detail in Chapter 6. There is, however, also a second assumption in the plan rational logic: that master models of development, often embedded in development plans, are equally applicable across the globe. Do such universal models of human behaviour, built on the experience of the West, have explanatory purchase in non-Western cultures and society? Gunnar Myrdal, in his epic *Asia Drama*, writes of the tendency towards building 'master models' and notes that 'the very concepts used in their construction aspire to a universal applicability that they do not in fact possess' (1968: 16, and see the quotation at the beginning of this chapter). Scholars of East Asian culture not infrequently challenge the very basis of the rational model that underpins development planning. East Asian (i.e Confucian) cultures stress familistic (affective) relationships, emotional bonds and group (rather than individual) orientation, and these sometimes rub up against the rational Western model, which emphasizes efficiency, individualism and social dynamism (see Tai 1989).[13] This is not to say that Asia is an unconducive place to pursue modernization, as Max Weber argued in *The Protestant Ethic and the Spirit of Capitalism* (1930);[14] recent experience has shown quite the reverse. It may, however, raise questions about the efficacy of development plans that apply 'universal' models, and which assume that capitalism is singular rather than plural (see Woodside 1996). It may also lead one to rather different conclusions as to the roots of development and growth. A related argument has been pursued by Evans (2004: 30–1) in his critique of 'institutional monocropping', the 'method of trying to build institutions that will promote development [by] imposing uniform institutional blueprints on the countries of the global South'. This, of course, is founded on the premise that institutional structures will have equal purchase across geographical and sociocultural contexts.

Planning experiences in Asia

The discussion has so far focused on broader debates about the coherence and efficacy of development planning. The chapter now turns to consider how these general critiques and concerns are reflected in particular planning experiences, namely: national development planning in Thailand; city planning in Vietnam; river basin development planning in the Mekong; and participatory planning in Indonesia.

These cases may be varied in their geographical location and reach but, as we will see, the lessons of each resonate to a surprising degree.

Development planning in Thailand (1959–present) Development planning in Thailand can be dated to 1957, when General Sarit Thanarat became prime minister and created the National Economic Development Board (NEDB), renamed the National Economic *and Social* Development Board (NESDB) in 1971.[15] It was also at this time that, not coincidentally, the Thai word for development – *kaanpattana* – came into widespread usage (Rigg et al. 1999). The motivation for the creation of the NEDB was not just political and tied to the desire of a new prime minister to make his mark; it also reflected a wish to rationalize development (Muscat 1994: 92), something that the World Bank was all too keen to support.[16]

With the guidance and support of the World Bank, this led to the release of Thailand's first five-year national economic development plan in 1961, ushering in the *samai pattana* or 'development era'. Since 1961 Thailand's development has been marshalled and guided, on paper at least, by twelve five-year plans, the Twelfth Plan spanning the years from 2011 to 2015. These have become increasingly sophisticated documents as the skills base and capacity of the NESDB have grown. They have also tended to reflect prevailing development wisdoms, even when these may have been dressed up in a cloak of localism (as with, for example, the Ninth [2002–06] and Eleventh [2011–15] plans' emphasis on the King of Thailand's *sethakit phor piang* or 'sufficiency economy').

The First Plan (1961–66), even with the World Bank's support, was an extremely thin document and contained very little economic analysis, let alone planning. Muscat (ibid.: 96) claims that there were only 'half a dozen' young professionals in the NEDB who were tasked to produce a national development plan in just four months. There were other reasons for the parsimonious character of the First Plan, however, and these resonate with the situation in many other developing countries in the 1960s. There were few statistics on which to base a plan and those that were available were of dubious accuracy. Even vital statistics (i.e. births and deaths) were of doubtful veracity. Individual ministries lacked planning capacity even to match the level of the NEDB, and there was duplication in responsibilities between individual departments and ministries. Furthermore, ministries tended to operate as micro-kingdoms in competition with each other, making the coordination of planning almost impossible (Demaine 1986). Unger pithily sums up the situation as follows: 'limited skills, lack of autonomy from political meddling, and particularly the absence of reliable data precluded effective regulation, much less any more ambitious roles' (1998: 72–3). An evaluation of the First Plan by the Thai government may have expressed satisfaction that 'in spite of inexperience, imperfection in the planning process, project formulation and implementation and the many problems encountered, the main purposes of the Plan were accomplished', but this was clearly by coincidence rather than design (quoted in Muscat 1994: 97). As seems to be so often the case when plan targets are met, there were real questions whether 'planning' had any role in this.

Since the First Plan, the capacity of the NE(S)DB has grown enormously, and by the Third Plan (1972–76)[17] the Board had become a fully fledged planning agency.[18] But the Third and Fourth (1977–81) plans, while they were undoubtedly much more sophisticated documents, suffered from a different problem: a lack of engagement and enthusiasm on the part of the government, which was distracted by other issues, not least security concerns and political instability at a time when the conflict in Indochina was intensifying and the Communist Party of Thailand was a significant threat. As a result, the Thai government 'had little interest in the plans or the planning machinery' (ibid.: 135), and the NESDB found itself marginalized. The World Bank, in a confidential review of the Thai economy, stated:

> There is ... little evidence that Thailand's development plans systematically guide or govern the actions of departments or, for that matter, the cabinet itself, in the day-to-day conduct of government affairs. Although national development plans should never be treated in mixed economies as binding and inflexible statements of government intentions, the frequency and extent to which development plans appear to be disregarded in the allocation of administrative and financial resources and in the introduction of new policies, programs and projects is indicative of a lack of full commitment to the concept of development planning. In recent years it has become increasingly difficult to discern a sense of direction and purpose in public sector behavior that is in any way comparable to its stated intentions and objectives. (World Bank 1978: 28)

The Fifth Plan (1982–86) represents, in many respects, the zenith of planning in Thailand in terms of the ambition of what it sought to do: redistribution, decentralization, stabilization (i.e. structural adjustment), cautious intervention, and diversification (NESDB 1981). When the plan was drawn up at the end of the 1970s, national development planning worldwide had not completely lost its gloss, and the NESDB was sufficiently well resourced and staffed that the plan which resulted was an impressive document, particularly compared to those that preceded it. The problems with the Fifth Plan lay not so much in the plan itself, but in the wider political economy. First, over the plan period other programme policies and plans were drawn up that conflicted with the Fifth Plan and, often, superseded it (Unger 1998: 86). A second problem was that the priorities which informed and shaped the Fifth Plan, particularly in terms of its social objectives, shifted. At the end of the 1970s, the threat posed by the Communist Party of Thailand (CPT) to the country's political stability was still very real, and this shaped and justified the policies aimed at tackling rural poverty and inequality. There is a dedicated section in the Fifth Plan addressing the issue of 'National economic and security development', and a chapter within this section on the 'Development of security sensitive areas' (NESDB 1981: 295–318). With the problem of communist insurgency rapidly receding in the early 1980s as the CPT lost membership and influence, however, and with growing concerns over macroeconomic stability in the light of the second oil price shock (from 1979), the investments needed to meet the social objectives of the Fifth Plan were quietly overtaken by events and, therefore, quietly shelved.[19]

Looking at the experience of over half a century of national development planning in Thailand, one sees an increasingly well-resourced and skilled planning agency developing ever more sophisticated national development plans informed by a growing abundance of baseline statistics. We also see, however, a planning agency which over time became increasingly marginalized in the battle between ministries for power and influence;[20] plans which, as they became more complex and ambitious, were at growing risk of being overtaken by events; and of interventions that were frequently upset by political meddling. It is hard to escape the conclusion that, by the Sixth Plan (1987–91), these documents had become little more than paper plans, or at best a series of good intentions. The preface to the Eleventh Plan (2011–15) sets out the following vision:

> The Plan has adopted the Philosophy of Sufficiency Economy as a guiding principle together with a holistic people-centered development approach. The vision of the Eleventh Plan is to create 'a happy society with equity, fairness, and resilience', where people can live peacefully, be well-prepared for change, within a society that has consolidated social foundations, quality economic growth, sustainable natural

resources and environmental management, and good governance.
(NESDB 2010, refined from Thai translation)

While it may be hard to disagree with the sentiments of such a vision, as a basis for planning it lacks precision, substance and a sense of direction.

City planning in Vietnam One of the threads running through critiques of development planning in Thailand is the disjuncture between the rationality of planning theory and the cultural practices of planning. We can see this reflected in abundance in the experience of urban planning in Vietnam.

Vietnam, notwithstanding the economic reforms progressively introduced since the mid-1980s, remains a country where a complex and multilayered system of administration permeates almost all areas of life, filtering down from the central government to individual households through a mosaic of mass organizations, line agencies and units of spatial (territorial) administration, which together give the impression of strong central control (Leaf 1999: 300–302; and see McGee 2009). The planning of Hanoi sits within this administrative framework and has been guided, in theory, by two twenty-year visionary master plans, the first running between 1990 and 2010, and the second from 2010 to 2030, the second complemented by an underpinning Hanoi Vision for 2050 (Labbé 2010).[21]

These master plans focus on the development of Hanoi's infrastructure and a series of ambitious projects (industrial zones, residential developments), many on the city's periphery, such as the mega-housing development of Ciputra (Illustration 2.1). Yet, as Leaf notes (Leaf 1999, 2002; and see Leaf 1998 on China), these plans are only partially reflected in the actual development of the city. He highlights four countervailing tendencies. First, Vietnam has insufficient financial resources and institutional capacity to achieve its planning goals, echoing the point made earlier. Secondly, the growing reliance of Vietnam on inward flows of private capital to achieve its planning goals has meant the country is increasingly dependent on investment conditions regionally and globally.[22] Thirdly, at the same time as it has instituted these visionary plans, the Vietnamese government has also largely lost its formerly quite rigid control over people and their activities. In particular, the household registration system, or *ho khau*, which used to stem migration, has much less purchase, leading to a substantial and largely uncontrolled migration of people from rural

Illustration 2.1 The Ciputra housing development in Hanoi, Vietnam (2010)

to urban areas, such as Hanoi. And finally, Vietnam's administrative system, on to which Hanoi's urban plans are grafted, are flexible and ambiguous, rather than centralized and rigid as they appear at first glance. 'The formal processes of planning', Leaf writes, 'do not recognise the capacity of households to engage the local administrative system successfully, in order to permit the construction of their own homes and shops' (1999: 306). The planned city is, in reality, largely an informal city where interpersonal relations, loopholes, regulatory ambiguity, under-the-counter deals and haphazard micro-developments trump the overarching visions and administrative formality of the Hanoi Master Plan. There exist national planning standards for parks and green spaces issued by the Ministry of Construction, but these are rarely adhered to and, in any case, the authorities do not fine developers who ignore the planning criteria (Labbé 2010: 19). More dramatically, during the 1990s as much as 70–90 per cent of urban construction in the city was undertaken without formal, official approval or oversight (Leaf 2002: 27). Indeed, most houses did not have proper land use right certificates and building was undertaken even without construction permits (Labbé 2010: 28; Labbé and Boudreau 2011). While over the course of the 2000s the proportion of housing construction undertaken by individual households decreased to around one half, developers also found numerous avenues to get around or ignore planning requirements:

In sharp contrast to the clear, modern vision of Hanoi's master plan, the physical emergence of the *doi moi* city – the rebuilding of inner-city sites from one-storey shophouses to three- four- or five-storey apartments and the rapid transformation of farmers' peripheral plots into urban construction sites – has occurred with virtually no planning or construction controls. (Leaf 1999: 305)

Hanoi's master plans provide sanitized and prescriptive twenty-year visions of the future of the city, but are fundamentally problematic in both their approach and their philosophy. Three particular issues can be highlighted. To begin with, there is the sheer formality of the plans, which can be set against the informal operation of cities like Hanoi.[23] As the examples above show, the reality of administration in Vietnam demonstrates the importance of understanding the everyday practices and interactions of people and administrators. In his review of urban transitions in Vietnam, Douglass (2002: 1.53) notes the 'degree to which these accommodations occur in day-to-day practice', leading him to conclude that formal urban planning in Vietnam pays 'insufficient attention to the real face of urban development'.[24] The plans take little note of the views of the public, and public participation is notably absent. A second major shortcoming is the time frame of the plans – twenty years – and the lack of attention to the inevitability of changing circumstances and how these can be incorporated. And the third issue relates to the administrative architecture of Vietnam, the place of the plans within the context of national and regional goals, and the planning capacities available. Labbé concludes her report by writing that 'what is required is a fresh look at different planning mechanisms', including 'thinking about what kind of institutional engineering is needed to implement a new planning approach, what financial and human resources are required, and how professionals in the built environment and urban administration fields must be trained in order to ensure the ongoing implementation of such an approach' (Labbé 2010: 40).

River basin development planning in the Mekong[25] River basin development planning has a long history – dating back to the latter half of the eigteenth century.[26] The early desire to manage river basins was due partly to their importance in terms of water management for farming (irrigation and flood control) and, slightly later, for hydro-power; what also made river basins attractive locales for early attempts at rational planning was their status as 'natural' regions.

Before decolonization, almost all attempts at river basin management were undertaken in Europe, North America and Australasia, the most famous being the Tennessee Valley Authority (TVA), which was established in 1933, and became a high-profile attempt at large-scale, regional planning at the level of the river basin (Molle 2009: 487). In the wake of Truman's 1949 exhortation to embark on a 'bold new programme' to bring science and development to underdeveloped countries, the hydraulic paradigm of the TVA was exported across the world and 'TVA-like river-basin development plans mushroomed' (ibid.: 489). Large-scale, multi-purpose dams became the signature edifice of this era of river basin development, reflecting a confidence in the technological prowess of humans and their ability to control nature in a rational manner. Like comprehensive development planning, with which there are clear echoes, river basin planning embodied a number of assumptions that have, often, subsequently proved to be flawed: the assumption that it is possible to rationally plan and orchestrate at the level of the river basin; an assumption that planning models permit a full understanding of the interdependencies in the system; a belief in the power and efficacy of science and technology to deliver development gains; and the assumption that human populations can be planned, managed and modelled as if they are rational decision-makers. More importantly, and unlike comprehensive development planning, river basin management has not lost its gloss for both governments and multilateral agencies:

> IWRM [Integrated Water Resources Management] and river-basin planning and management now appear as consensual concepts, from water experts to international banks and from NGOs to multilateral agencies, despite serious doubt on the effectiveness of the approach, whether and how it can be operationalized, and whether it is not sometimes a solution looking for a problem. (Ibid.: 491)

The criticisms that are levelled at river basin management are those of comprehensive development planning, writ small: the absence of sufficient baseline data; a lack of flexibility; an excessive degree of optimism regarding deliverables; a shortage of community participation and engagement; a tendency to overlook the politics of planning; and a failure to understand the independencies between biophysical and socio-economic systems.[27] In their review paper, Gregory et al. (2011) propose a 'middle ground' framework for sustainable river management governance. This, they suggest, will allow an effective articulation across scales and representation between actors, helping to reconcile the tensions between bottom-up and top-down approaches.

TABLE 2.5 Planned versus realized impacts and returns of the Pak Mun Dam

Planned, promised, predicted	Realized	Over-/under-estimation
Cost US$135 million	Cost $233 million	Over 70 per cent higher than projected cost
Mitigation $11 million	Mitigation $32 million	Three times projected cost
Dry season HEP: 136 Megawatts	Dry season HEP: 40 Megawatts	Less than one third of projected output
Economic Internal Rate of Return: 12%	Economic Internal Rate of Return: 5%	Less than one half projected rate of return
Irrigation: 29,500 hectares	Irrigation: none	
Displaced families: 241 households	Displaced families: 1,700 households	Seven times more displaced households than projected
Reservoir fisheries: 100 kg/hectare/year	Reservoir fisheries: 10 kg/hectare/year	One tenth projected fisheries production
Natural fisheries: fish ladder first for a Mekong tributary dam	Natural fisheries: 169 of 245 species disappeared upstream of dam	

Note: Data for this table have been extracted from a Thai Development Research Institute report

Sources: Hirsch (2010: 315); and see WCD (2000), TDRI 2000

They also warn, however, against seeing any particular approach as offering a 'panacea'; all management structures, in their view, need to be decentralized, reflexive, adaptive and experimental if they are to be sensitive to difference, both human and biophysical. The challenge, and it may be an insurmountable one, is whether such an ethos can be aligned with a planning mentality.

In the context of river basin management, large, multi-purpose dams, for many activists, have taken on an emblematic significance, embodying the arrogance of the state, multilateral agencies and 'experts' who have overlooked their costs and overestimated their returns. This is all too clear in the experience of north-east Thailand's Pak Mun Dam, where returns were consistently overstated, and costs/impacts either understated or ignored (Table 2.5). The executive summary of the Thai Development Research Institute's (TDRI) assessment of the dam is illustrative of this planning gap:

> A re-examination of the premises that were used to justify the construction of Pak Mun on economic grounds does no one credit. It is evident that EGAT over-stated the case of project benefits ... The National Economic and Social Development Board (NESDB), responsible for vetting infrastructure investments, failed to challenge the critical assumptions underlying the project's economic feasibility ... Its given title as a multipurpose development project is misleading. The attribution of its irrigation benefits was at best conjectural ... (TDRI 2000; see also Foran and Manorom 2009)

Across the rich and poor worlds, social activists are empowering local communities, furthering bio-regionalism, and challenging the authority of governments and scientists to shape river basins according to the designs of planners. In the introduction to their volume on the Mekong basin, Molle et al. (2009a: 12) note the way in which the planning and development of this vast river basin, encompassing six riparian countries (Cambodia, China, Myanmar, Lao PDR, Thailand and Vietnam) and dating back to 1951 with the establishment of the Mekong Committee, have increasingly been fashioned, not by an ever more informed and effective planning apparatus, but by the actions of national and transnational civil society groups. The failures of planners and planning, and the fractured power of local groups, can be seen reflected in the experience of river basin development in Vietnam.

All river basins in Vietnam have been influenced by human activity and there are tens of thousands of reservoirs, tanks, dams and weirs across the country. However, it is in the country's multi-purpose dams that the planning dilemmas noted earlier in the chapter can be seen manifested at the grass roots. As elsewhere, dams are seen in Vietnam as essential for the country's modernization and industrialization, while, at the same time, also being justified as a means to improve the livelihoods of those living in the river basins concerned (Dao 2010: 326). As Hirsch (2010) points out in his review paper of dams on the Mekong, there has emerged in recent years an 'intricate interplay between geopolitics and eco-politics' which defines the shifting thinking over dams. Even in one-party states like Vietnam and the Lao PDR, not to mention China, the views of new stakeholders have to be taken into account, both local and non-local, such that decision-making has become rather more deliberative and inclusive (ibid.: 313; and see Käkönen and Hirsch 2009). In the 1960s and 1970s, dam building and river basin development were firmly embedded within a development planning milieu. The 'value' of dams was viewed in terms of their contribution to national economic production, whether in the form of power (electricity) or agricultural outputs or, preferably, both.[28] Increasingly from the 1980s, developmental concerns framed in terms of aggregate economic returns to dams in particular and river basin development more generally have come to be matched by five other sets of issues which have immeasurably complicated the planning process: by a growing eco-political awareness; by a growing cognizance of the social impacts of river basin development; by a growing recognition of the important of the voice(s) of local people and groups in affected areas; by a growing acceptance of the legitimacy of the roles of stake-holder in wider civil society; and by a transnationalization of advocacy. Taken together, these have provided a powerful countervailing force to the modernist current that has tended to inform the actions of planners and governments.

The planning framework for river basins in Vietnam has been transformed since the turn of the millennium. In 2002, River Basin Planning Management Boards (RBPMBs) were created for the country's three major river basins (the Mekong – or Cuu Long – Dong Nai and Red River-Thai Binh) to manage and coordinate development, and River Basin Organizations (RBOs) were also established as cross-cutting entities to join up the various competing interests (see Molle and Hoanh 2007). But RBOs have proved to be relatively toothless, positioned as they are under the auspices of the Ministry of Agriculture and Rural Development (MARD). A cascade of institutional developments has sown confusion rather than improved coordination and planning, notwithstanding the government's attention to many of the changes to the understanding of and approaches to river basin planning. The Ministry of Natural Resources and Environment (MoNRE, established in 2002) and MARD both have roles in strategic water management, with the result that inter-ministerial conflict has escalated (ibid.: 4–5). In addition, within each of these two ministries, confusion over their roles and respective planning responsibilities has grown.

Dao (2010) compares resettlement policies and experiences in relation to two large, multi-purpose dams in Vietnam built twenty-six years apart, the Hoa Binh and Son La dams. In the intervening years the government of Vietnam has embraced many of the lessons of 'best practice' from elsewhere: listening and engaging with local people (to a degree); considering the social and environmental impacts of dam constructions and associated developments; and drawing in stakeholders from wider society, nationally and internationally. Even so, a 'gap remains between improved policy and planning and implementation processes, which demonstrates the difficulties of turning policy into practice' (ibid.: 330).

While for Dao the reasons for resettlement failure lie in the difficulties of 'turning policy into practice' (which certainly should not be underplayed), Hirsch highlights something rather more fundamental and which is situated in the very underpinning logic of planning. He writes that 'affected people's lives and livelihoods *are planned for them* by a wider group of resettlement experts, agronomists and others, but more in the spirit of beneficence than of empowerment through deferral to the rights of people to decide their own futures' (Hirsch 2010: 322, emphasis added). Planning pays lip-service to participation and stakeholder engagement, and remains a technocratic exercise formulated by experts who continue to believe that their rational visions are the 'right' ones, if only people would listen and learn. Taking this view, the very idea of 'participatory planning' becomes almost a non sequitur. Perhaps the most incisive critique of participatory planning in South-East Asia comes in the work of the anthropologist Tania Murray Li, drawing mainly on her research in upland Sulawesi, Indonesia.

Participatory planning in Indonesia For Li (2002a, 2007), sustained state and market failures have created the context for the emergence of community-based alternatives in natural resource management (and much else besides). These have become mainstreamed as Community Based Natural Resource Management (CBNRM), a more effective, efficient, engaged, empowering and environmentally sustainable alternative to the top-down approaches that have gone before. But while CBNRM may provide a powerful alternative framing of development intervention, it does so in a way that also engenders a problematic simplification of people, places, histories and livelihoods. Upland people often do not fit the template that CBNRM marks out; longstanding patterns of discrimination become reproduced in the form of participatory exclusions (see Mosse 2005); and 'community' is reified as a positive counterpoint to the state, when in reality they are mutually constituted.[29]

Given the mainstreaming of participation, the concern for community engagement and the need to include stakeholders at all levels, the optic of state-led development structured by way of overarching development plans has been supplanted by more decentralized, less hegemonic and seemingly more democratic approaches. This is not just reflected in the work of NGOs but also in that of multilateral agencies such as the World Bank and the Asian Development Bank. As Li writes of the ADB's work in Sulawesi:

> Alert to the critiques of clumsy top-down interventions, the Asian Development Bank's massive Central Sulawesi Integrated Development and Conservation project was very thoroughly researched by anthropologists, ecologists, agronomists, and other experts. It included components for community development, participation, and micro-credit – and the leading edge of 1990s development thinking. It failed, one might argue, because it was not executed according to plan. (Li 2007: 274; and see Li 2005)

Li calls this attempt to fine-tune development the 'improvement of improvement', but is not convinced that the endless tinkering with development to find the correct, magic combination of ingredients – the 'witches' brew' (Li 2007: 271), as she calls it – really addresses the core limitations of development planning and intervention. Instead she highlights three issues which point to a more fundamental set of limiting issues (ibid.: 275–6). First, the character of the ruling regime. If a state regime, such as Indonesia's, routinely ignores people's rights and orchestrates violence against the subjects of development then we cannot blithely assume that they wish the best for their citizens. Development, as she says, works within power's matrices. Following on from this and secondly, development is about power relations and, more particularly, the power of those who 'do' development (including its design), and those who are the targets of such interventions. Participatory and community-based approaches cannot escape the 'paradox of government through community', wherein the perceived deficiencies of local people and communities, and the absence of particular capitals – such as human (skills, knowledge) and financial (credit) – are met by expert advice and targeted interventions (ibid.: 237). Participation operates within a developmental space that is quite tightly demarcated.[30] And thirdly, the new ethos of participatory, empowering and locally sensitive development tends to overlook the structural roots of inequality, placing the locus of development intervention on the objects of development (i.e. villagers, workers) and not on the way the agents of the state operate (ibid.: 267). This is a major oversight. All in all, it means that the endless tinkering of development interventions as each era's development insight is incorporated fails to make much difference. Even major paradigmatic shifts, such as that towards community-based, participatory development, characteristically end up as disappointments: 'new programs routinely retain the limitations of the programs they replace' (ibid.: 275).

Alternatives to planning: a conclusion and a beginning

National development planning has, as this chapter has set out, produced consistently disappointing results. This is not restricted to South-East Asia. The experience from other developing regions is much the same (see Boettke 1994; Byrd 1990). The chapter has also suggested that the reasons for this only partly lie in a lack of articulation and support. In other words, correcting the disappointments of the past does not mean more and better planning. Rather, the contention of the chapter is that development planning as an exercise is a fundamentally flawed and therefore futile project.

The lesson to be drawn from a half-century of development planning is one of multiple and layered failure. The plans themselves are not infrequently based on faulty or incomplete data; the analysis of the data is problematic; the plans themselves, far from being 'objective', technocratic documents, are resolutely political and not infrequently highly overambitious; implementation is characteristically partial and held hostage to interest groups; and the assumptions on which all plans are based are quickly overtaken by events. Perhaps the biggest planning assumption of all is that planners are in a position to understand the complexities of the development process, have a firm grasp on the current situation (*what* it is, and *why* it is as it is), and can see even a handful of months over the event horizon. When plan targets are met – and in Asia they often have been – it is more by accident than design, and it is hard to find convincing examples of plans that have *caused* growth. Given the number and range of fundamental barriers impeding the effectiveness of development planning, it would seem reasonable to conclude that the challenges are insurmountable.

Of all the market and quasi-market economies of Asia, the country which has had the longest love affair with planning is India.[31] The failures that have been highlighted in the Indian case resonate with the discussion in this chapter. For Byrd (1990) – writing in 1990 and therefore before the liberalization of the Indian economy – four sets of factors can be highlighted to explain the failure of planning in India: (1) misperceptions ('problematic premises') about the nature of economic development reflected in export pessimism, market distrust and over-optimism about the efficacy of the public sector and the planning mechanism; (2) faulty or inappropriate implementation mechanisms; (3) the power of interest groups that have blocked reform and appropriated resources; and (4) lack of flexibility and slowness to learn from experience.

This is not to say that the objectives of planning in India and in South-East Asia are undesirable. We can point, for example, to the need to meet certain social objectives (health, education, poverty); to avoid uncontrolled environmental decline; and to anticipate problems and avoid or minimize them. However, planning in the manner in which it often continues to be pursued across the global South is not the means to achieve these desirable ends. National planning is best distilled into a *national development strategy* – a statement of desirable ends that explicitly recognizes the politics of development, which acknowledges the limited capacities governments have at their disposal, and which accepts that events will be unsettling.

This, then, returns to a point noted earlier and which can be traced back over almost half a century of planning debates: what is the proper role for government in managing development? There is no question that governments have to do some things; this is desirable and necessary. There are market failures as well as fallible states, and the former is explored in the next chapter (Lall 1996: 23). The trick is to know what things to do, what not to do, and when and how to do them. As the economic history of Asia demonstrates, in addressing these questions, governments have tended to be more wrong than right. There are four main alternative avenues to comprehensive development planning:

1 Sustained and structured investment in social goods such as education, health and social security, and in environmental protection
2 The creation of an 'enabling' environment for economic development through investment in roads and the infrastructure of a modern economy
3 The setting out of an industrial policy such as that associated with the East Asian developmental states
4 Instigating a process of devolved, participatory grassroots planning.

Regarding the last of these, Rodrik (2007) and Sen (1999a) propose that rather than development plans being devised from above (the 'blueprint' approach), based on a set of plan-rational assumptions about what is best, what is desirable, what is logical and what is possible, plans should be built from the bottom up through the creation of participatory political institutions that are 'thickly democratic', in Sen's phrase. This makes the production of institutions and their policies and programmes not a means to an end, but an end as well as a means. Planning, in this way, becomes part of a process of deliberative development (Evans 2004). This is similar to radical or insurgent planning, which is action-oriented and provides diverse social, ethnic and political (e.g. labour) groups with a role and a stake in planning (see Friedmann 2003). A point to bear in mind is that, as Tania Murray Li has shown, even taking this approach to planning seldom breaks power's matrices. The disappointing experience of even participatory development planning should not, however, lead us to think that the 'answer' is to turn to the market for a corrective. As the next chapter will show, market failures are at least as prevalent and problematic as the government failures just discussed.

3 | State and market perfections and imperfections

The central economic paradox of our time is that 'development' is working while 'development policy' is not. On the one hand, the last quarter century has witnessed a tremendous and historically unprecedented improvement in the material conditions of hundreds of millions of people living in some of the poorest parts of the world. On the other hand, development policy as it is commonly understood and advocated by influential multilateral organizations, aid agencies, Northern academics, and Northern-trained technocrats has largely failed to live up to its promise. We are faced with the confluence of two seemingly contradictory trends. (Rodrik 2007: 85)

Introduction: from Asian miracle to Asian crisis

The Asian economic crisis broke in Bangkok on 2 July 1997 when the Bank of Thailand gave up its efforts to support the Thai baht in the face of concerted speculative pressure, and the value of the currency collapsed by 20 per cent overnight, and continued to weaken through the course of the remainder of the year. On 30 June 1997, one US dollar would buy 24.7 baht; six months later, at the end of the year, it bought 48.1 baht. Domestic companies that had borrowed foreign currency on the expectation of a stable exchange rate found they were unable to meet their obligations. Hundreds of firms were bankrupted. In consequence, the proportion of non-performing loans held by domestic banks climbed to unsustainable levels, causing the government and then the IMF to step in and support the Thai financial system. Millions of workers were laid off as companies went under, construction projects were abandoned, and the economy contracted by over 10 per cent in 1998. These laid-off workers, many of them poor migrants from rural areas and more often than not ejected from their jobs with barely any severance, retreated to their villages as urban livelihoods evaporated. What began as a currency crisis quickly became a wider banking and economic crisis, and as this hit the real economy so it became a human crisis as people struggled to sustain their livelihoods with no state social security net to speak of and a traditional moral economy fractured by years of modernization. Levels of poverty rose dramatically for the first time in a decade and Thailand's miracle was thrown into reverse (Figure 3.1). Before the end of the year there was a change of government, and a coalition administration led by Democrat leader Chuan Leekpai came to power.

The Thai 'contagion' spread quickly spread to Malaysia, South Korea, the Philippines and, most dramatically, to Indonesia (see Table 3.2). The Indonesian economy shrunk by 13 per cent in 1998, poverty rose from 15 per cent at the onset of the financial crisis (or *krismon*) in 1997 to 33 per cent by the end of 1998, and 36 million additional Indonesians were propelled into poverty (Suryahadi et al. 2003a, 2003b, 2009; and see Dhanani and Islam 2002). With President Suharto's reputation largely built on his ability to deliver improving living standards as *Bapak Pembangunan* – the Father of Development – there was a breakdown in civil order in Jakarta, and he was tellingly ousted from power in May 1998 after thirty-two years as president.

While each country's crisis was, necessarily, *sui generis*, it was in-evitable that they should come to be viewed as part of a collective experience, with some general lessons. The Asian economic miracle had come off the rails, and had done so in spectacular fashion. Within days, headline writers were writing epithets to replace the miracle talk of a few weeks earlier: Asian flu, Asian contagion and Asian debacle, among them. Just as the miracle induced scholars and policy-makers to search for a model – the 'essentials' – that might underpin growth, so the crisis also led to a desire to learn general 'lessons' and to mark out an explanatory model.[1] Of the short-term lessons, the one that should have induced a degree of humility was the failure of almost everyone to predict the Asian crisis (see below). Of the longer-term lessons, the most important was: what is the 'proper' role of the market and the state in industrialization and economic development?

The East Asian financial crisis can be seen as a turning point in the development consensus. Until that time, the eight High Performing Asian Economies (HPAEs) were regarded as role models for the rest of the global South. This, it seemed, was how to 'do' development, as the World Bank so influentially outlined in its *East Asian Miracle* (EAM) report (World Bank 1993). While some commentators may have seen in the experiences of the East Asian economies the invisible hand of the market at work, and others the machinations of the state, to a very large extent both sets of protagonists agreed that there were positive lessons to be learned; the question was: exactly what lessons? The East Asian miracle and the Asian economic crisis represent, therefore, a 'clash of capitalisms' (to use Johnson's [1998] phrase), and a profound difference of opinion over the conditions that led to growth and, then,

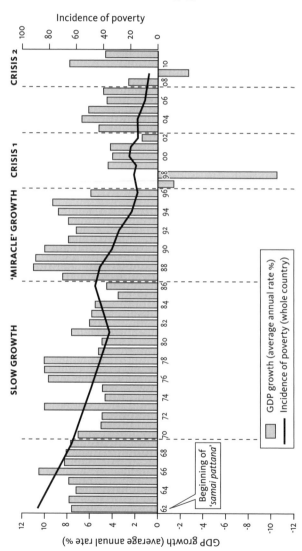

Figure 3.1 Growth and poverty, Thailand: 1962–2011

those that led to collapse. As we will see, while some scholars see in the Asian economic crisis a failure of East Asian capitalism, others view it as indicative of the shortcomings of Western capitalism.

This chapter uses the lens of the two great economic events to have shaped East Asia over the last half-century – the economic 'miracle' of circa 1965–97 and the economic crisis of 1997–99 – to explore three core debates: the difficulty of 'explaining' developmental success and failure even in retrospect and, seemingly, with mountains of evidence; the lamentable inability to anticipate, predict or forecast key economic events; and the question of the proper role of the market and government intervention (the state) in development.

The East Asian miracle, industrial policy and the Asian developmental state

... anyone who predicted in 1950 that within a generation 'miracles' would occur in the [South-East Asian] region would have been regarded as an idle dreamer. (Anderson 1998: 3)

The East Asian miracle: a primer[2] There is little question that something quite remarkable happened in East Asia over the course of the three decades from the mid-1960s through to the mid-1990s. Over this period, a broad swathe of countries experienced rapid and sustained economic growth, and sharp falls in poverty (Table 3.1 and Figure 3.2).

TABLE 3.1a East and South-East Asia: average annual growth of GDP, 1960–97 (%)

	1961–70	1971–80	1981–90	1991–97
East Asia				
China	5.6	6.2	8.9	11.2
South Korea	9.1	9.3	9.1	7.1
Taiwan	–	9.7	8.0	6.5
South-East Asia				
Indonesia	3.9	7.2	5.6	6.8
Malaysia	6.5	7.9	6.0	8.4
Singapore	10.0	9.0	7.4	8.9
Thailand	8.2	6.8	8.0	7.0

Sources: 1961–97 data drawn from Baer et al. (1999: 1736); Quibria 2002; online ADB statistics (beta.adb.org/data/sdbs) and ADB *Key Indicators of Asia and the Pacific* series (see www.adb.org/documents/books/key_indicators/)

TABLE 3.1b East and South-East Asia: average annual growth of GDP, 1997–2010 (%)

	1997	1998	1999	2000	2001	2002	2003
East Asia							
China	8.8	7.8	7.1	8.0	7.3	8.0	10.0
South Korea	5.0	−6.7	10.7	9.3	3.1	6.3	2.8
Taiwan	6.7	4.6	5.7	5.9	-2.2	3.5	3.7
South-East Asia							
Cambodia	3.7	1.8	5.0	7.0	5.7	5.5	8.5
Indonesia	4.7	−13.2	0.2	4.9	3.4	3.7	4.8
Lao PDR	6.9	4.0	5.2	5.8	5.8	5.9	6.2
Malaysia	7.5	−7.5	5.4	8.3	0.4	4.2	5.8
Philippines	5.2	−0.6	3.3	4.4	3.0	4.4	5.0
Singapore	8.4	0.4	5.4	9.4	-2.4	2.2	4.6
Thailand	*−1.7*	−10.2	4.2	4.6	1.9	5.2	7.1
Vietnam	8.2	5.8	4.8	6.8	6.9	7.0	7.3

	2004	2005	2006	2007	2008	2009	2010
East Asia							
China	10.1	11.3	12.7	14.2	9.6	9.2	10.3
South Korea	4.6	4.0	5.2	5.1	2.3	0.3	6.2
Taiwan	6.2	4.7	5.4	6.0	0.7	−1.9	10.8
South-East Asia							
Cambodia	10.3	13.3	10.8	10.2	6.7	0.1	5.9
Indonesia	5.0	5.7	5.5	6.3	6.0	4.6	6.1
Lao PDR	7.0	6.8	8.6	5.9	7.8	7.6	7.9
Malaysia	6.8	5.3	5.8	6.5	4.8	−1.6	7.2
Philippines	6.7	4.8	5.2	6.6	4.2	1.1	7.6
Singapore	9.2	7.4	8.7	8.8	1.5	−0.8	14.5
Thailand	6.3	4.6	5.1	5.0	2.5	−2.3	7.8
Vietnam	7.8	8.4	8.2	8.5	6.3	5.3	6.8

Note: Crisis countries (Indonesia, Malaysia, South Korea and Thailand) and years (1997, 1998, 1999), in *italic*.

Sources: 1961–97 data drawn from Baer et al. (1999: 1736); Quibria (2002); online ADB statistics (beta.adb.org/data/sdbs) and ADB *Key Indicators of Asia and the Pacific* series (see www.adb.org/documents/books/key_indicators/)

While there were scholars and activists who highlighted the widening inequalities that seemed to be going hand in hand with this economic expansion in East Asia (see ADB 2007), not to mention the environmental costs of fast-track industrialization (Bryant and Parnwell 1996), it is

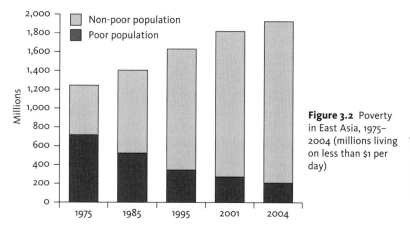

Figure 3.2 Poverty in East Asia, 1975–2004 (millions living on less than $1 per day)

nonetheless still the case that more people were lifted out of poverty during this period of a little more than a generation than ever before in human history, some 370 million between 1975 and 1995, and a further 163 million between 1995 and 2004 (Figure 3.2) (World Bank 1998: ix).[3] That this was a remarkable achievement – and in developmental as well as economic terms – I regard as clear; that the experience was 'miraculous' is rather more questionable; and why it occurred when it did and with what policy implications yet more questionable still.

There are also two caveats to note here, which are discussed in detail in Chapter 5 (see p. 113): first, data such as those depicted in Figure 3.2 give the impression that there is a fixed stock of poor people and that with growth some of the individuals that make up this stock are lifted out of poverty; as Chapter 5 explores, there is much more movement between the poor and non-poor populations than this view permits. The second caveat concerns where we draw the poverty line. If we draw it at $1 a day then between 1990 and 2005 the population of poor people shrank by 36 per cent in the Asia Pacific region at a time when the population as a whole grew by almost a quarter. If we take a $2-a-day line, however, then the poor population declined by just 15 per cent (Figure 3.3).[4]

The Asian miracle is associated most clearly with the *East Asian Miracle* (EAM) report of the World Bank (1993) noted above. This report identified eight High Performing Asian Economies (HPAEs) and wrote of them:

> The eight HPAEs are highly diverse in natural resources, population, culture and economic policy. What shared characteristics cause them to be grouped together and set apart from other developing economies?

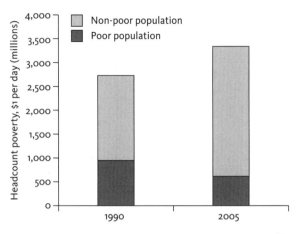

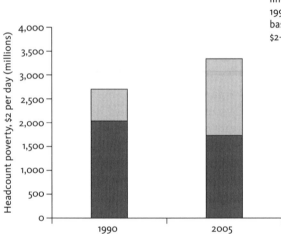

Figure 3.3 Drawing lines: poverty in Asia, 1990 and 2005 (millions) based on $1-a-day and $2-a-day poverty lines

First ... they had rapid, sustained growth between 1960 and 1990. ... The HPAEs are unique in that they combine this rapid, sustained growth with highly equal income distributions. They also all have been characterized by rapid demographic transitions, strong and dynamic agricultural sectors, and unusually rapid export growth. (Ibid.: 8)

Since the publication of the original report two follow-up studies have been published by the World Bank, *Everyone's Miracle?* (Ahuja et al. 1997) and *Rethinking the East Asian Miracle* (Stiglitz and Yusuf 2001). The first of these implicitly widened the HPAE grouping to include a further tier of miracle economies, consisting of Vietnam and China. In fact, in terms of the periodization of their growth, we can identify four groupings of East Asian 'miracle' economies (Table 3.2). The original East Asian growth economy of Japan; the first-tier NIEs of East Asia (Hong Kong, Singapore, South Korea and Taiwan); the second-tier growth economies of South-East Asia (Indonesia, Malaysia and Thailand); and a third tier of late-industrializing East Asian economies, namely China and Vietnam. While all these countries are East Asian in terms of their geographical setting, in other respects they could be said to be more different than they are alike. Their growth experiences stretch across half a century; they range from the city-state of Singapore with a population of 5 million to China's 1,300 million; they span the Confucianist cultures of Japan, South Korea and Taiwan, the Muslim-dominated countries of Indonesia and Malaysia, and the Theravada Buddhist countries of mainland South-East Asia; they include single-party communist states through to putative democracies; and they encompass a diverse assortment of institutions and policies from among which it is hard to pick out many common features. Nonetheless, there has been a persistent desire to search for commonalities or shared experiences that might link these diverse places. Nor is this an effort rooted in the past. The Dutch Ministry of Foreign Affairs-funded 'tracking development' project (2006–12) has taken four South-East Asian and four African countries with the aim of 'seek[ing] answers to the question of why Southeast Asia and Sub-Saharan Africa have diverged so sharply in development performance in the last 50 years' (www.trackingdevelopment.net/, and see p. 179) This debate over the 'essence' of the Asian miracle, in summary and at risk of collapsing a wide-ranging discussion, reflects six sometimes overlapping positions.

To begin with, there are those scholars who have explained East Asia's success in terms of the operation of the market, sometimes reduced to the term 'getting the fundamentals right'. This has been largely associated with the neoliberal establishment in Washington, hence spawning the expression the 'Washington Consensus' to encompass the views of the World Bank, the IMF and the US Treasury (see Berger and Beeson 1998: 494–5; World Bank 1993: 82–3).[5] With reference to Hong Kong, South Korea, Singapore and Taiwan, Chen, for example, argues that 'What the state has provided is simply a suitable environment for the entrepreneurs to perform their functions' (Chen 1979: 183–4, quoted in World Bank 1993: 82, and Baer et al. 1999: 1738–40). At its crudest, this position is that even when governments have intervened in Asia, these interventions have been ineffective, even negative in their effects (see Yusuf 2001: 20–5).

TABLE 3.2 Tiers of East Asian miracles

Country	Periodization of onset of rapid growth	Population (millions, 2010)
Original East Asian developmental state		
Japan	1954–80	127.4
Tier 1: First-generation East Asian NIEs		
Hong Kong	1961–80	7.1
Singapore	1969–85	5.1
South Korea	1961–90	48.9
Taiwan	1961–90	23.1
Tier 2: Second-generation South-East Asian NIEs		
Indonesia	1987–97	234.2
Malaysia	1988–97	28.3
Thailand	1986–95	67.3
Tier 3: Third-generation East Asian late developers		
China	1990–present	1,339.7
Vietnam	1992–present	86.5

Note: The 'periodization of growth' column refers to the period when industrial expansion 'took off'; several of these countries have had more than one period of rapid growth

Source for statistics: ADB (2011)

Secondly, there are those scholars and policy-makers who see in Asia's growth a critical role being played by the state in shaping the miracle that occurred, mainly through state-orchestrated industrial policies. This group are sometimes termed the 'revisionists'. The policy-makers who took this view were largely based in Asia and particularly in Japan, where the Ministry of International Trade and Industry (MITI) was particularly influential in pursuing an alternative explanation for Asia's success to that emanating from Washington.[6] From this line of argument emerged the thesis of the Asian 'developmental state', which is explored in greater detail later in this chapter. Even among those who took this line, however, there were substantial differences of opinion over the sorts of state interventions that were positive and necessary, and those that might impede and even hinder economic growth. Nonetheless, all saw an important role being played by the state in East Asia's economic development and therefore in explaining the region's economic success.

A third line of discussion focuses on the role of culture in accounting for Asia's economic transformation. After all, it has been plausibly reasoned, all these countries are Asian and therefore could there be something about the nature of Asian culture and society that has provided particularly fertile ground for economic growth – a 'magical' cultural ingredient? From this emerged the thesis of Asian values or the Asian way, which came to be particularly associated with two influential former prime ministers, Dr Mahathir Mohamad of Malaysia (prime minister from 1981 to 1993) and Singapore's Lee Kuan Yew (prime minister from 1959 to 1990). When Lee Kuan Yew was asked to comment on the EAM report following its publication in 1993, he said the most glaring omission was the failure to address the issue of culture. It was the unique cultural context of East Asia which made, he suggested, the transferability of the miracle to other developing countries so difficult (Zakaria 1994: 116–17).

The fourth line of explanation focuses on the historical conditions, regionally and globally, which existed at the time of the Asian miracle. The role of the Korean War and then the wars in Indochina; the place of US policy in the context of the Cold War, whence Asian allies were given both generous infusions of aid and an umbrella of security; and, rather later, the way in which the forces of globalization led to the active search by multinationals for investment opportunities in the countries of the global South where they could take advantage of the emerging global divisions of labour. This particular historical conjuncture of factors, which benefited first Japan and the East Asian NIEs, and then rather later the second-tier growth economies of South-East Asia, created the enabling conditions for economic expansion.

A fifth line of argument relates the miracle to one-off demographic factors and is particularly linked to the influential economist Paul Krugman. In his paper 'The myth of Asia's miracle' (1994), Krugman argued that East and South-East Asia's economic growth had been based on a massive mobilization of human resources linked to the region's stage in the demographic transition. In Singapore, for instance, the economically active proportion of the population rose from 27 per cent in 1966 to 51 per cent in 1990 (ibid.: 70). In addition, governments made very substantial investments in physical and social infrastructure. 'These numbers', Krugman wrote, 'should make it obvious that Singapore's growth has been largely based on one-time changes in behaviour that cannot be repeated' (ibid.: 71). A similar increase in the economically active proportion of the population also coincided with the economic growth periods of the other countries of the region, delivering a 'demographic dividend' (ADB 2002: 1, and see p. 191). As this demographic dividend has worked its way through the age

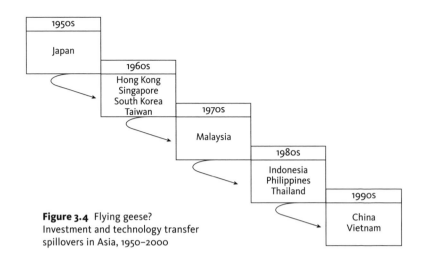

Figure 3.4 Flying geese? Investment and technology transfer spillovers in Asia, 1950–2000

cohorts, so it is being transformed, some scholars and practitioners believe, into a considerable demographic burden, already evident in Japan and shortly to be so in the other countries of East Asia and – later – South-East Asia.

Finally, and least extensively articulated, is a line of explanation which focuses on geography. Not in the sense of Asia being a cultural region (as the Asian values argument would suggest) but in terms of the propinquity of the countries concerned – their proximity to one another. In this argument, which has links to the earlier 'flying geese' metaphor of regional economic growth, Japan – and more latterly the East Asian NIEs – has acted as the linchpin of growth in the wider region, with Japanese firms being the critical actors in propelling Asian foreign-investment-driven, export-oriented industrialization (see Jomo 1996: 56).[7] There have been industrial 'spillover effects' as investment and technology have been transferred from Japan and, rather later, the first-tier East Asian NIEs to the other emerging economies of the region (Ito 2001: 61–2; Yamazawa 1992). The sequencing, as the periodization in Table 3.2 indicates, was as follows: Japan → Hong Kong, Singapore, South Korea and Taiwan → Malaysia → Indonesia and Thailand → China and Vietnam (Figure 3.4). Yamazawa argues that the 'main mechanism underlying ... increasing interdependence in the Asia Pacific region is the transfer of industries, particularly manufacturing industries, from early starters to late comers' (ibid.: 1523).

The purpose of this brief summary of the various positions that scholars and policy-makers have adopted in explaining the Asian miracle is to highlight that even though 'the facts' may be before us, and even with decades of hindsight, there is no consensus on quite what happened to Asia during those remarkable years, quite what the causal linkages were, and quite what the lessons for policy might be. It seems that agreement is achieved only when the lessons are reduced to broad statements such as 'getting the fundamentals right' (World Bank 1993: 347), or emphasizing the role of 'good governance' in achieving economic growth (Berger and Beeson 1998; Thompson 2004a). There can scarcely be anyone who suggests that the route to growth is bad governance and getting the fundamentals wrong (see Lall 1996: 108).[8] Even with regard to bland statements such as these, however, and as we will see when it comes to the Asian crisis, they are often only identified retrospectively. Furthermore, such high-order principles are not infrequently achieved through an array of policies which are quite different country to country and, often, quite unconventional (Rodrik 2007: 39). When we move beyond these general observations to analyse in more detail the correspondence between the ideal of economic success set out in the various models of Asian growth and the experiences of individual countries, there are revealed more anomalies than areas of conformity. This is all too clear when it comes to interpreting Vietnam's recent growth experience, the latest Asian 'success' story.

Interpreting the lessons of Vietnamese growth Vietnam has been the most recent entrant into the pantheon of Asian miracle-growth economies. Since the country embraced *doi moi*, or 'renovation' (economic reform), in 1986, and particularly since the early 1990s, the country's economic expansion has been truly spectacular, turning a stagnant and slow-moving socialist state into a vivacious and fast-changing market economy in little more than a decade (Illustrations 3.1 and 3.2). On the basis of the Vietnamese government's own measures, the incidence of poverty has fallen steeply, from 58 per cent in 1993 to 16 per cent in 2006 (JDR 2007: 4). This decline has been most pronounced in urban areas, where the respective figures are 25 per cent (1993) and 4 per cent (2006) (ibid.: 4).

To what extent has Vietnam's experience conformed to the Washington Consensus, the Post-Washington Consensus, the East Asian Miracle or, for that matter, the explanatory model of the developmental state? While discussions of this kind can get bogged down in detail, there are many more reasons to be sceptical of any clear association than there are to be convinced. Indeed, a checklist (Table 3.3) reveals that, for the large majority of the characteristics of *all four* of these explanatory 'models', the anomalies outnumber those areas of correspondence. The

Table 3.3 Mapping the Vietnamese experience onto growth models

Model	Vietnamese experience
Washington Consensus (1980s)	
Fiscal discipline and austerity	Weak financial sector regulation
Public expenditure priorities	Yes, in physical and social infrastructure
Tax reform	Partial
Financial liberalization	Non-tradable currency, restricted entry, controlled by government
Exchange rate reform	Non-tradable currency
Trade liberalization	Partial; protected state-owned sector geared to domestic market
Openness to foreign direct investment	Yes, but limited to certain sectors and restricted, especially in early years of reform
Privatization	Partial; large and influential state-owned sector
Deregulation	Partial; limited to export and foreign invested sectors; state-owned sector highly regulated
Secure property rights	Only partial
East Asian Miracle (1990s)	
Fundamentally sound macroeconomic policy	Weak financial sector regulation
High levels of domestic saving and investment	Yes
Tax policies favouring investment sectors	Yes, but targeted and channelled to identified industries and sectors
Secure, bank-based financial system with strong regulation and supervision	Weak regulation
Competitive real exchange rates	Non-tradable currency
Pro-export trade incentive structure	Yes, but only for identified industries
Openness to foreign technology and investment	Partial; mostly limited to export industries

Efficient public administration	Inefficient and often corrupt and opaque administration
Disciplined government intervention	Tendency for interventions to be shaped and captured by special interest groups
Investment in building human capital	Yes
Investment in physical capital	Yes
Developmental state (1990s)	
A determined developmental elite	Partially fulfilled
Relative autonomy	Only partial insulation from special interest groups
A powerful, competent and insulated economic bureaucracy	No
A weak and subordinated civil society	Yes, to a significant extent
The effective management of non-state economic interests	No; economic interests and management characterized by moral hazard, rent-seeking, corruption and cronyism
Repression, legitimacy and performance	Yes
Post-Washington Consensus (2000s)	
Good governance	No; moral hazard and rent-seeking widespread, corruption and cronyism endemic
'Get the institutions right'	No; institutional weaknesses still evident in terms of both operation and capacity
Selective regulation	Yes; but these do not always map on to those recommended
Broad set of objectives and instruments	Yes; but instruments often unorthodox
Context-sensitive policies	Yes; but shaping context is often political, reflecting the needs of a one-party communist state
Economics + focused	Yes; but the 'plus' is often political rather than social

Sources: Adapted from Standing (2000), World Bank (1993), Rodrik (2007), Leftwich (1995), Rigg (2003)

Illustration 3.1 Hanoi's streets (and market economy) in 1990

same would be true of the world's greatest recent economic miracle, China. Both China and Vietnam are examples not of any particular 'model', therefore, but of heterodox reform. 'It is difficult to identify', Rodrik writes, 'cases of high growth where unorthodox elements have

Illustration 3.2 Hanoi's streets in 2010

not played a role' (2007: 40). In the case of Vietnam (and this likewise applies to China), perhaps the most significant unorthodox element is the pursuit of what has been termed a 'two track' approach to reform. Vietnam has a vital and internationally competitive, foreign-invested export sector alongside a protected, regulated and inefficient state-owned sector geared to the domestic market. Moreover, state interests span this divide, having representation in both of these two industrial tracks. While after a quarter-century or so of 'marketiza-tion' one might expect some of this to have impacted on the nature of the Vietnamese state, Gainsborough is of the view that 'the state in Vietnam remains little changed in terms of its underlying political philosophy and many of its practices' (2010: 157; and see Beeson and Hung forthcoming).[9] Even in agriculture, which like China's was the first sector to be reshaped by the reform policies of the late 1980s and early 1990s, the rapid growth of exports (rice, fish, coffee) was achieved in the context of continuing regulation of property rights. There is also, when it comes to interpreting rural reform, an important difference between those who see reform being generated from above – in other words, being led by the state – and those who see it as driven from below, by the 'everyday' actions of ordinary women and men.

Kerkvliet's work (1995, 2005 and 2009) has done most to draw our attention away from assumed perspicacious leaders in the Politburo and other organs of the central state to the individual, low-profile, quiet and mundane actions of ordinary women and men in Vietnam's countryside and towns. As he explains when trying to account for the apparently unproblematic implementation of economic reforms in the north Vietnamese countryside in the mid-1980s:

> Everyday politics matters. ... It can have a huge impact on national pol-icy. Consider what happened in Vietnam. Collective farming, a major program of the Communist Party government, collapsed without social upheaval, without violence, without a change in government, without even organized opposition. Yet national authorities were pressured into giving up on collective farming and allowing family farming instead. To a significant degree, that pressure came from everyday practices of villagers in the Red River delta and other parts of northern Vietnam. To a significant extent, those practices were political because they involved the distribution and control of vital resources. Those everyday politi-cal practices were often at odds with what collective farming required, what authorities wanted, and what national policy prescribed. (Kerk-vliet 2005: 234)

This has led some scholars to wonder whether, in fact, Vietnam is not the 'strong', one-party communist state one might expect but, in fact, a weak state that has surprisingly little capacity to control events and direct its population (see Painter 2003, 2005). Gainsborough (2010) finds this strong/weak state debate rather unhelpful and instead regards the Vietnamese state as *both* strong and weak, depending on where and how we look. The key point in the context of the discussion here, however, is that the Vietnamese state, far from being highly centralized and embodying a strong and effective bureaucracy, is, in practice, characterized by a 'highly decentralised, fragmented and sometimes incoherent set of state institutions' (Painter 2005: 267). This opens up the possibility, and not only in Vietnam, for the actions of ordinary people significantly to shape country-level events. While the developmental state thesis explored in the next section suggests that the East Asian experience was one of strong states and weak societies, the Vietnamese case raises questions regarding whether such a formulation truly describes the nature of state–society relations in Vietnam, and by extension in other places too.

Notwithstanding the range of arguments that have been deployed to account for the Asian economic miracle, the core of the debate can be distilled down to a twin-faceted question: was the miracle largely market based, or was it state orchestrated? This is intimately linked to the debate over the role of industrial policy in Asian economic success, and the emergence of what became known as the East Asian developmental state. It is to these concerns that the chapter now turns.

Industrial policy and the Asian developmental state

> Economists enamoured of the neo-liberal Washington Consensus may have written it off, but successful economies have always relied on government policies that promote growth by accelerating structural transformation. (Rodrik 2010)[10]

There are innumerable examples of planning failures and planning disappointments across the developing world, as the previous chapter outlined. East Asia also has, however, what is often trumpeted as the world's best and most successful example of planning success in the guise of industrial policy and the East Asian 'developmental state'.[11]

Chalmers Johnson's *MITI and the Japanese Miracle: The growth of industrial policy* (1982) was seminal in making this case. In it he argues that the Japanese state prioritized economic development above all else, thus making it a 'developmental state' (rather than a welfare state, a revolutionary state, or a regulatory state). Later, Alice Amsden's *Asia's Next Giant: South Korea and late industrialization* (1989) and Robert Wade's *Governing the Market: Economic theory and the role of government in East Asian industrialization* (2004 [1990]; and see Wade 1988, 1992) extended Johnson's ideas to the East Asian NICs (South Korea especially, but also Hong Kong, Japan and Taiwan). Building on these studies, other scholars have also drawn Singapore into the developmental state paradigm, arguing that it too reflects many of the characteristics of the East Asian NICs. Foremost among the publications to make this case was Rodan's (1989) *The Political Economy of Singapore's Industrialization* (see also Huff 1994, 1995a, b). More recently still, other countries in the wider East Asian region have been labelled developmental or semi-developmental states, including China (Baek 2005), Indonesia (Vu 2007), Malaysia (Beeson 2000), Thailand (Dixon 2001), Vietnam (Beeson and Hung forthcoming) and the South-East Asian economies more broadly (Hayashi 2010).

Whether different countries in Asia are counted as developmental (or 'semi-developmental') states depends in part on how the term is defined – and whether, on that basis, a particular country's experience can be shoehorned to fit. In some instances, as Stubbs (2009) observes, no definition is provided, simply a checklist of characteristics (Table 3.4). For Weiss this is not altogether helpful, with 'nowadays, the term "developmental state" [being] so loosely applied that it has become virtually synonymous with "the state is East Asia"' (2000: 23). Lying at the core of most (but not all) accounts of the developmental state, however, are two elements: the presence of an insulated (or autonomous) elite developmental bureaucracy; and a society that can be shaped and directed in line with developmental state policies and whose legitimacy emerges from the success of these policies.[12] We can add a third element to the mix, which not all scholars explicitly mention, but which is usually tacit: an international political and economic environment conducive to such policies. This introduces an important historical component to understanding the emergence and success of developmental states.

While central and comprehensive planning may have fallen into disrepute, the industrial policies associated with these developmental states have remained attractive and persuasive, not least because of the evident economic success of the high-performing Asian economies, and the temporal association of that success with sustained government intervention. While there are many things that separate the countries of East and South-East Asia, as noted above, they all had industrial policies – even Hong Kong in the sense that its industrial policy was

TABLE 3.4 Pinning down the developmental state

Themes	Johnson (1982)	Leftwich (1995)	Deans (2004)	Öniş (1991)	Wade (2004 [1990])
State autonomy	Political system in which the elite bureaucracy can take the initiative and operate autonomously	A determined developmental elite	The blurring of the public/private	Strong and autonomous state	
Political/civil society context		A weak and subordinated civil society	State ideology		Disciplined rent-seeking achieved by authoritarian or illiberal democracies
Market intervention	Use of market-conforming approaches to state intervention in the economy	The effective management of non-state economic interests	Developmental legitimacy	'National rationality' over 'market rationality'	Transfer of resources from 'productive' to 'unproductive' sectors
International (and domestic) environment	Situational imperatives		Favourable international context		Favourable Cold War international context
Industrial policies	An overarching agency that directs industrial policy – in Japan's case, MITI	Legitimacy based on economic performance*	Plan rationality	Focus on rapid industrialization over profitability	Distorting markets through targeted industrial policies
Bureaucratic elite	Small, elite state bureaucracy staffed by the best managerial talent	A powerful, competent and insulated (autonomous) economic bureaucracy	Autonomous economic technocracy		

Note: * In Singapore this is sometimes referred to as a 'prosperity consensus', while in Indonesia, former President Suharto's (1965–98) position was intimately linked to his ability to deliver on the promise of development. In this interpretation, the failure of the Indonesian economy during *krismon* (1998–2000) led, inevitably, to his ousting from power.

Sources: Information extracted from Stubbs (2009), Leftwich (1995), Wade 2004 [1990], Johnson (1982), Deans (2004), Öniş (1991)

China's (Stiglitz 2001: 519). The 'revisionist' view of East Asian success can be contrasted with that of those scholars who emphasized the role of the market in explaining the region's economic success. Out of this debate emerged what has often been presented in rather stark, even binary, terms: was Asian economic success directed and stage-managed by the state or was it an outcome of the invisible hand of the market? This, needless to say, oversimplifies a discussion which reveals fine gradations along a spectrum from state to market (Table 3.5).[13]

For Wade, the key issue is not so much state intervention, as state leadership. The state, through a skilled, independent and autonomous bureaucracy,[14] had the opportunity to shape and pursue policies that would enhance industrial performance. He termed this 'governing the market', which, in East Asia at the time, meant by relatively authoritarian and corporatist states (Wade 2004 [1990]: 297). Wade identifies two key characteristics of the East Asian developmental states and their industrial policies. To begin with, they were sufficiently strong or 'hard' relentlessly to pursue the industrial policies identified and in the process 'not only to resist private demands but actively to shape the economy and society'. And secondly, the industrial policies sought to 'make' winners, and not simply to 'pick' them. He summarizes his argument as follows:

> ... the central economic mechanism of the capitalist developmental state is the use of state power to raise the economy's investible surplus; insure that a high proportion is invested in productive capacity within the national territory; guide investment into industries that are important for the economy's ability to sustain higher wages in the future; and to expose the investment projects to international competitive pressure whether directly or indirectly. (Ibid.: 342)[15]

What is important and different is not that these East Asian development states discovered industrial policy – which has a long pedigree (see Grant 1995) – but that they were able and in a position to pursue such policies in a coordinated, consistent and commanding manner.

There are many reasons to see the East Asian NICs' success – and their *ability* to govern as they did – as historically contingent. Korea and Taiwan were authoritarian states, operating during the Cold War under conditions of considerable military threat and benefiting massively from US largesse; Japan, Korea and Taiwan had to contend with enormous dislocations in society following division and/or conflict, almost legitimizing a strong role for the state; Singapore was coming to terms with its ousting from the Federation of Malay States in

TABLE 3.5 State to market, and points between

Term	Position
Free market (laissez-faire)	A minimalist state, limited to upholding the law, protecting property and rights, representing a country abroad, and protecting a country and its people from external threats
Simulated free market, or 'market enhancing'*	An interventionist state that *simulates* the free market through policies that bring prices very close to those that would prevail in a free market
Indicative planning	The setting, usually, of sectoral targets which may be guided by grants, taxes and incentives but which the private sector is not compelled to meet
Rent-seeking+	Government restrictions on economic activity (common even in market-oriented economies), leading to rent-seeking as people and companies compete for the rents that such restrictions can bestow
Following the market	Government adopts policies in line with proposals or pressures emanating from the private sector, and in that sense 'follow' the market
Guided capitalism	Enterprises are free to operate but the government will either directly participate in and/or guide certain industrial activities
State leadership (leading the market)	Government takes initiatives and designs policies to promote certain industries or activities in line with state-identified strategic objectives. In this form of intervention, governments 'lead' the market
Governing the market	Policies, incentives and controls govern market processes such that investment and support are channelled in line with government-set priorities
Commanding the market	The market is virtually redundant; the state owns the means of production, sets targets and determines the nature, direction and character of industrial growth

← More market

More state →

Notes: * The term 'market enhancing' is used in Aoki et al. (1997) + See the separate discussion of rent-seeking, as distinct from corruption, in this chapter

1965; and Hong Kong had a revolutionary China under Mao Zedong on its doorstep actively exporting revolution during the early years (1966–68) of the Cultural Revolution (1966–76). The role of the USA in providing a security umbrella, delivering military and economic aid, and in opening its markets to imports from East Asia was critically important. Johnson writes of Japan that 'it would be to reason in an ahistorical and ill-informed manner to fail to note that Japan's high growth system was the product of one of the most painful passages to modernity any nation has ever had to endure' (1982: 306–7). In focusing on the historical conditions that accompanied the emergence of East Asia's developmental states, history becomes not just the backdrop *of* change, but the context *for* change (see Vu 2007).

There are also scholars (e.g. Hill and Chu 2006: 47) who, while accepting that the East Asian NICs have experienced rapid growth and have adopted highly interventionist industrial policies, question whether there is any convincing demonstration of causality. It has been suggested that the tendency in South-East Asia, with the exception of Singapore, has been for promotional industrial policies to be hijacked by interest groups and lobbies, and to be inconsistently rather than consistently pursued. Hill and Chu (ibid.: 48) claim that industrial policies in Indonesia during the 1970s and 1980s, in Thailand between 1970 and 1989, and in Malaysia over the period from 1978 to 1986 were ineffective in generating growth and shaping development, and show little evidence of causality between government assistance and performance. Thailand may have been one of the fastest-growing economies in the world from the mid-1980s to the early 1990s (see Figure 3.1), and labelled a 'semi-developmental' state on the basis of the country's industrial policies and their partial adherence to the East Asian paradigm (Dixon 2001), but it is hard to identify a connection between these policies on the one hand and performance on the other (Warr 1994: 220–222, Warr 1999). While there was certainly a shift to export promotion in the mid-1970s, which can be seen reflected in the Third Five-Year National Economic and Social Development Plan (1972–76), the industry interventions that were targeted are *negatively* correlated with sector performance. To put it another way, the industries that the Thai government sought to promote actually performed less well than those that it left alone. Critics of industrial policy in Asia have also highlighted the tendency for industrial policy to be subverted into rent-seeking behaviour – colloquially termed crony capitalism – as the Asian economic crisis (1997–99) illuminated (see below).[16]

Furthermore, the discussion of the high-performing East Asian developmental states, in many respects more different from each other than they are alike, tends to divert attention from so-called 'failed' developmental states, such as India (Maswood 2002: 41). Virtually every developing country has had industrial policies, to the degree that they have promoted or protected particular sectors; for the most part these are said at least to have failed, and even to have harmed prospects for development (Rowen 1998: 5). It is, therefore, important to highlight the limits of the East Asian experience – beyond historical contingency – not least because the experience of the countries of South-East Asia (not to mention South Asia) raises questions about the exportability of such an approach.[17]

All that said, it does seem perverse to ignore the experience of the East Asian NICs in considering the potential to 'plan' for development, providing as they do apparently convincing evidence for the efficacy of embedded autonomy in shaping and guiding the development process through a powerful industrial policy. As outlined in this section, there is a strong case to suggest that industrial policy in the East Asian NICs has been strong, effective and, it would seem, successful. Certainly, the balance of power and influence between what Stubbs (2011) terms the developmental state coalitions and the neoliberal coalitions in each East Asian economy has shifted over the years (with the former in the ascendancy from the 1960s to the 1980s, and then again from 1998 onwards, and with the latter being dominant from the 1980s to the late 1990s), but even so the role of the state has been highly influential at critical development junctures. This does not detract from the argument that in the context of wider Asia, not only were the NICs successful because of the historical intersection of a particular and unrepeatable set of economic and political factors and forces, but the experience of other countries should warn against seeing the East Asian NICs as 'exemplars', notwithstanding the World Bank's desire to set them up as such (World Bank 1993). Creating an enabling environment for economic and social development – 'getting the prices right', 'getting the fundamentals right', creating a 'market-friendly' environment – is one thing; to seek to 'pick winners' in the form of an industrial policy is quite another.[18]

From miracle to crisis The Asian economic miracle came to an end, as the opening of this chapter outlined, on 2 July 1997. While the economies of Asia did recover and China, above all, has been transformed in the years since with global ramifications, talk of 'miracles' is muted, the notion that there is some silver bullet for achieving development dulled, and the search for a checklist of development 'do's and don'ts' subdued. This is not surprising in the light of some of the steepest falls in economic output in a century. Instead, the crisis caused scholars and practitioners to reflect on their interpretations and predictions, although not – it should be noted – often in a manner that is resonant of any great sense of humility.[19]

The lessons of the Asian economic crisis

In short, I was 90 per cent wrong about what was going to happen to Asia. However, everyone else was 150 per cent wrong – they saw only the 'miracle', and none of the risks. So while nobody predicted what actually happened, I guess in that sense I came closest. (Krugman 1998)

Hindsight and foresight: predicting crises, predicting miracles As Paul Krugman observes in his characteristic comment above, very few scholars or practitioners predicted the Asian financial and economic crisis.[20] In his paper of 1994, Krugman may have suggested a slowdown in Asian growth, but certainly not the calamitous fall from grace that occurred. Various other commentators had noted certain structural weaknesses in the Thai economy, not least a fall-off in returns to investment, a slowdown in exports, concerns that the property bubble might burst, and an overvalued baht but, again, not to such an extent that these weaknesses might induce a financial and economic crisis of the geographical breadth and economic depth that occurred (see Table 3.5). Baer et al. (1999) suggest that the warnings were there; it is just that people were 'blinded by the miracle' and did not see the writing on the wall (ibid.: 1746). The newly industrializing economies (NIEs) of East Asia contracted by 2.9 per cent while those of South-East Asia (minus Singapore, which is included in the NIE grouping) shrunk by 9.0 per cent (Table 3.6). For the countries most severely affected – Indonesia, Malaysia, South Korea and Thailand – it was their first economic contraction for decades (see Tables 3.1a and 3.1b).

In May 1997, just two months before Thailand's economic collapse, the IMF, the ADB, the World Bank and most independent commentators were predicting continued healthy growth for Malaysia, Indonesia and Thailand (Table 3.6). The expectation was that these economies would expand by between 6 and 8 per cent in 1998. After all, they had been growing through to 1997, and the safe bet seemed to be that they would continue to do so. The Asian Development Bank published a major report in May 1997 entitled *Emerging Asia* which had, as its starting point, the region's economic and social transformation 'unrivaled

TABLE 3.6 GDP growth in Asia, 1998, forecast and actual

| | Actual GDP growth (%) | Forecast GDP growth (%) | | | | | |
| | | IMF | | ADB | | Consensus Economics | |
	1998	1998 (as of May 1997)	1998 (as of April 1998)	1998 (as of April 1997)	1998 (as of April 1998)	1998 (as of June 1997)	1998 (as of April 1998)
Indonesia	−13.2	7.4	−5.0	6.0	−3.0	7.6	−6.3
Malaysia	−7.5	7.9	2.5	5.4	3.5	8.0	1.1
Philippines	−0.6	6.4	2.5	5.4	2.4	6.3	2.2
Singapore	0.4	6.1	3.5	6.0	3.0	7.3	2.7
South Korea	−6.7	6.3	−0.8	4.5	−1.0	6.1	−1.6
Thailand	−10.2	7.0	−3.1	4.0	−3.0	5.9	−4.1
East Asian NIEs	−2.9	–	–	–	–	–	–
South-East Asia	−9.0	–	–	–	–	–	–

Notes: The East Asian NIEs and South-East Asia grouping figures are the simple weighted arithmetic means based on the size of each economy in 1995/96 in current US$. The East Asian NIEs include Hong Kong, Taiwan, South Korea and Singapore. The South-East Asian group includes all the countries of South-East Asia excluding Singapore (which is included as an East Asian NIE) and East Timor (which had not yet achieved independence from Indonesia in 1998).

Sources: Ormerod (1998); Goldstein (1998: 3); ADB (1997b, 1998, 2000)

in history' (ADB 1997a: 1). The report took the position that Asia's future could be 'gleaned from its recent past' and that there was every reason why the underpinnings of economic success should be 'durable and replicable' (ibid.: 54).[21] In Asia, the ADB saw the operation of 'effective institutions' and 'open economies' playing a leading part in the region's successful economic transformation ... If only the Bank had waited two months.[22] A similar absence of prescience, of course, can be discerned in the charted prospects of the countries of East and South-East Asia on the eve of the economic miracle – 'idle dreamers', as Anderson describes those who might have been so foolhardy (see the quotation towards the start of this chapter).

While foresight is remarkably thin on the ground, the scholarly landscape is thickly blanketed with hindsight. In the months and years following Asia's fall, economists and commentators produced an avalanche of books and papers deftly identifying the causes of the crisis, reflecting on its implications, and mapping out the lessons to be learned (e.g. Brooks and Queisser 1999; Goldstein 1998; Stiglitz and Yusuf 2001). Relatively few of these commented, let alone reflected, on the elephant in the room: that almost none of these experts was sufficiently expert to see the crisis coming.

There has been a tautological vein to much of the analysis of Asia's miracle growth and then crisis decline. When things were going well, the governments of these countries were doing the right things – getting the fundamentals right, in the wording of the EAM report; when the crisis hit, good governance quickly became reframed as crony capitalism: 'In light of the events of 1997–98, it is impossible to find an observer who will argue that the Asian tigers have benefited from prudent government' (Baer et al. 1999: 1744; and see Jomo 2003: 4).[23] Neoliberals, who were happy to play up the role of the market rather than government during the boom years, deftly shifted tack to emphasize the distorting effects of the state as the central cause of the crisis. In fact, however, the role of government in resource allocation was actually declining over the course of the 1990s so that the role of the state was diminishing in the years leading up to the crisis. As Stiglitz (2001: 517) says, the evidence is in fact contrary to those who saw the market driving success, and the state determining failure. If anything, it was the other way around.

In the early months after the crisis there was a stark difference of opinion between those economists who explained the crisis in terms of 'crony (Asian) capitalism' and those who instead focused on excessive liberalization of the afflicted countries' capital markets. For the market purists, there was a certain satisfaction in thinking that the model of the developmental and interventionist state had failed. It is now broadly accepted, however, that one of the key reasons for the Asian financial crisis was not excessive state action but the excessive liberalization of financial and capital markets – a degree of liberalization that helped fuel a real estate bubble in Thailand and left the baht, and other Asian currencies, open to speculative attack when the flow of short-term capital reversed (see Stiglitz 2000). It is this view which led to the emergence of what quickly became termed the Post-Washington Consensus (PWC, see below), and which re-energized the debate over the proper role of the state in economic development (see Öniş and Senses 2005). It is seen as no accident that those Asian countries which were not afflicted by the crisis – China particularly, but also India, Taiwan and Sri Lanka – were those which had not liberalized (opened) their financial and capital markets. But before turning to these two concerns, it is worthwhile first considering market herd instincts.

The epidemiology of crisis: the Asian contagion and herd mentalities One of the reasons why it became normal to talk of *an* Asian crisis was because of the way in which Thailand's economic collapse reverberated through the region, making it tempting to draw epidemiological parallels and to see the crisis as a 'contagion', with shocks-as-infection being transmitted from one country to another (Baig and Goldfajn 1999). The fact that these countries were so different has led some analysts to see in the crisis an irrational, herd mentality in operation. For Radelet and Sachs (1999: 3) the Asian financial crisis was, therefore, as much a crisis of *Western* capitalism as it was a crisis of Asian capitalism, because it exposed the inherent instability of markets. In their study of the wild fluctuations in markets during the Asian financial crisis, Kaminsky and Schmukler (1999) conclude:

> Our main results indicate that some of the largest one-day swings cannot be explained by any apparent substantial news, economic or political, but seem to be driven by herd instincts of the market itself. ... Moreover, as the crisis deepens, daily reactions in the absence of relevant news become more pronounced perhaps indicating an increase in uncertainty and asymmetries in information, which can magnify the contagion effect ...

In this way, understanding the crisis and, in particular, the progress of the crisis requires an understanding of its subjective, psychological and pathological underpinnings, as well as its 'objective' causes. For Jomo

(2005: 18) it was 'incredible' that the IMF did not appreciate this fact; had it done so, then the Fund might not have instituted the austerity measures it did, an approach which in the eyes of many analysts made a serious situation even more so by undermining investor confidence at a critical juncture (e.g. ibid.; McLeod 1999; Lim 2004; Chandrasekhar et al. 2004). Terms such as 'market jitters', 'panic behaviour', 'positive feedback trading', 'trend chasing' and 'irrational exuberance' have been used to describe the market atmosphere of the moment (Lim 2004: 64–6; Ito 2001; Wade 2004 [1990]: xxviii). This interpretation of the progress of the Asian economic crisis opens up a debate about the role of government intervention in such systemic crises, and the risks inherent in leaving any resolution to market forces.[24]

Off-the-shelf remedies in a world of difference It was not just that the IMF failed to appreciate the subjective and psychological factors driving the Asian contagion; it was also criticized for instituting rescue packages that overlooked the particular conditions that existed in the crisis countries. Having failed to understand the causes of the crisis, the IMF '... was also incapable of designing optimal policies in response to it' (Jomo 2005: 16). Stiglitz describes an approach to financial management by the IMF that regarded financial problems as generic and which treated countries as if they are all alike. Moreover, the pressure of time left little room for developing a framework for intervention that was sensitive to specific country conditions and contexts:

> When the IMF decides to assist a country, it dispatches a 'mission' of economists. These economists frequently lack extensive experience in the country; they are more likely to have firsthand knowledge of its five-star hotels than of the villages that dot its countryside. They work hard, poring over numbers deep into the night. But their task is impossible. In a period of days or, at most, weeks, they are charged with developing a coherent program sensitive to the needs of the country. Needless to say, a little number-crunching rarely provides adequate insights into the development strategy for an entire nation. Even worse, the number-crunching isn't always that good. The mathematical models the IMF uses are frequently flawed or out-of-date. Critics accuse the institution of taking a cookie-cutter approach to economics, and they're right. (Stiglitz 2000)

The Post-Washington Consensus[25] Even in the aftermath of the Asian financial crisis, there was continuing disagreement over why it occurred and what lessons might be learned from the experience.

TABLE 3.7 From Washington to Post-Washington Consensus

Original Washington Consensus (as it was, based on Williamson 1990)	Modified Washington Consensus (as it came to be seen)	Post-Washington Consensus (PWC)
Fiscal discipline	Macro	Micro
A redirection of public expenditure towards fields offering both economic returns and potential to improve income distribution (e.g. primary healthcare, primary education and infrastructure)	Fiscal discipline	Good governance
Tax reform (to lower marginal rates and broaden the tax base)	'Get the prices right'	'Get the institutions right'
Interest rate liberalization	Deregulation	Selective regulation
A competitive exchange rate	Narrow set of objectives and instruments	Broad set of objectives and instruments
Trade liberalization	One-size-fits-all policies	Context-sensitive policies
Liberalization of inflows of foreign direct investment	Washington-centred	Developing world engaged
Privatization	Theoretically shaped	Empirically informed
Deregulation (to abolish barriers to entry and exit)	Economics focused	Economics + focused
Secure property rights	Role of international institutions	Role of national institutions

Sources: Expanded based on Vestergaard (2004), Williamson (1990, 2000)

The mainstream view from Washington – encompassing the US Federal Reserve and the IMF, rather less so the World Bank – was that the crisis occurred because states had excessively intervened in market affairs and that this, at its worst, had taken the form of cronyism. 'In country after country', Chanda wrote, 'the story was remarkably similar. Corruption and crony capitalism had weakened solid economies built on years of hard work and prudent investment' (Chanda 1998: 46–7). In this view, the operation of market forces had been fatally impeded by government interventions which had created economies founded on 'know who' rather than 'know how', characterized by rent-seeking or, to give this its more pungent equivalent, crony capitalism. The IMF, most notably of all, ascribed the crisis to a failure of *East Asian* capitalism (Radelet and Sachs 1999), highlighting failures of corporate governance, insider dealing, cronyism, and so forth. Among the conditions that the IMF imposed for their financial support was continuing financial market liberalization.

A second view, which is particularly associated with Joseph Stiglitz, the then chief economist at the World Bank, was that the crisis occurred because of excessive liberalization of crisis economies' financial markets. Stiglitz directly criticized the IMF interpretation of the Asian crisis and even more so its approach to dealing with it, labelling the IMF's policies 'market fundamentalism' and seriously flawed.[26] This led to the emergence of what became termed the 'Post-Washington Consensus' or 'augmented Washington Consensus', at first glance a toned-down and less doctrinaire version of the Washington Consensus (Table 3.7). But on second reading, the Post-Washington Consensus is much more than business as usual: it represents a revisitation of a much-discussed issue: namely, the proper role of the market and the state in development. As Stiglitz has written:

> What is at issue then is not just the size of government, but its role – what activities should it undertake – and the balance between government and the market. The post Washington consensus recognizes that there is a role for a market; the question is to what extent do the neo-liberals recognize that there is a role for the state, beyond the minimal role of enforcing contracts and property rights. (Stiglitz 2004: 3)

The 'proper' role of the market (and the state)

The discussion in this chapter has explored several themes in Asia's growth experience which are germane to the wider thrust of the book. To summarize:

- first, looking back over the last half-century, there is little evidence that analysts, policy-makers or scholars foresaw the key turning points in the region's economic history;
- secondly, the factors behind both the miracle and the crisis continue to be hotly contested;
- and thirdly, attempts to search for commonalities between countries are confronted by the intractable problem of difference.

But of the arguments and differences of opinion that the Asian miracle and the Asian crisis induced, perhaps the most profound was the question of the 'proper' role of the market and the state in economic management. To put it simply, and with the debate over Asia's growth in mind: what should governments do and what should governments leave to market forces, and how should they do these things? This is not a matter just of economics. Even were it possible to arrive at an optimal economic role for the state, there might be compelling reasons – social, political and environmental – to do otherwise.

Plans in the real world: the 'proper' role for the state and for the market

> Though the profusion of government must, undoubtedly, have retarded the progress of England towards wealth and improvement, it has not been able to stop it. ... notwithstanding ... a hundred impertinent obstructions with which the folly of human laws too often encumbers its operation. (Smith 1776, quoted in Harris 2002: 41)

Among the commonly highlighted reasons for the poor performance of development plans and development planning is the assumption, prevalent in the three decades from the early 1950s, that planning was necessary to correct for market failures. It was assumed that the state should both spend and intervene more, and planning was part of this effort. From the early 1980s, however, confidence in the ability of technocrats to rationally plan an economy faltered spectacularly, and a 'Washington Consensus' emerged based on the belief that markets are better than states at allocating resources (see the left-hand column in Table 3.7). This coalesced around the assumption that the smaller the state's role in the economy, the better (see Stiglitz 1998a, 1989, 2004). This assumption then led, in turn, to an equally misplaced confidence in the ability of the market to efficiently and unproblematically allocate resources, sometimes termed a position of market fundamentalism.

The key questions for planners became: what should and what can markets do best; and what should and what can governments do best? Or to put it another way, what is the 'proper' role of government (Stern 1991; Stiglitz 1998a) and where does government have a comparative advantage (Krueger 1990)?

What makes this debate particularly complicated is that there are both market failures and government failures and, not unusually, both occur at the same time. The Asian economic crisis was just such a case. The challenge is to identify the pattern of failure across the market and government spectrum, and to respond accordingly. While both neoclassical economists and developmental state theorists would agree that there is evidence of both these forms of failure, they disagree on how such failures should be tackled. Aoki et al., for example, argue that in the context of market failures 'the government's role is to facilitate the development of private-sector institutions that can overcome these failures' (1997: 9). Stiglitz is more pragmatic, proposing that we should not be too focused on the relative sizes of the state and the market in the overall economy (i.e. their respective shares of GDP) but rather pay close attention to *how* the state is involved in the economy (1998a: 25). Given that there are both market failures and socially desirable outcomes that may be market inefficient, there is little question that there is a necessary – and therefore proper – role for the state in development. The state needs to be thoroughly engaged in social investment (education, health), in providing physical infrastructure (roads, water, power supplies – an enabling environment), in protecting vulnerable groups and the environment, in ensuring law and order, in the delivery of good governance (minimizing corruption, rent-seeking, improving the functioning of government departments), and in raising savings and investments (see Stern 1991; Stiglitz 1989; Jomo 2003: 2–3). This, as one can see, is no minor enterprise.

These are so-called functional government interventions which help to mitigate the effects of market failures, and which the World Bank came to view as positive. There are other interventions, however, which are market distorting (rather than market correcting), and therefore which have to be avoided. These are termed 'selective' interventions. Industrial policy, for many neoclassical economists, falls into this second category of market-distorting interventions, as discussed above. The World Bank took the view that market failures, while they did occur, were almost always less costly than government failures (Lall 1996: 126–7), and therefore such decisions should be left to the market rather than second-guessed by government. Applying this schema of 'good' (market-conforming) and 'bad' (market-distorting) interventions to the East Asian miracle highlights the quagmire that the World Bank found itself in when trying to account for Asian growth. It is clear, as the discussion of industrial policy in this chapter shows, that these interventions were important in shaping development in East Asia and cannot be discounted as ineffective at best, and negative in their effects at worst.[27] At the same time, the 'embedded autonomy' (Evans 1989) that is meant to have been characteristic of the first-tier East Asian NIEs cannot be seen to be operating in the second-tier South-East Asian economies, let alone the third tier of China and Vietnam, where corruption, the power of vested interests and rent-seeking (of the illegal kind) are all very much in evidence.

Conclusion

That the developing economies of East Asia have something to say – lessons to impart – to the rest of the world is clear. What, exactly, those lessons are, however, is less evident. When it became apparent in the 1980s that a select group of countries in East and South-East Asia had experienced some of the most rapid and sustained economic growth in history, the World Bank took it upon itself to tease out the 'specific policies [that] contributed to growth, [and] to under-stand the institutional and economic circumstances that made them viable' (World Bank 1993: 7). The World Bank also considered that the Asian experience would have relevance to developing economies across the world, and sought to distil this in its highly influential *East Asian Miracle* report, which in short order became known among the cognoscenti simply by its acronym – the EAM report.

As this chapter has shown, however, there is little agreement over what these growth-inducing policies might have been, perhaps best reflected in the debate over the role of industrial policy in Asian growth. Were the Asian growth economies market-conforming or state-led? The slate of shaping factors variously highlighted to 'explain' Asian growth extends from the nature of the Asian family and the value attached to education in Confucian societies through to the role of US policy during the Cold War and the selective interventions made possible by embedded autonomy. The Asian economic crisis of 1997–99, as unheralded as the miracle of the previous decades, provides a sec-ond insight into the disagreements that characterize both scholarly and policy debates. Not only were the sources of the crisis vigorously disputed, but so too were the solutions put in place by the IMF. As Rodrik writes, the question over what these countries were doing right (and, for that matter, wrong) is one 'of the greatest economic puzzles of our time' (2007: 1).

The discussion above leads away from any existential view as to the 'right' or 'wrong' way to pursue development and shape policies (Aghion et al. 2011). It is not, therefore, whether governments *should* embrace industrial policies, but rather what form those policies should take if they are to achieve desirable social and environmental as well as economic goals; it is not *whether* the state should be involved in such policies, but *how*. The answer to these questions will vary between countries and time periods. A vitally important consideration here is that such policies should not simply enrich business and empower bureaucrats, but serve the interests of society broadly drawn (Rodrik 2010). If the question is not whether but how, then this should lead us to expect a degree of heterodoxy (or eclecticism) in terms of policy when we look across East Asia. The reason why, perhaps, academics have been so loath to define the East Asian developmental state is that it defies definition: no single definition quite captures the evident differences between countries. Hence the tendency to identify 'characteristics', rather than specifying defining features, because no country ticks all the boxes. When we also factor in the role of economic history in continually reworking the spaces of developmental opportunity, then heterodoxy becomes not yet another 'model' (albeit one that is hard to pin down), but an inevitability. Perhaps it is for this reason that the state failure versus market failure debate is never satisfactorily reconciled (see Datta-Chaudhuri 1990). The construction of such a strategic economic development policy 'prescribes free trade, protection, and subsidies in various combinations depending on a country's circumstances and levels of industrialization' (Wade 2004 [1990]: 1). It does not ideologically favour and follow any particular approach, bar one of pragmatism based on the recognition that historical and geographical contexts truly matter when it comes to formulating an appropriate policy mix.

More widely, the debate over the roots of the Asian miracle and the causes of the Asian crisis brought to the fore an area of discussion that can be traced back to the eighteenth century: the role and place of government action in a market economy. Being doctrinaire about this question of the respective role of government and the market in economic management and growth is just as problematic. It is not unusual for the issue to be reduced to the respective size of the public sector as a proportion of GDP. It is not, however, size that matters but rather *the nature* of the state's role: or, to put it another way, *how* it intervenes. And investigating this issue requires that we get our boots muddy in the empirics and specifics of country experiences. Context – environment – really does matter.

There is a further issue which has informed, but not directly, a good deal of the discussion in this chapter: history. Above all, perhaps, what the miracle/crisis diptych has done is highlight the difficulty of second-guessing the passage of history. It is to the problem of history that the next chapter turns.

4 | The teleology of development: history and technology

Introduction

Time's arrow suggests temporal directionality: that the modelling of events possesses a logic of cause and effect such that events can be modelled backwards, as well as forwards. In this scheme of thinking, history is just 'one damned thing after another'.[1] But:

> Lumpiness, rather than smoothness, is the normal texture of historical temporality. These moments of accelerated change ... are initiated and carried forward by historical events. While the events are sometimes the culmination of processes long underway, events typically do more than carry out a rearrangement of practices made necessary by gradual and cumulative social change. Historical events tend to transform social relations in ways that could not be fully predicted from the gradual changes that may have made them possible. What makes historical events so important to theorize is that they reshape history, imparting an unforeseen direction to social development and altering the nature of the causal nexus in which social interactions take place. (Sewell 1996: 843)

This chapter is about the events that Sewell draws our attention to – moments, both grand and seemingly small; events which have had the effect of causing a temporal break in the apparently smooth trajectory of history. We may be able to track back and *attempt* an explanation of the sequence of changes experienced but, characteristically, we lack the ability to look forward and over the time horizon and anticipate when such events might occur, the form that they will take, and the outcomes that will result. This is because those events which characteristically turn one era into the next – wars, environmental disasters, stock market crashes, technological innovations, currency failures, civil unrest, the death of key political leaders – cannot, in the main, be neatly linked to past experience and nor can they, therefore, be mathematically modelled even should economists agree on which model is the right one. The discussion of the Asian miracle and Asian crisis in the last chapter highlighted this important point: that some of the great moments in history – the historical breaks that, with hindsight, have turned one era into the next – come with little warning.[2] The discussion also showed that even looking back and attempting an explanation is none too easy. Just because an event, an intervention for example, appeared to lead to a particular outcome, this does not mean that *ex ante* it will do so again. There are many reasons for this: the fact that historical moments do not repeat themselves; that small changes can have large effects; that causalities are difficult to pin down; and that humans are eccentric, their actions sometimes perverse, and their behaviour notoriously difficult to model. As the Greek philosopher Heraclitus (c. 535–475 BCE) said, 'it is not possible to step into the same river twice'.

It is for these reasons that forecasting, possibly among all the tasks of economists, has been the least successful. At the 2011 World Economic Forum in Davos, a session was convened on the 'perils of economic prediction'. Raghuram Rajan, former director of research at the IMF, admitted that 'we [at the IMF] always failed to predict the [economic] turning point' and 'we were always wrong on Africa', not least because wars and civil unrest have tended to turn things on their head.[3] And it is not just sub-Saharan Africa. The Arab Spring, which blossomed in December 2010, has transformed the Middle East and North Africa. Scholars and commentators were surprised and unprepared in a region which, hitherto, they had often characterized as immune to change. Such surprising political events are not exceptions that prove the rule; arguably, they are the rule. A second difficulty with forecasting is what might be termed the tyranny of the consensus – the tendency among forecasters towards a group mentality whereby forecasts converge on a narrow range of outcomes, quite similar to the herd instincts of investors discussed in the last chapter. This means that it is normal – and it should be expected – for forecasts to be wrong.

This chapter addresses and illuminates the passage of history, and its important interruptions and turning points, using four entry points, from the grand to the apparently inconsequential. First of all, the chapter examines perhaps the greatest development teleology of all: modernization theory and the idea that all countries have embarked on the same historical road, towards 'high mass consumption' founded on capitalism. This section unpicks the modernization discourse to identify three interleaved strands: modernization as theory; modernization as blueprint; and modernization as desire. This threefold distinction is then geographically grounded through a discussion of modernizing the uplands in mainland South-East Asia. This section is followed by an examination of the role of the Plaza Accord of September 1985 in forging the Asian miracle in South-East Asia. While it has become normal to view Asia's success as natural and, therefore, inevitable (a little like the collapse of the Soviet Union), a consideration of the Plaza Accord offers the possibility that the miracle, at least for the late developers in South-East Asia, followed in the wake of a decision taken in Tokyo and Washington which was underpinned by concerns of a very different character. The chapter ends with a discussion of the minutiae of historical events, tracking the emergence of 'boom crops' in South-East Asia and the role of the shrimp-tail pump in revolutionizing farming in the Mekong Delta.

This may appear an uncomfortable mix, from Rostow's non-communist theorizing to why and how Pangasius came to be such an important fish in the lives of farmers in the Mekong Delta. The intention, however, is to reveal the degree to which the passage of history is less a highway of change, which it can appear as we look back over our shoulders, than a maze of dark corners, dead ends and unexpected doorways. History is time spent, but immersing oneself in a historical context is to reveal how 'particular combinations of actors, structures and events coalesced or not (for whatever reason or reasons) at a particular moment to give rise to the outcome that did occur rather than another' (Woolcock et al. 2011: 78). This process creates an 'openness to alternatives' and highlights the indeterminacy of historical paths today. Writing of path dependence in the study of politics, Pierson says that the

> ... prominent modes of argument and explanation in political science ... attribute 'large' outcomes to 'large' causes and emphasize the prevalence of unique, predictable political outcomes, the irrelevance of timing and sequence, and the capacity of rational actors to design and implement optimal solutions (given their resources and constraints) to the problems that confront them. If path dependence arguments are indeed appropriate in substantial areas of political life, they will shake many subfields of political inquiry. This essay argues that they are. (2000: 251)

To state what may seem obvious, but which is often overlooked in the social sciences, events are: partly random; can lead to a range of possible outcomes; are differently sequenced or variously path dependent;[4] and therefore, the history and the *order* of such events matter. Furthermore, even when events are strongly path dependent – i.e. they have a high degree of sequential lock-in – the event(s) that may have initiated the process will be contingent and therefore inexplicable in historical terms (Mahoney 2000: 507–8).

The grandest teleology: modernization theory, modernization thinking

One of the grandest attempts to trend-set the developing world was Walt Whitman Rostow's *The Stages of Economic Growth* (1960). This, more than almost any development text, has been attacked for its teleological presumptions, made all the easier because of Rostow's role as an adviser to US president Johnson during the American war in Vietnam, his links with the CIA, and the way in which the text was used to justify a particular approach to pacification and the securing of order in that and other developing countries at a particularly tense period in world history (see Fisher 2006; Berger 2003: 438; Ish-Shalom 2006). Rostow opens his précis article of 1959, writing:

> This article summarizes a way of generalizing the sweep of modern economic history. The form of this generalization is a set of stages of growth, which can be designated as follows: the traditional society; the preconditions for take-off; the take-off; the drive to maturity; the age of high mass consumption. (Rostow 1959: 1)

The subtitle of the book is at least as important as its main title: 'a non-communist manifesto'. For Rostow, communism is 'a kind of disease which can befall a transitional society if it fails to organize effectively those elements within it which are prepared to get on with the job of modernization' (Rostow 1960: 164). Like many other scholars and development practitioners of the period (see p. 13), Rostow expected governments to take the lead in planning development through direct intervention if they were to avoid the communist trap.[5] Critics of Rostow's stages of growth have been correct to highlight the theory's reductionist and simplifying approach to the development process – seeing the complexities of social and economic change in almost mechanical terms: the traditional society → the preconditions for take-off → the take-off → the drive to maturity → the age of high mass consumption (→ beyond consumption).[6] In critiquing its problematic simplifications, however, these critics have often overlooked its wider significance.

The obvious inheritor of Rostow's mantle is Francis Fukuyama with his highly influential – and almost equally contentious – book *The End of History and the Last Man* (1992), written at the end of the Cold War with the collapse of the Soviet bloc. Not unlike Rostow, Fukuyama has been criticized for what are seen to be his book's teleological simplifications and political undertones. In particular, critics have rounded on his presumption that history has ended in the victory of capitalism and liberal democracy. In response, Fukuyama has clarified that his suggestion that history has ended was not meant as a simple empirical statement (clearly, history has not ended), but a normative one: the combination of free markets and liberal democracy is the best (or the least worst) system we have (Fukuyama 1995: 28–30):

> The assertion ... that liberal democracy constitutes the 'end of history' does not depend on the short-term advances or setbacks to democracy world-wide. It is a normative statement about the principles of freedom and equality that underlay the French and American revolutions, to the effect that they stand at the end of a long process of ideological evolution, and that there is not a higher set of alternative principles that will in time replace them. (Ibid.: 30)

More important in terms of the discussion here, however, is Fukuyama's interest in 'directional history' (ibid.: 31–2). At its core he sees directional history being driven by economic modernization, with the 'only parts of humanity not aspiring to economic modernization [being] a few isolated tribes in the jungles of Brazil or Papua New Guinea, and they don't aspire to it because they don't know about it' (ibid.: 32). He accepts that some societies may choose to modernize differently, often for cultural reasons, but the broad framework within which it occurs is common to all societies and peoples. Even those countries which may have rejected capitalism subscribe to economic modernization. It is on this basis that he makes his defence of modernization theory:

> Modernization theory collapsed in the 1970s under the weight of ... attacks [from its critics], but it should not have. The transition from a premodern to an industrial society is one that affects virtually every other 'story' in a fundamental way, and it affects virtually all societies in some manner, whether or not they have modernized successfully. (Ibid.: 34)

While Rostow's book has come to be seen as seminal in setting out a trend line of development as modernization in the global South, the idea of progress – based on a European teleology – is of considerably greater antiquity. What was notably different between the pre- and post-1945 eras was the way in which ideas of progress became inscribed into the development 'project' (Berger 2003). Progress, therefore, changed from being an immanent or natural process of social, economic and political transformation, on which the hand of the state rested only very gently, to a project to be intentionally engineered, managed and achieved through state policies and sometimes through state fiat (see Cowen and Shenton 1995, 1996). Hart denotes this shift by referring to what she terms 'Big D' development, and 'Little d' development (Hart 2001). It was the Big D development project – the trend-setting of the developing world – rather than the idea of progress itself, which should be counted as new, and in many ways it is this which is the more problematic.

Looking across Asia, there is little doubt that a yearning for development as modernization informs and structures not just what governments do and set out to achieve, but also how people act, and what they believe and hold dear. As Ferguson explains in his account of failed development in Zambia, the modernist meta-narrative and the dualisms that underpin it ('modern' versus 'traditional', 'civilized' versus 'primitive', 'capitalist' versus pre-capitalist, sedentary versus mobile) may constitute a dubious theoretical model but they are, at the same time, an 'indubitable ethnographic fact' (1999: 16, 86).[7] The irony is that while Rostow's neat blueprint for the achievement of the desirable end state end of capitalist modernity has been thoroughly rejected by many scholars, the desire for this end among the subjects of development has actually hardened over time.

States, almost without exception, have marked out courses of development – not infrequently encapsulated in national development plans (see p. 17) – that seek to bring modernity to their populations. This may not have worked out in quite the way envisaged, and policies may have brought hardship rather than affluence to some (see below), but the aims of states and the desires of most people not infrequently intersect. Key words in local lexicons of development are often shorn of the blurred edges that students of development studies are expected to acknowledge. In Indonesia and Thailand, the words for development, *pembangunan* and *kaanpattana* respectively, are replete with the sense of the state-orchestrated achievement of modernity; a gift from government to the people, something to be delivered to a grateful population through various 'interventions' (Demaine 1986; Rigg et al. 1999; Vandergeest 1991; Antlöv 1995: 43). These deliverables are, more often than not, the hardware of development: irrigation schemes, roads, schools, electrification, potable water, and so forth. A slogan of Field Marshal Sarit Thanarat's, the prime minister of Thailand who established the National Economic Development Board and charged it with producing Thailand's first five-year national development plan, was *nam lai, fai sawang, thang di, mi ngan tham, ban daan suk*, or 'running water, widespread electricity, good roads, jobs, [these] create happiness'. The software of modernization has also been inculcated and instilled – rather than delivered – through education, various other avenues of communication and by the media, whether state-controlled or not. In Thailand, young women ache to be *than samai* or up to date (Mills 1997, 1999), while in Indonesia *maju*, modernity, is a largely uncontested goal and people talk disparagingly of ethnic minorities as backward (*masih di belakang*) and lacking progress (*belum maju*) (Elmhirst 1997: 226). The 'left behind' in Asia are those who have been, for whatever reason, left out of the quest for development-as-modernization:

> ... there is much in common in the tales of modernisation and the experiences of modernity across the globe. The 'failed' Zambian migrant worker, the cash cropping peasant cultivator in Guatemala, the young, female factory operative in China or Malaysia, and the pedicab driver in Dhaka, Bangladesh may be separated by geography, history and culture; but they are united in their quest for a better life which is channelled and structured in ways which they would all find familiar. (Rigg 2007: 58)

With this in mind, in discussing and thinking about modernization it is useful to make a threefold distinction between:

- modernization as teleology (modernization theory);
- modernization as blueprint (the development project – means);
- modernization as end state (modern living – ends).

The first of these is a theoretical teleology, with myriad attendant generalizing tendencies and shortcomings; the second constitutes the means by which states set out to achieve modernization, through the intentionalities inscribed in plans and planning, the shortcomings of which have been outlined in Chapter 2; the third is the wish and desire to be modern, deeply embedded and which is no less sought after even when it is not achieved. The failure of development should be read, therefore, as the failure of the development project; this is rarely, however, translated into alternatives to development-as-modernization. The theory is flawed; the blueprints (intentionalities) not infrequently fail to deliver (quite) what is intended or promised; but the ends (modern lives and living) often remain an aching desire even in the context of failure. In this way, the separation of modernization as blueprint and modernization as desirable end state opens up space for a consideration of historical ruptures or breaks. We can see this clearly in the often heated debates between academics, policy-makers and development practitioners over the effects of sedentarization, state land settlement policies, and pioneer incursions into the highlands of mainland South-East Asia.

Modernizing the uplanders and the uplands

> The westerners have been here for so long, building one bridge, one hospital, one school ... villagers are still poor, still living the way they did ten, twenty, fifty years ago. What we bring is *real development, real modernity*. (A senior manager at a Chinese rubber company in Laos, promoting rubber in the upland province of Luang Namtha, quoted in Shi 2008: 72, emphasis added)[8]

One of the most durable geographical, ecological, economic, cultural and political divisions and distinctions in South-East Asia is between the uplands and the lowlands, or between hill and valley. The uplands, traditionally, were beyond the purview and the control of the state (see Scott 2009), inhabited by ethnic minorities with their own distinctive ways of living, who characteristically used various forms of shifting cultivation to sustain a livelihood in forested areas. There may have been a tendency to exaggerate the isolation of such peoples and to see too close an intersection between the highlands as a geographical space and the minorities (hill 'tribes') as the inhabitants of that space ('hill tribes'). It is evident, for example, that there was considerable commercial and cultural intercourse between hill and valley as well as the settlement of lowland peoples in the uplands (see Walker 1999; Forsyth and Walker 2008). Nonetheless, it remains the case that the uplands and their populations were viewed – by governments and low-landers alike – as distinct and different, an ethnic 'other' beyond the geographical frontiers of civilization (Wittayapak 2008; Friederichsen 2012; Winichakul 2000).

Since 1945, and coinciding with the intensification of the moderniza-tion project, the states of mainland South-East Asia, often with the determined support of external agencies, have seen one of their key roles as bringing these uplands areas and their minority populations into the mainstream. Physically, by constructing roads; economically, by bringing 'development' through various projects; culturally, by extending state education and promoting a national language; and politically, by seeking to ensure that highland peoples think of them-selves, first and foremost, as citizens of the Lao PDR, Thailand or

Vietnam. Even before the achievement of independence in 1954, the Vietnamese state in both the north and south of the country saw one of their central tasks as being that of bringing the highland minorities into the mainstream:

> A big part of this responsibility has meant introducing the highlanders to a modern way of life. Later, this modernization imperative would develop into an ideological progression, with the ultimate objective of creating a new 'socialist man' out of the 'primitive highlander'. In the Republic of Vietnam [South Vietnam], Ngo Dinh Diem's government pursued a similar modernization imperative through the rubric of 'Improving the Livelihood of the Highlander Compatriots'. These policies of the Vietnamese state (through its various embodiments) aimed at introducing 'modern' material living (clothing, cooking, entertainment, sports, etc.), planned residential patterns, and modern agricultural techniques to the highlands. (Tan and Walker 2008: 126)

These efforts can be seen visually and verbally reproduced in propaganda posters and state exhortations (Illustration 4.1), where traditional upland living is not infrequently portrayed as primitive, where livelihoods are necessarily fragile and meagre, and where methods of production are regarded as inherently environmentally destructive. As a UNDP report on an integrated rural development project in the highlands of the Lao PDR put it: 'The main type of agriculture in the district is shifting cultivation, which provides only a marginal subsistence and is, as far as the Hmong variant is concerned, extremely destructive to the forest and hence to restoration of soil fertility' (UNDP 1986: 5; see also Forsyth and Walker 2008: 76–84). In Thailand latterly, in Vietnam until recently and in Laos at the present time, governments have pursued policies directed at eradicating shifting cultivation and settling or sedentarizing the hill peoples (Rigg 2005; Souvanthong 1995: 19).

Critiques of such assimilationist and totalizing policies have been many and varied, often highlighting the fact that while development interventions may have brought modernity to the highlands, they have not always brought development to the peoples of the hills (see, for example, Rambo et al. 1995; Santasombat 2003; Chamberlain and Phomsombath 2002; ADB 2001; Laungaramsri 2000). They have been criticized on a range of grounds: on developmental grounds for their often deleterious effects on livelihoods and the well-being of uplanders; on political grounds for their controlling tendencies; on sociocultural grounds for their assimilationist intent; and on environmental grounds for their simplistic and often erroneous interpretations of the causes of

Illustration 4.1 'The route to a new life': modernizing the uplands and uplanders in the Lao PDR

The upland minorities are brought down from their villages in the hills (left, headed 'present') to be provided, through the beneficence of the Lao state, with medical care, electricity, sanitation, schooling and clean water, as well as an abundance of food (right, headed 'future')

environmental decline. There is little doubt of the often crude ways in which development has been extended to the highlands. Some scholars and alternative development practitioners have interpreted this not just as a failure of development – which it no doubt frequently has been – but also a rejection of development-as-modernity. Here the evidence is more contentious and links back to the discussion regarding the teleology of development.

The Karen are often presented in the academic and activist literature as forest farmers par excellence, their knowledge of the trees and the land, their rotational shifting cultivation practices, their accumulated wisdom and – of most relevance for the discussion here – their cultural preference for subsistence and self-sufficiency over market and profit marking them out as different from lowlanders and from some other uplanders, such as the Hmong. The Karen are valorized, in this way, as forest-friendly, subsistence-preferring and self-sufficiency-leaning hill peoples who have been drawn, largely against their will, into commodity production, and with disastrous results: debt, despair and decline are said to have been associated with this forcible incorporation of the Karen into the market mainstream:

> The winds of change exert a powerful force on the Karen. The elders are now worried that their children will lose their ways of life, their identity as children of the land and children of the water, and their ecological knowledge of the forest. 'We never get lost in the forest … But we will get lost in the city …' (Santasombat 2004: 111)

This is what Walker terms the Karen 'consensus' (Walker 2001; and see Walker 2004; Forsyth and Walker 2008). At the other end of the spectrum are the Hmong, who are, in contrast to the Karen, presented as 'forest destroyers' because of their farming practices. Rather than the rotational shifting cultivation of the Karen (seen as sustainable), they are pioneer shifting cultivators who mine virgin forest, often on or close to environmentally sensitive watersheds. Their characterization as forest destroyers is accentuated and given political resonance by their association with opium cultivation, a crop which is not only illegal but also notoriously draining of the land and the soil.

While the Hmong are derided as forest destroyers and the Karen lauded as forest guardians,[9] both have been stereotyped. But, as Walker explores (2001; and see Walker 2004; Forsyth and Walker 2008: 72–6), the evidence reveals that the Karen are not averse to engaging in market relations, and that far from the 'hyper anxiety' that Santasombat (2004) identifies, there is a substantial proportion of Karen who are living comfortably as middle-class peasants and 'for whom agricultural modernisation has generated enhanced security and more diverse opportunity' (Walker 2004: 262). Similarly, those scholars who see the Hmong as having being dragged into market relations through the influence of state-directed policies of monocropping (e.g. Laungaramsri 2000) contribute to the 'persistent theme that commercialization in the uplands is socially and environmentally inappropriate' (Forsyth and Walker 2008: 83):

> ... the image of the Hmong as victim, rather than villain, is problematic. It has to confront the considerable evidence that agricultural transformations such as the adoption of cabbages [as a commercial monocrop] are the result of internal Hmong initiative rather than external interventions. (Ibid.: 83)

In this way, the uplands of mainland South-East Asia have become contested landscapes in a number of overlapping ways. The role of the uplands in livelihoods is contested as lowlanders increasingly see hill peoples as the cause of environmental decline through 'destructive' practices of shifting cultivation. The ownership of land and the resources of the uplands are contested as the state, hill peoples and lowlanders struggle over land, forests, forest products and rivers, where their interests in each diverge. And the wider place of the uplands in the national economy, and in the national psyche, is contested as 'wild' places to be avoided become reconstructed as centres of biodiversity to be protected and managed. These struggles and conflicts, real though they no doubt are, should not be translated into a struggle over the meaning of development-as-modernization; they are, rather, a struggle over who gets to cut the cake, and how the slices are distributed. This is, therefore, partly an argument about equity and partly one about means; the contention here is that it is not, at root, an argument about development versus alternatives-to-development, although it might sometimes masquerade as such.

Historical breaks

> There's one thing we all know. The Soviet Union isn't going to change. (Summary of proceedings at a high-level international conference voiced by the conference chair and former UK ambassador to the Soviet Union, 1985)[10]

One the greatest historical breaks of the last 100 years was the collapse of the former Soviet Union in 1991. From the perspective of today it seems all too obvious: the Soviet empire was economically, ideologically, politically and socially bankrupt, or so we have come to believe. But, as Dallin observes with regard to this monumental break, and which applies to much of this chapter, 'We must take care not to introduce retrospectively a clarity let alone inevitability, where there was contingency and complexity' (Dallin 1992, quoted in Brown 2009: 584). The Soviet Union in the mid-1980s was strong and powerful and its leadership, seemingly, firmly embedded. The usual structural reasons paraded for the collapse of the Soviet empire are not fully convincing; instead, it is soft issues such as 'legitimacy' and 'morality' to which we need to look, and these are, almost by definition, hard to grasp. Something fundamental did change, but not in a manner that could be counted, graphed and calculated. Things could have worked out very differently, and at the time 'virtually no Western expert, scholar, official, or politician foresaw the impending collapse of the Soviet Union' (Aron 2011). The British ambassador quoted above was, therefore, in very good company.

We can seek to identify, with hindsight, the turning points of history: those moments when a different decision, a different action or a different coincidence of characters or events would have led, in all probability, to a very different present. These are the moments of historical lumpiness that Sewell writes about in the extract in the introduction to this chapter. Of course, the counterfactual or 'what if' genre has been popularized by films and novels such as *Sliding Doors* and Robert Harris's *Fatherland* but also extends to virtual histories by academics such as Ferguson's edited *Virtual History: Alternatives and counterfactuals* (1997b).[11] The point here is not to observe that the world might have been a very different place had the Prussians under Blücher not decisively intervened at the Battle of Waterloo on the evening of 18 June 1815; or that those who died and those who survived the Indian Ocean tsunami of 26 December 2004 would have been different had it occurred a few hours earlier while most of Asia was in bed. Rather, it is to highlight that occasionally, at critical junctures, history's progress, time's arrow, is disturbed in flight. Thinking back to the discussion in the two previous chapters, one such turning point concerns the apparent reproduction of the Asian miracle in the late-developing South-East Asian economies, and the Plaza Accord of 1985.

The Plaza Accord and the Asian miracle In 1985, James Baker was appointed US Treasury Secretary, coming to the post with a less doctrinaire view of economic intervention than that of his predecessors

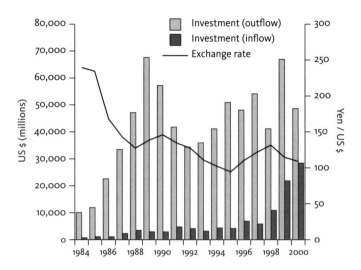

Figure 4.1 Japanese foreign direct investment, 1984–2000

(Berger 1999: 239). With this intellectual outlook, he actively pursued international economic cooperation, not least to lower the value of the US dollar against the Japanese yen as a means to address the growing US trade deficit with Japan.[12] This culminated in the Plaza Accord signed in New York's Plaza Hotel on 22 September 1985. At that time, one US dollar would buy 238 yen; by the end of 1985 it was worth 201 yen, and one year on from the Accord in September 1988 a dollar bought 128 yen. This not only made US exports more competitive but had the parallel effect of making Japanese exports significantly less competitive in world markets. This spurred a geographical reorientation of Japanese investment as companies sought to escape the effects of the now high-cost yen by investing overseas and moving their production offshore.

Japanese investment in East and South-East Asia had grown significantly prior to 1985, as the Japanese economy became the second largest in the world. From the mid-1980s, however, the rate of increase accelerated as Japanese multinational firms, burdened by the strong yen and growing labour shortages (and rising wage rates) at home, sought to move their production overseas to maintain their competitiveness (Figure 4.1). It has been suggested that Japanese firms saw this appreciation not as cyclical, but as a permanent revaluing of the currency against the US dollar and other major currencies (Fung et al. 2002: 6). Asia was the logical site for these investments. Geographically, the countries of East and South-East Asia were close at hand; the region had already benefited from large amounts of Japanese overseas development assistance; and many of the countries had relatively cheap and abundant workforces that could be drawn into factory work. In addition, the countries concerned were pursuing policies that were favourable to foreign investment, creating a congenial investment climate (Quibria 2002: 5). During the late 1980s there was a surge in Japanese manufacturing investment in Asia, and particularly in the countries of Asean (especially Indonesia, Malaysia and Thailand) which 'resulted in an unprecedented shift in productive capacity within the region' (Thomsen 1999: 13).

There is the danger in this sort of discussion of holding too much store by single events, such as the signing of the Plaza Accord, and to be drawn into the post hoc fallacy of assuming causality:[13] 'after this, therefore because of this'. There is, certainly, a statistical link – a correlation – between the Plaza Accord and patterns of Japanese and US investment and activity in Malaysia and South Korea (Chua et al. 1999). But this need not mean causality. That said, most scholars do see the surge in Japanese investment in South-East Asia after 1985 as causally linked to the appreciation of the yen following the Plaza Accord, with a slight lag reflecting the time needed for companies to make and act on these sorts of strategic decisions (e.g. Berger 1999; Chua et al. 1999; Fung et al. 2002; Thomsen 1999; Quibria 2002: 20). For Fung et al. (2002: 5), the Plaza Accord, and the appreciation of the yen that followed directly from the agreement, was 'the most important macroeconomic factor explaining the expansion of Japanese direct investment during the latter half of the 1980s'.

It was the increase in foreign direct investment into the second-tier NIEs of South-East Asia (see Table 3.1 in the previous chapter) during the mid- to late 1980s, much of it from Japan, which did most, in Quibria's view (2002: 5), to drive economic growth. In 1986, the Asean-5[14] received US$2.8 billion in FDI, representing 3.6 per cent of the total for developing economies; in 1991 these figures were US$12.9 billion and 8.1 per cent (Urata 2001: 414–15). In addition to the transfer of funds that this flow of FDI represents, it also had associated spillover effects in terms of technology and managerial skills transfers. In other words, if the Plaza Accord led to the surge of Japanese investment, then this in turn was a highly important factor explaining growth. We can take this farther, because even more scholars would link the sharp falls in poverty in South-East Asia to economic expansion, notwithstanding the continuing unequal distribution of the benefits of growth. It would be wrong to assume that growth would not have happened in the absence of FDI; domestic investment by a substantial class of domestic entrepreneurs was at least as critical in the development of these countries' manufacturing base. Furthermore it is not just the level of FDI but the uses to which it is put. Natural-resource-rich countries in Africa, for example, have also experienced high FDI inflows, but these have mostly been concentrated in the natural resource sector where, arguably, their spillover effects have been narrow and therefore their effects on poverty limited.

The Plaza Accord is a historical event with high visibility as well as, arguably, a very significant impact on the direction and progress of Asian modernization and development. There are other events and interventions which have such a low profile as to be almost invisible in international terms. These, likewise, can have large effects. One such intervention was the introduction of the shrimp-tail pump into the fields of the Mekong Delta.

Small innovations with big outcomes in the Asian countryside The term 'agrarian transformations' gives the impression of grand sweeps of change, shaped by overarching historical processes. This, in itself, is problematic given the degree to which local rural studies reveal a mosaic rather than a clear and neat trajectory of transition (see Rigg and Vandergeest 2012). Looking across the South-East Asian region, we can see reversals, counter-movements, surprising twists and un-expected outcomes. But equally significant and less commented upon is the way in which rural transformations are sometimes quite pro-foundly influenced by small innovations and developments, such that micro-events can shape broader histories.

The headlines of technological change range from railway networks and large-scale, multi-purpose dams to state-orchestrated irrigation schemes, wide-span suspension bridges, container ports and ships, and scientifically bred modern varieties of rice. These are emblem-atic of high modernism and the modernization process (Adas 1989). But it is sometimes in the footnotes of technological innovation and change that we find explanatory purchase, particularly insofar as they affect everyday lives. These micro-innovations may be overlooked and ignored, shaded from sight by official histories and grand scientific advances; yet it is just such low-visibility, low-cost and sometimes low-technology innovations that redefine life and living: the bicycle, motorcycle, sewing machine, radio and two-stroke engine, for example (Arnold 2011).[15] Such everyday technologies 'helped to displace or trans-form traditional craft practices; they refashioned changed gender roles and customary modes of work; and they made their own contribution to cultural change and political mobilization'.[16] One such technology is the shrimp-tail pump in the Mekong Delta.

FROM RICE SOCIETIES TO RICE ECONOMIES The history of Vietnam's Mekong Delta has often been described as the opening up of a former wilderness by means of French imperial power allied to technological muscle. From the 1890s monstrous steam-powered dredges turned a wild and empty space (as it was seen) into a site for settlement, acting as 'the catalyst that permitted millions of Vietnamese migrants to head southwards and build rice fields out of marshes and mangrove forests' (Biggs 2012: 55) (Illustration 4.2). In his speech at the inauguration of a new canal in 1930, Governor-General Pierre Pasquier said: 'yesterday [these expanses] were dismal, vast solitudes, but today they are rich

Illustration 4.2 Steam dredge used to dig the canals of the Mekong Delta

These pictures were taken in 1915 when this dredge, the *Loire*, was being used to excavate the Vinh Te canal. Reproduced in Biggs (2003: 95)

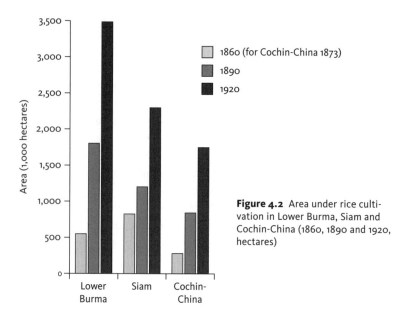

Figure 4.2 Area under rice cultivation in Lower Burma, Siam and Cochin-China (1860, 1890 and 1920, hectares)

Legend:
- 1860 (for Cochin-China 1873)
- 1890
- 1920

Y-axis: Area (1,000 hectares)

X-axis categories: Lower Burma, Siam, Cochin-China

patchworks, sumptuous *cloisonnés* in which the golds and emeralds of the peaceful fields are set as far as the eye can see ...' (quoted in Biggs 2003: 77). Over some half a century to 1930, 165 million cubic metres of earth and mud were dredged,[17] the cultivated area expanded by 2.2 million hectares, and the delta was settled by millions of migrant Vietnamese (ibid.: 79; Biggs 2012: 54–6). A similar process has been described for the other great river basins of South-East Asia, including the Irrawaddy in Burma (see Adas 1974) and the Chao Phraya in Siam (Thailand) (see Brummelhuis 2005).[18] In these three deltas combined, the area under rice cultivation almost quintupled in the three decades between 1890 and 1920 from 1.6 million to over 7.5 million hectares (Figure 4.2). This was achieved by the Chakri dynasty and the British and French colonial authorities, albeit not without resistance, by applying Western knowledge and expertise to a considerable technical challenge. For centuries, rice may have been the staple crop of Burma, Cochin-China and Siam, but the transformation of these countries from rice-growing 'societies' to rice-growing 'economies' took place in tandem with the opening up of the vast lands of the Irrawaddy, Mekong and Chao Phraya deltas. At this time, rice was transformed from being (just) a staple crop to becoming a commercial commodity that required the attention and intervention of the state.

This is the formal, official and muscular history of development in the great rice-growing deltas of the South-East Asian region. It emphasizes the complementary roles of (Western) science, finance, engineering and the state. In this history, migrant farmers become pawns on a paddy-field chequerboard where they either merely respond to the opportunities that are provided by a benevolent state, or are actively and sometimes coercively forced into such a role. 'What brighter proof', Governor-General Pasquier said in his speech, 'of the continuity and benefit of our policies than this hydraulic management of Cochinchina?' (quoted in Biggs 2003: 77). It is easy to forget when reading such self-congratulatory statements that the real champions of this geographical transformation were the millions of pioneer peasant cultivators who were willing to settle these frontier zones and, in so doing, turn wildernesses into productive lands. Just like the millions of young women and men who left their homes to throng the factories of Asia in the decades from the 1970s, so these farming households quite literally took their lives into their hands and ventured into the deltaic wildernesses of mainland South-East Asia.

A HISTORY OF SMALL INNOVATIONS IN THE MEKONG DELTA: THE SHRIMP-TAIL PUMP The technical innovations that transformed these deltas were not just the steam dredges depicted in the illustration reproduced here. Offstage and almost out of sight were other (micro-) innovations, which have had, arguably, an even greater impact. One such was the motorized water pump, the shrimp-tail pump, which arrived in the Mekong Delta in the 1960s (Illustration 4.3). As Biggs writes (2012: 60), this was a 'silent revolution', insofar as its arrival was unheralded, the moment of 'take-off' none too clear and its distribution, though widespread, fuzzy. The most thorough examination of the shrimp-tail pump's development and transmission through the Mekong Delta during the 1960s, and its revolutionary impact on rice production, is Sansom's 1969 paper (and see Sansom 1970). The dredging of the deltas provided the agrarian space that could be settled and developed by millions of pioneer cultivators from the mid- to late nineteenth century; with their bravery and perseverance, however, was allied a remarkable degree of ingenuity as these peasants and their descendants sought to increase the productivity of their lands.

The shrimp-tail pump was invented, according to Sansom, by a farmer – Mr Van Nam of Song Binh village – in 1962 (Sansom 1969: 111). Mr Van Nam had worked for a French dredging company in Saigon, and he brought his engineering skills and experience to bear when he, like other farmers in the area, was facing the effects of a severe drought in 1962. Adapting the impeller principle of French dredges,

Illustration 4.3 Low-visibility revolution: the shrimp-tail water pump (*source*: Reproduced from Sansom 1969: 111)

and after several months of experimentation, he encased the impeller in a simple metal sleeve and attached this to a 4.5 HP Clinton engine imported from the USA (ibid.: 111–12). The pump (or adaptations of it[19]) was a great success and was taken up almost instantaneously across the Mekong Delta, in the process 'transforming' the economy of the upper delta (ibid.: 109). Up until this point, machines were used for *no* farm tasks; yet within four years, the shrimp-tail pump had *completely* replaced the pedal-powered water wheel as a water-raising device in the areas where Sansom was working. By 1966, around 40 per cent of farmers owned such a pump, and all the remainder rented them. When Sansom asked one farmer about his water wheel, he replied, 'I burnt it' (ibid.: 113).

A similar process of inventive adaptation of small engines to pump water also occurred in Thailand and Laos. As Biggs says (2012), while these pumps, adapted by entrepreneurial farmers and merchants, were rapidly spreading across the Mekong Delta, official responses were dismissive. American advisers thought them inefficient while the Vietnamese state's response 'ranged over the years from non-enthusiastic to obstructionist' (ibid.: 66).[20] Biggs concludes his paper:

> The rapid proliferation of small engines in such post-colonial 'gardens' points to deeper concerns on the horizon about the role of states in promoting effective technologies that respond immediately to economic needs, especially in developing rural areas. The small engine in the post-colonial garden signifies a new middle space, one where national and international development experts play catch up to local entrepreneurs racing past, engines roaring. Elite engineers and once powerful state agencies cannot keep up with millions of individual modifications across a river delta. Nevertheless, it will remain the state's responsibility to respond to any emergent ecological crises as the 'silent revolution' grows noisier. Ultimately, the small machine in the garden may

elicit two kinds of nostalgia, one for the old countryside animated with water buffalo, manual labour, and sail, and the other for the old state with a single agency and its experts responsible for keeping the water flowing. (Ibid.: 70)

There are three important points that follow from this account of the development and spread of the shrimp-tail water pump. First, its diffusion across the delta in remarkably short order was achieved without official support, indeed often with institutional resistance, and without the advantage of modern communications. Word-of-mouth and personal observation drove the diffusion of the innovation (Sansom 1969: 116–17). Secondly, it was not just the individual invention of the shrimp-tail pump which was important, but all that flowed from it. The pump was the catalyst for a cascade of associated developments that provide, collectively, an alternative narrative of the Green Revolution very different from the usual one with its focus on the work of the International Rice Research Institute in Los Baños in the Philippines allied to official government programmes and policies. Thirdly, the story of the pump encourages us to look under the stones of history to identify the factors contributing to progress. The innovations and developments that have been prominent in the progress of irrigated rice agriculture across Asia over the course of the latter decades of the twentieth century were not, arguably, the grand gravity irrigation schemes that have received so much attention, but a 'groundswell' of micro-developments as small (less than 5 HP), cheap pumps became available to individual small farmers across the region (Barker and Molle 2005: 7). As Molle et al. (2003) contend, the dissemination of cheap pumps has 'probably [been] as crucial a transformation' as the Green Revolution itself. Such micro-innovations continue to play a leading role in forging the waterscapes of the Mekong and other river basins in Asia.

BOOM CROPS AND BOOM FISH The final examples of historical turbulence in the development histories of South-East Asia come in the guise of 'boom' crops (see Hall 2011). These encompass some of the more remarkable developments in the region's agricultural sector and include coffee and Pangasius in Vietnam, rubber in the Lao PDR (Baird 2011; Cohen 2009) and cocoa in Sulawesi (Li 2012). To understand the development and dispersal of such crops, it is not possible to illuminate a particular innovation (like the shrimp-tail pump) or event (like the Plaza Accord); rather one has to consider the agency of poor farmers who have seized an opportunity and, in so doing, forged new

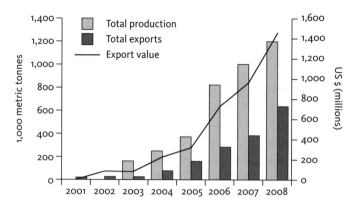

Figure 4.3 Pangasius production, exports and value, Vietnam, 2001–08

– and unheralded – geographies of development and livelihood pathways. Once again, and as we will see, these narratives of development provide an alternative insight into the development process, one that encourages us to pay attention to people and communities rather than to the state, to micro-developments rather than macro-initiatives, and those elements of development which tend to be shaded from sight in the face of the grand edifice of the Development Project.

The shrimp-tail pump revolutionized rice farming in the Mekong Delta before the communist victory and reunification in 1975/76; the Pangasius catfish (*Pangasius bocourti – ca basa* in Vietnamese – and *Pangasianodon hypophthalmus – ca tra*) has similarly revolutionized fish farming and rural livelihoods in the delta in the period since, and especially in the provinces of An Giang, Dong Thap, Can Tho and Vinh Long, and has significantly contributed to the rapid economic expansion of the delta. The similarity between the two developments lies in the disjuncture between the intentionalities of the state and the actions of the 'target' populations; and in the sheer speed with which Pangasius spread across the delta.

Pangasius production in Vietnam expanded by 35 per cent *per year* between 2001 and 2008 (Bush et al. 2009: 271; Bush and Duijf 2011; and see Figure 4.3). This, like the shrimp-tail pump, was largely spontaneous and uncontrolled, notwithstanding attempts by the Vietnamese state to control events. Vietnam's Ministry of Agriculture and Rural Development (MARD) sets production targets and provincial governments produce elaborate land-use plans, but these are rarely reflected on the ground. Pangasius has expanded with little regard to the directionalities of state policy, and even when the police have visited ponds to stop excavation, farmers have been said to have continued digging, but at night (Bush et al. 2009: 281). The result has been that the Vietnamese government has been playing 'catch-up' as farmers have run ahead of targets. In 2006 production of Pangasius was 'capped' at 600,000 metric tonnes by 2010; in 2007, as farmers' action made this target fanciful, the cap was almost doubled to 1 million metric tonnes (ibid.: 281).

During the early years of the Pangasius boom in Vietnam, much of the exported production – close to 80 per cent in 2001 – made its way to the United States, where it challenged the established catfish industry. The Catfish Farmers of America (CFA) brought an anti-dumping case against Vietnamese producers, and when the US Department of Commerce found in favour of the CFA, import tariffs of between 37 and 65 per cent were imposed (ibid.: 273). In response, Vietnamese producers reduced costs and diversified their export markets to the EU, the other countries of Asean, the Middle East and South America. 'The result', Bush et al. conclude, was far from stagnation or decline but 'a reinvigoration of the industry as a whole' (ibid.: 274).

The remarkable story of Pangasius in the Mekong Delta reveals a 'developmental' state (see p. 62) unable to control or to anticipate development, instead illuminating farmers who have innovated and responded with such alacrity that the Vietnamese government has been forced to play governance catch-up. Part of the reason for this state of affairs is that government plans and regulations cannot adequately address the interpersonal nature of governance in Vietnam. Paper plans, regulations and laws exist, and to a considerable degree the means (capacities) to implement them also exist; however, as Kerkvliet has argued in his work on 'everyday' politics in Vietnam (1995, 2005) drawing on fieldwork in rural sub-districts south of Hanoi, policies in Vietnam have been shaped by the everyday political practices of ordinary rural folk, rather than by the state. The most remarkable example of this was the collapse of collective farming owing to the everyday political practices of villagers in the Red River Delta, practices which 'were often at odds with what collective farming required, what authorities wanted, and what national policy prescribed' (Kerkvliet 2005: 234). The story of Pangasius is yet another insight into the limits of state power, regulatory control and the dictates of planning in Vietnam. This story from the southern Mekong Delta also has its counterpoint in coffee in the central highlands.

Coffee has been grown in Vietnam since the late nineteenth century – there was a coffee plantation in Son Tay in the 1890s – and urban coffee 'culture' has been present for many decades. But the explosion

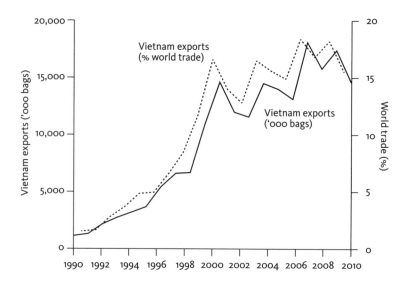

Figure 4.4 Vietnam's and world coffee exports, 1990–2010

of coffee production for export in Vietnam dates from the early 1990s when the country emerged – in an extraordinarily short period of time – as a major producer and exporter of low-grade robusta coffee, mainly for the instant coffee market (Figure 4.4).[21] In 1990, Vietnam accounted for 1.5 per cent of world trade in coffee; by 1997, this had risen to 8.5 per cent and in 2000 was almost 17 per cent (Figure 4.4). Over this period, the country was transformed from being an also-ran in the world coffee stakes, to becoming the world's second-biggest coffee producer and exporter after Brazil. Like that of Pangasius and the shrimp-tail pump, the expansion of coffee in Vietnam is not to be revealed through the careful sifting of government planning documents and interviews with high-level ministerial officials ('key informants'), but through seeking to understand how and why individual farmers and low-level commercial intermediaries came, collectively, to embark on an enterprise that had the cumulative effect of reshaping the world market in coffee.

Of Vietnam's coffee, about 60 per cent is grown in the Central Highlands province of Dak Lak, although Buon Me Thuot, Dalat and Lam Dong are also significant producers. Unlike some other major coffee exporters, such as Brazil, the country does not have a plantation system and most coffee farms in Vietnam are small, extending to just one or two hectares, with some one million small farmers being reliant on coffee as their main source of income (Ha and Shively 2008).

The story of Vietnam's coffee 'rush' is often presented in value (or commodity) chain terms, in which global demand for a commodity (in this instance, coffee) inextricably leads to a sequence of causes and effects which can be understood simply by following the links in the chain. But, as Tan (2000) describes, pioneering Vietnamese coffee farmers in frontier areas of Dak Lak province were engaged in a process of self-enrolment (ibid.: 60). The state and global firms were relatively distant from this process. Farmers took the initiative to make plots of coffee bushes in the forest, working outside the sight-line of the state. They sourced their own seeds; they developed and extended their own networks of knowledge to successfully cultivate the coffee bushes, exchanging experiences and lessons; and they '"walked" their way into the coffee marketing networks of the traders' (ibid.: 60). They even instituted their own approaches to quality control.[22] From one end of the coffee telescope, we see quality controllers, multinational firms, chains of coffee shops and state marketing boards; from the other end, we observe individual coffee producers working outside and sometimes against the state, operating in league with petty coffee traders, creating a 'disjuncture' in the chain:

> ... the consolidation of coffee frontier fronts – connecting a frontier to the global economy – cannot be attributed to a process of deliberate enrolment by either the State or transnational corporations. The precipitate peasants initiated the expansion of the frontier and linked up with local markets already developed by earlier waves of colonisation. (Tan 2000: 62–3; see also Tan and Walker 2008: 122)

Tan does not see in Dak Lak's coffee rush the shadow of capitalist globalization but the distant actions of 'precipitate' peasants. There is, of course, a historical backdrop to Dak Lak's precipitate peasants. The expansion of coffee had to be enabled in some way, and a number of adjustments in Vietnam's political economy were highly important in this regard. We can highlight, for example: the imposition of the reforms of *doi moi* from the mid-1980s and their deepening through the early 1990s; the willingness on the part of the state to permit, if not to encourage, forest settlement and clearance, which it had previously actively opposed; and the loosening of the formerly quite tight controls over personal mobility in Vietnam enshrined in the *ho khau* or household registration system, which, until the 1990s, effectively 'fixed' people in space. But that all of these changes, broadly linked to reform, would make Vietnam the world's second-largest coffee producer and cause a million farm households to become dependent on the crop for their livelihoods and well-being was scarcely contemplated. Furthermore, the fact that most of the incipient coffee farmers are majority Kinh lowlanders who have migrated to the uplands has led to development-induced displacement for the minority uplanders. Where minorities have embraced coffee, their returns have not matched those of the Kinh, with the result that they have become relatively poorer, exacerbating already deep inequalities in Vietnamese society (Doutriaux et al. 2008).

Conclusion: from state optics to parochial politics

In his book *Seeing Like a State* (1998), James Scott memorably shows how states have sought to make people and spaces 'legible'. The state that Scott describes is one with considerable vision and latitude, able to exert its will through mechanisms of statecraft, even though outcomes may be harmful to its population.[23] This chapter, however, has focused on a series of locally, regionally and nationally important developments and events over which the state has had, apparently, very little control and which it has sometimes actively attempted to shape, but with little effect.[24] This raises questions about how and where state policies operate, and what operates in addition to the state.

Kerkvliet (1995, 2005), as noted above, draws our attention to the everyday practices of ordinary people, in his case in Vietnam. He endows his Vietnamese peasants with agency and power so that the state's role becomes muted and occasionally beholden to the collective 'will' of the people. This does not, however, manifest itself either in turbulent politics or in largely futile attempts at 'resistance', but rather in a powerful yet understated groundswell that can either ferment change or prevent it. Tania Murray Li (2005) also challenges the notion that the state is all powerful and all seeing (p. 384), directing our gaze instead at the myriad of agencies and organizations that lie 'between' the state and the people, most obviously non-governmental organizations but also religious groups, philanthropists, 'experts' and political activists.

This chapter, at one level, could be viewed as unhelpful. The art of social science is to bring meaning to the patterns of the world; to seek to understand processes of change and the imprint that they leave in people's lives and on social and economic history. Here the argument has been that some of the key social and economic transformations in South-East Asia have been lumpy in terms of their genesis, and surprising in their ensuing trajectories. History may be 'one damn thing after another', but what technologies or events are taken up and what are not, and how these then ricochet through time and space, is not obvious:

> Technology has the power to reconstitute society but to do so in different ways in different places – the reconstitution of domesticity with the arrival of the sewing-machine or the reframing and revisualization of marriage through photography might be vastly different from their uses and effects in other social spaces and cultural settings ... It is precisely by addressing ... the spatial location and physical mobility of the machine that we begin to see, technologically speaking, if not the fragility, then at least the permeability, of the late-colonial and even the post-colonial order. The time and place of the everyday thus helps us to de-centre the state from the histories of South and Southeast Asia and to bring other temporalities and spatialities into prominence. (Arnold and DeWald 2011a: 15, 16)

This process of events taking histories in new directions and technologies altering relationships and behaviours in surprising ways continues. The latter can be seen, for example, in the role of motorbikes and mobile phones, which have spread far more quickly and disseminated far more widely than anyone expected and been used in creative ways that do not emulate their patterns of use in the rich world.

5 | The power of ordinary events in shaping development

But little Mouse, you are not alone,
In proving foresight may be vain:
The best laid schemes of mice and men
Go often askew,
And leave us nothing but grief and pain,
For promised joy!

(Robert Burns, 'To a Mouse, on Turning Her Up in Her Nest,
with the Plough', 1785)

Life is what happens to you while you're busy making other plans.
(John Lennon, 'Beautiful Boy [Darling Boy]', 1980)

Introduction

This chapter deals with the ways in which everyday histories get caught up in the unexpected and unplanned: 'the best laid schemes of mice and men'. Often this is dismissed as 'noise'; exceptions to the rule which do not detract from the march of history and structures of living. The chapter seeks to decouple individual life histories and household livelihood pathways from the wider sweep of history to show how, particularly when we move from the aggregate and the regional to the specific and the local, experiences and stories are more different than they are alike. To put it another way, ordinary people often live extraordinary lives. Moreover, the extraordinary character of so much living is not just because people bring to their lives unique combinations of skills, aptitudes and personality traits; it is also because unexpected (but ordinary) events disturb and unsettle livelihood trajectories. This chapter, then, is about the power of the ordinary.

For East and South-East Asia we can collectively – and convincingly – show how rapid economic growth has raised incomes, improved material well-being and reduced poverty, notwithstanding the sometimes unequal distribution of growth (see Figure 3.2, p. 51). How this came about may remain a matter of conjecture, as discussed in Chapters 3 and 4, but that the effect was substantially to raise incomes and therefore reduce income poverty, and to do so across a broad swathe of society, is not seriously disputed. Where the apparently neat translation of economic growth into poverty reduction becomes less clear, particularly in relative terms, is when we track the experiences and performance of individuals and families. This has implications for our understanding of how lives progress; it also requires a reconsideration of 'higher'-level attempts at planning and, in particular, policies that seek to tackle poverty. It is easy to overlook the point that economic growth, in terms of GDP, is an aggregate measure of national economic expansion; poverty, on the other hand, is experienced individually or at a family or household level. As Ravallion writes:

> People are often hurting behind the averages. Panel data and observations from the ground can reveal this, but the aggregate statistics cannot. It is important to know the aggregate balance of gains and losses, but it will be of little consolation to those suffering to be told that poverty is falling on average. (Ravallion 2001: 1811)

The role of chance, luck, fate, serendipity, failure, tragedy, happenstance and misfortune in shaping individual and family pathways is a familiar one. From John Dryden's observation that '... seldom three descents continue good' (Dryden 1745: 294)[1] to Bob Dylan's 'simple twist of fate', the ability of unforeseen events to turn life upside down and inside out is a current that runs through novels, proverbs, songs, plays and poetry – as well as everyday lives.

John Dryden and Bob Dylan may both be highlighting the turbulence of history. The former, however, is paying attention to the inter-generational (family) transfer of wealth and the latter to the unsettling effects of chance events on individual (personal) life chances and courses. This chapter considers both the inter-generational and the intra-generational transfers of wealth and poverty, how they occur and what interrupts their progress. *Intra-generational mobility* concerns movements, in this instance of wealth or poverty, within or between social classes during an individual's lifetime or life course. *Inter-generational mobility*, sometimes shortened to IGT poverty (inter-generational transmission of poverty), on the other hand, refers to the transfer of wealth or poverty between the generations. Beyond such transfers of wealth and poverty, a series of other related questions also weaves its way through the chapter. Have economic development and social change altered the patterning of untoward or serendipitous events? How do communities and individuals act and behave to minimize or thwart their effects? And what is – and what might be – the role for government in such contexts both to support and enable upward movements and to protect families who might be propelled downwards?

So far this book has mostly concerned itself with debates over national economic growth, development planning and historical transitions. Much of this chapter and the next, however, will focus on individuals and households and how they respond to and are buffeted by larger-scale processes and events. A particular concern is with the predictability of such events, the transfer of their effects through the life course and across generations, and the ways in which people 'cope' and governments 'manage' in the face of assorted shocks and disturbances.

Conceptualizing the poor in time: the inter- and intra-generational transmission of poverty

We know a good deal about poverty characteristics and trends over time, particularly in relation to monetary poverty; the economics of poverty is a mature industry with a wealth of supporting data. As Sen writes in the Preface to *Poverty and Famines* (1981: vii), 'much about poverty is obvious enough'. Intuitively, we also know who the poor are. We know far less, however, about poverty dynamics and the intra- and inter-generational transmission of poverty, and especially those personal characteristics that might explain the dynamics that panel studies[2] reveal (Hulme and Shepherd 2003: 407; Baulch and Davis 2008: 1; Krishna 2010: 29; Krishna and Shariff 2011): 'The task of explaining social mobility patterns', Krishna writes, 'remains as yet substantially incomplete' (2010: 124). Moreover, the comparative absence of longitudinal studies (as opposed to cross-sectional studies) is particularly acute in the global South (Bird and Shinyekwa 2005). At the start of the millennium, only twelve out of 110 low- and medium-income countries had household-level data on poverty dynamics (Harper et al. 2003: 538). While this situation is continually improving, it is still the case that most panel data sets are relatively short run (less than five years) and/or restricted in terms of their number of waves or sample points.

John Dryden and Bob Dylan were referring to the disturbing and unsettling effects of events in family lives, and how these can throw normal progress off track. In academic studies of poverty, however, it is normally the *continuities* in patterns of poverty which are highlighted, rather than the *discontinuities*. People are, variously, caught in poverty 'traps' (Dasgupta 1997; Carter and Barrett 2006; Krishna 2011), there are 'cycles of disadvantage' (Boggess et al. 2005), families face 'unequal chances' (Bowles et al. 2005), and poverty is 'persistent' (Carter and Barrett 2006), 'enduring' (Harper et al. 2003) and 'chronic' (Hulme and Shepherd 2003; CPRC 2009; Aliber 2003). Studies frequently emphasize that poverty, and also prosperity, is reproduced in quite predictable ways; the children of the rich of one era become the adult rich of the next. Intuitively, we would expect this to be the case; the children of more prosperous families, particularly when that is allied to stable household conditions, will inherit the wealth of their parents and, in turn, transmit that prosperity to their children. What is transmitted from one generation to the next is not only positive (land, savings, livestock, education and various other assets) but can also be negative (debt, undernutrition or, more contentiously, cultures of poverty). The question, then, is: what explains the patterns that can be discerned in both the intra- and inter-generational transmission of poverty?

In considering the relationship between poverty and the temporal dimension, three broad hypotheses present themselves: the persistence hypothesis; the life cycle hypothesis; and the individualization hypothesis (McDonough et al. 2005: 1797). The persistence hypothesis leans towards a structural interpretation of the reproduction of poverty, seeing it as linked to institutional and individual factors that perpetuate poverty. These include, for example, social exclusion and labour market rigidities that make it hard for the poor to escape their condition, through to individual (or neighbourhood) characteristics that create a culture of poverty and dependency which is transmitted from generation to generation. So-styled 'deviant' values and behaviours are seen to be reproduced inter-generationally through familial and neighbourhood experiences (Corcoran 1995: 238). Critics of this culture of poverty interpretation of the inter-generational transmission of poverty maintain that it is not due to the passing on of deviant cultures and behaviours, but because of racial discrimination and social exclusion. This relocates 'blame' from the poor and the neighbourhoods that they create to wider society.

The life cycle hypothesis builds upon the early and seminal work of Seebohm Rowntree (1901) in the northern British city of York and focuses on the way in which poverty is linked to stages in the life course: young families with dependent children are constrained in terms of what they can do, while individuals in older age also face particular – but different – difficulties in making a living. Rowntree noted that 'the wages paid for unskilled labour in York are insufficient to provide food, shelter, and clothing adequate to maintain a family of moderate size in a state of bare physical efficiency' (ibid.: 133). 'The fact remains', he continued, 'that every labourer who has as many as three children must pass through a time, probably lasting for about ten years, when he will be in a state of "primary" poverty; in other words, when he and his family will be underfed' (ibid.: 135). Finally, the individualization hypothesis proposes that late modernity is causing the sources and trajectories of poverty to be unsettled, disturbing any patterns and regularities that might, once, have been evident.

While there are important continuities in the production and reproduction of poverty, and these structural features need to be addressed if the 'cycle' of poverty is to be broken, the degree to which there are discontinuities is surprising. As Harper et al. state, the 'most striking features of the body of evidence on poverty transfers are its ambiguity and highly context dependent conclusions ...' (Harper et al. 2003: 537). Drawing on data from the Panel Study of Income Dynamics (PSID), a continuing study of some five thousand households in the United States,[3] McDonough et al. (2005) highlight the turbulence of the poor. While 70 per cent of the sampled households were never poor over a sixteen-year period from 1967 to 1982, of the 30 per cent who were poor, a little more than one third were poor throughout the period; around the same number left poverty; and around a quarter became poor. Based on these panel data, McDonough et al. (ibid.) identify four broad classes of poor: the non-poor, the always poor, the declining poor and the rising poor.

Even within these classes, however, there is diversity. The chronically poor, for example, include those who are poor through their social exclusion (highlighting societal and institutional barriers to progress) and those who are long-term deprived. The former may be best conceptualized through the persistence hypothesis and the latter through the individualization hypothesis. In addition, the two categories of declining poor and rising poor can also be subdivided. The former into those who decline into poverty and become chronically poor, and those who decline but then return to their prior non-poor status; and the latter into those who rise but then return to poverty, and those who rise to become non-poor. A further complication is that countries exhibit different balances between chronic and transient poor, and this requires different policy responses. In those where most of the poor are only occasionally poor, interventions might best be concentrated on providing adequate social safety nets; where it is chronic poverty which is the issue, then asset redistribution and sustained investment in social and physical infrastructure might be the preferred policy intervention (Hulme and Shepherd 2003: 404).

Using the same PSID data set, it is possible to track what happened to the children born into poor and non-poor families in 1968 and their early adult outcomes recorded in 1988. The first point to note, once again, is the degree of mobility: more than three-quarters of poor black children in 1968 were living as non-poor early adults twenty years later. The proportion for white children, however, was nine-tenths. At the same time, the study also revealed the degree to which poverty is transmitted inter-generationally: poor black children were two and a half times more likely to be poor in early adulthood than non-poor children. The figures for white children are even starker: those living in poverty in 1968 were almost eight times more likely to be poor in 1980. There is, on the basis of these data, an important (but far from deterministic) element of path dependence in the trajectories of the poor and the non-poor through their life course. The study also, and thirdly, draws attention to the marked differences between black and white children in terms of their chances of being poor in the first place, and remaining poor in the second. All this is significant and interesting. There is still, however, a puzzle in the data. This relates to the question of *why* growing up poor is significantly more likely to lead to poverty in later life, which may seem intuitively obvious but is in fact less clear than one would imagine. The data reveal that the effects of parental poverty, even when controlled for education, family size, family structure, maternal schooling and neighbourhood effects, are large and significant. This leads Corcoran (1995: 250) to conclude that 'poverty is clearly not just a proxy for measured parental and neighbourhood disadvantages'. Growing up poor in the United States clearly matters; why it matters is less clear. It is also evident from these data and the other studies noted in this chapter that poverty is not preordained.

There are distinct links between how poverty is produced intra-generationally and inter-generationally, with each drawing on similar explanatory frameworks. In seeking, however, to illuminate the discontinuities and contingencies that characterize life and living for those in or close to poverty, this chapter will separately consider the poverty dynamics that concern the experiences of individuals and individual households over time on the one hand, and the poverty dynamics that relate to the inter-generational transmission of poverty on the other.

Intra-generational twists

Poverty traps and intra-generational mobility

A small peasant and a landless labourer may both be poor, but their fortunes are not tied together. In understanding the proneness to starvation of either we have to view them not as members of

TABLE 5.1 Four approaches to framing poverty and counting the poor

Framing	Categorization		
Division	Poor (those who fall below the poverty line)	Non-poor (those who lie above the poverty line)	
Demarcation	Breadth of poverty (the multidimensionality of poverty)	Depth of poverty (the poverty gap, how far people individually or collectively fall below the poverty line)	Duration of poverty (how long people or households remain in poverty)
Distinction	Transient poor (the occasionally or 'churning' poor)	Chronic poor (the long-term poor, consisting of the always poor and the usually poor)	Ultra or severely poor (the destitute, who may also be chronically poor)	Non-poor
Dynamics	Poverty trends (the change in the headcount measure of poverty from year to year)	Poverty dynamics (the poverty experiences, over time, of individuals and households)	Poverty turbulence (the oscillation of people across a poverty line)	IGT poverty (the intergenerational transmission of poverty)

the huge army of 'the poor,' but as members of particular classes, belonging to particular occupational groups, having different ownership endowments, and being governed by rather different entitlement relations. Classifying the population into the rich and the poor may serve some purpose in some context, but it is far too undiscriminating to be helpful in analysing starvation, famines, or even poverty. (Sen 1981: 156)

While broad sweeping theories have great intellectual interest there is no grand theoretical framework yet proposed that can explain the persistence of poverty in general, or the persistence of poverty for countries or social groups in particular. The nature of chronic poverty, and the causal factors that underpin it, differ from context to context, and so explanations must also vary. (Hulme and Shepherd 2003: 413)

'The poor', as Sen describes in the quotation above, are far from a homogeneous group. Individuals and households are poor for different reasons and to different degrees, and their experiences of poverty are different. The policies that might lift them out of poverty have, therefore, to be equally varied if they are to be sensitive to such differences. The headline poverty data – such as those reproduced in Figure 3.2 (see p. 51) – are politically important in drawing attention to the poverty challenges that still confront the world. But such data shield from view the diversity that Sen describes; they also hint that there might be a silver bullet to tackling global poverty.[4] As Table 5.1 rudimentarily sets out, beyond simply dividing the world into the poor and non-poor, we can demarcate the poor in terms of the depth, breadth and duration of poverty; we can draw distinctions between types (or categories) of poor; and we can focus attention on the dynamics that underscore poverty over time. It is the last of these with which this chapter is particularly concerned, although, as we shall see, what happens over time is intimately linked to why people are poor in the first place and the depths of poverty that they experience.

Shocks and resilience: latent and constructed How do families progress or decline? There is an assumption that the two processes mirror each other: that each is gradual, one of improvement and the other of decay. In addition, it is also commonly assumed that the factors that drive these upward and downward movements are much the same, just working in opposite directions. The evidence, however, is that upward and downward livelihood trajectories are different both in the

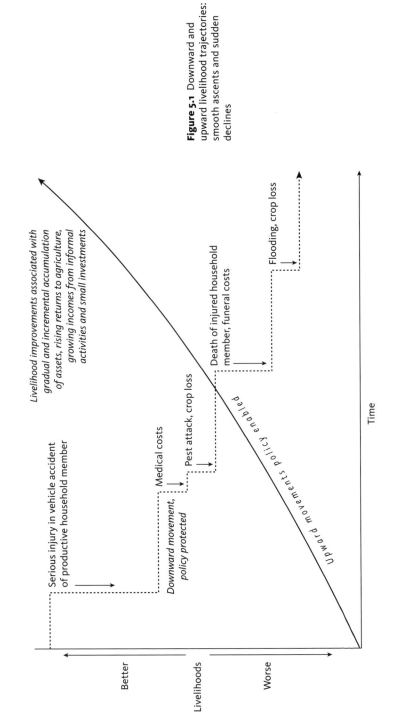

Figure 5.1 Downward and upward livelihood trajectories: smooth ascents and sudden declines

Livelihood improvements associated with gradual and incremental accumulation of assets, rising returns to agriculture, growing incomes from informal activities and small investments

Serious injury in vehicle accident of productive household member

Medical costs

Downward movement, policy protected

Pest attack, crop loss

Death of injured household member, funeral costs

Flooding, crop loss

Upward movements policy enabled

Better

Livelihoods

Worse

Time

paths that they take, and in the processes that propel or underpin the movements.

Figure 5.1 illustrates these differences, drawing on the work of Krishna (2010), Davis (2006, 2007), Hulme and Shepherd (2003), Sen (2003) and Baulch and Davis (2008). As Figure 5.1 shows (and see Table 5.3), upward movements tend to be gradual and cumulative as people find work, generate surpluses, and invest wisely or fortuitously; they are also linked to wider economic conditions and can thus be seen as 'enabled' by policy contexts. In expanding economies, the employment and investment opportunities that permit such upward movements are more numerous, as Box 5.1 describes in the case of Truong, a rural migrant in Hanoi.[5] There is also an important element of serendipity: poor or near-poor households must avoid the sort of shocks that propel downward livelihood movements.

Box 5.1 Downward mobility in north-east Thailand

I first met and interviewed Mrs Achara Wattana in the north-eastern Thai village of Ban Non Tae in 1983 (Illustration B5.1). At that time, Achara and her husband were relatively prosperous in village terms. They owned a good-sized area of rice land, marginal though it may have been (like so much rice land in this part of Thailand), and their livelihood was robust in village terms. When, with Albert Salamanca, we reinterviewed Achara in May 2008 and then for a third time in 2009, she had fallen significantly down the village wealth hierarchy and was regarded by other villagers as 'poor'.[6] The reasons for this decline in fortunes can be linked to the sort of events with which this chapter is concerned.

Achara's husband was struck by lightning and killed in 1983 when she was a young mother with three children and an adoptive son (her nephew) to support. Her husband's livestock trading business subsequently collapsed and, as a result, the household's main source of income dried up. In 1986, Achara was forced to sell a large part of her land to pay bills after she was hospitalized with a liver complaint. Of her three children, one son was killed in a road accident in Pattaya in 2006, a second son left the village to live in Phetchabun (another province in north-east Thailand), and Achara's only daughter later left home to live with

Illustration B5.1 House compound, Ban Non Tae, north-east Thailand, 1983

her husband in Bangkok.[7] By 2008, a reasonably robust rural livelihood in the early 1980s, at the time of the first interview, had become a progressively more marginal one. By the time we reinterviewed Achara in 2008 she was fifty-eight years old, a widow and in poor health, suffering from heart problems and hypertension (Figure B5.1).[8]

Unlike in Hulme's (2003) study of a single chronically poor household in Bangladesh, however, Achara had not fallen into destitution. This can be seen to be linked to two sets of factors. First of all, Thailand has begun to introduce a lattice of social safety nets that help to protect individuals at times of crisis, and cushion the effects of downward livelihood shocks. In particular, under former prime minister Thaksin Shinawatra, the Thai government introduced a universal healthcare programme in 2002,[9] bringing modern medical care within reach of almost everyone. The number of Thais without some form of medical insurance fell from 16.5 million in 2001 to 2.9 million in 2005, raising the proportion of Thailand's population covered from 73 to 96 per cent. The second reason relates to the scope for upward movements. Achara is not alone in her rural, village redoubt: she looks after the children of her daughter – her two

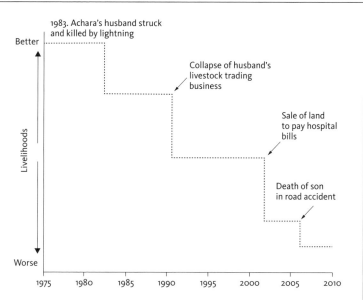

Figure B5.1 From stability to vulnerability in north-east Thailand

grandchildren. Achara's daughter and son-in-law work in Bangkok, the latter as a taxi driver, and remit around 3,000–4,000 baht (US$100–135) per month to Achara, so that she can care for their children. Thailand's industrialization has created the sorts of opportunities – in factories, in domestic work, and in a whole assortment of informal and semi-formal sector activities and settings – that have enabled rural Thais incrementally to inch up the prosperity ladder, even in a context of continuing, even enhanced, vulnerability.

Downward movements, in contrast to upward shifts, are often sudden, unexpected and, not infrequently, debilitating in livelihood terms.[10] They come out of the blue and are livelihood shocks in the real sense: a family member is seriously injured in a motorcycle accident; his income is lost and hospital costs are incurred; land is mortgaged to pay these hospital bills and then lost when falling incomes mean repayments are not met. In these ways, a non-poor family with a sustainable livelihood and a bright future can find its assets eroded, and become poor. It has been suggested (Horrell et al. 2001) that these downward movements exhibit *hysteresis* – in other words, their effects resonate through time, and sometimes across generations, even when the event itself is long in the past. An example might be a family that takes a child out of school following a livelihood shock, causing that child's life chances to be long-term impaired, which will then compromise the ability of that child to support its parents as they grow old and infirm.

Upward movements are gradual and incremental (Box 5.2); downward shifts are sudden and 'lumpy'. Importantly, such highly individual, idiosyncratic sequences (or chains) of unfortunate events are not explained by large-scale processes of social, economic or political change: 'Such monumental or large-scale factors can help explain differences in aggregate poverty among countries, but they shed little light on why some individuals were able to escape poverty while others in their neighbourhoods remained or became poor' (Krishna 2010: 14; and see Baulch and Davis 2008). Not only do these livelihood shocks impact on current generations, they can sometimes also be transferred inter-generationally, a theme which is considered below (see p. 131).

Box 5.2 Upward mobility in Hanoi, Vietnam

Mr Truong provides an example of how hard work and a smidgeon of luck can lever a family into a stronger livelihood position (Figure B5.2). We interviewed Truong in his motorcycle repair shop in Cau Giay in Hanoi in September and November 2010, at which time he was a married man of fifty-two, with three children, a son and two daughters. He was born and raised in a village in Thai Binh, a little over one hundred kilometres south-east of Hanoi, and arrived in Hanoi in 1989. He came to Vietnam's capital originally to find medical care for his son, who had been born with a cleft lip. He scoured the city for the best specialist, visiting five hospitals. His intention initially was to have his son treated, and then return to Thai Binh. But in the event he had to stay. His son underwent five years of treatment in Hanoi and was then transferred to a Swedish-funded children's hospital in Quang Ninh province.

In order to pay to have his son treated, as well as meeting their living expenses in the city, Truong sold a truck he owned in Thai

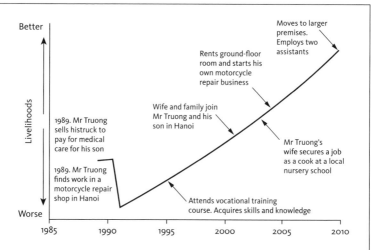

Figure B5.2 From vulnerability to prosperity in north Vietnam

Binh – his only significant asset. This might have been the first of a series of downward livelihood steps. Instead, however, he gradually established himself in the city, found work and enrolled his son in a city school (even though he was still registered as living in Thai Binh). At first Truong worked as an employee in a motorcycle repair shop, having pestered the owner to take him on. He attended a vocational training course in motorcycle maintenance in 2000/01, and gradually accumulated skills and knowledge. He noticed that there was an absence of repair shops in Cau Giay district. He rented a ground-floor room and opened his own repair business in the district in 2005, moving to new, larger premises in 2010. Situated close to a campus of the Vietnam National University, his business thrived. In 2001 his wife, Tam, joined Truong and their son in Hanoi, and she opened a tea stall. The following year his daughters followed, reuniting the family for the first time since 1989. In 2004 Tam became the cook at a local nursery school. In 2010, when we interviewed Truong, he was employing two migrants (from Hung Yen and Tuyen Quang). Truong still owned his house and land (4,000 square metres) in his home village in Thai Binh and returned around three times a year for festivals and to see his relatives. His intention is to retire to his homeland, but for the moment his life and livelihood, both seemingly secure and increasingly remunerative, are centred on Hanoi.

These differences between upward and downward movements mean that government interventions to protect people who fall into poverty will be different from those that might be engineered to lift people out of such a condition. To achieve the former it is necessary to provide social safety nets that support livelihoods at times of personal crisis, and protect family assets (especially land) from being disposed of (see Moser 2009: 252–5). Assets are often built up over years of frugal living and careful shepherding of resources, and can be lost in a moment of bad luck (Hulme and Shepherd 2003: 409).[11] Most important of all safety nets is universal healthcare: to use the subtitle of Krishna's (2010) book, many, many people in the poor world are just 'one illness away from poverty' and 'thousands more have become deeply indebted on account of burdensome health care costs' (ibid.: 73).[12] And for the poor, often their only asset is their labour and this is dependent on their continuing good health. Furthermore, good health is often complementary to other elements of human capital. For the poor and near-poor in the global South, therefore, ill health is the asset risk par excellence. The way that illness can impact on households is revealed in studies of HIV, which characteristically creates a vicious cycle of illness, leading to underproduction and thence to destitution, which is transferred inter-generationally as children are taken out of school, households become single parent headed and, if both parents die, children become orphans:

> The sickness of the main breadwinner adds the burden of care to the workload of women. Sooner or later, they are likely to become sick themselves. Frequent and long periods of sickness deprive the family of their means of production – for example, they are unable to tend the land. Lack of money because of inability to work further limits people's access to health services, and a vicious circle of illness and poverty develops, in which families sell their assets, borrow money and go further down the hill of poverty. (Smith 2002: 66; see also Hulme 2003; Hulme and Moore 2010)

Many illnesses are medically short term, but if they have led to the disposal of assets then livelihoods may become compromised in the long term. It is for this reason that families will often cut consumption to within a whisker of crossing the subsistence threshold (beyond which health and nutrition consequences become intolerable), rather than disposing of critical productive assets such as land and livestock (Barrett and McPeak 2003: 10–11). People, in other words, will accept current transitory poverty in order to protect themselves from chronic future poverty. More germane still, some health shocks are irreversible, leading to a profound and chronic decline in living conditions. These can propel not just the near-poor but also the far-from-poor into poverty (Krishna and Shariff 2011: 542–3). The different ways in which a shock might impact on a chronically and temporarily poor household are schematically set out in Table 5.2. For chronically poor Household A, there is very little room for manoeuvre and the effect is deleterious in the extreme; Household B, on the other hand, has some latitude to cut consumption, protect assets and recover. A third point to make is whether we should treat health spending as non-discretionary (see, for example, Wagstaff and van Doorslaer 2003 on Vietnam). Another study from Vietnam (Ensor and San 1996) showed that the poor delayed obtaining treatment for longer, they avoided more expensive health facilities (hospitals and health centres), instead preferring pharmacies and pharmacist advice, and they were more likely to borrow money to fund treatment, especially from moneylenders.

For South-East Asia, the countries of Indonesia, Malaysia, Singapore and Thailand have effective and reasonably broad-based healthcare schemes to counteract the sort of downward livelihood spiral described above. In the other countries of the region, the poor are less well protected from the depredations of illness. While protection in the form of safety nets may be the key means to protect families from destitution in the face of livelihood shocks, creating the conditions for upward mobility requires a rather different mix of conditions and interventions. In this instance, governments need to create vital, expanding, job-creating economies with efficient bureaucracies and transparent governance, supported by sustained improvements in physical (roads) and social (education, health) infrastructures.

TABLE 5.2 The chronic and transitory poor: shocks to the system

Household example	Why is a household poor?	Nature and depth of poverty	Response to shock	Effect of shock	Resilience/vulnerability status
Poor household A	Structural	Persistent, deep	Selling of productive assets	Profound	Vulnerable
Poor household B	Stochastic shock	Transitory, shallow	Cutting of consumption	Disturbing but short term	Resilient

A recurring theme in recent studies is an interest in 'resilience' (often paired with vulnerability). Building resilient communities, economies, societies and livelihoods has been a leitmotif of the last decade, linked to the challenges posed by climate change, regional and global economic and financial crises, and the War on Terror. Because resilience has been taken up by such a broad range of subject areas, it is not surprising that definitions also vary. However, key attributes of most definitions include: the capacity to withstand shocks and positively adapt; and the ability to return quickly to a pre-shock state ('bounce-back-ability'). What is less clear is what makes for resilience and, even more pertinently, whether it is possible to plan and govern for resilience.

Bumping along the bottom: shocks when you are close to the edge The discussion in Chapter 3 highlighted the remarkable decline in both the proportion and the number of people in the wider Asian region living on less than US$1 a day (see p. 51). Figure 5.2a reinforces this point, showing the number of people living on less than $1 per day by country in South-East Asia in 1990 and 2005. These data reveal that the number of poor shrunk by 70 per cent from close to 24 million in 1990 to just 7 million in 2005. In some countries such as Thailand and Malaysia it would seem that poverty had been eradicated by 2005, at least on the basis of these measures. What, though, if we raise the poverty line to $2 a day? Then, as Figure 5.2b illustrates, a large number of additional poor 'appear' and the record becomes rather less impressive, with a decline in the number of poor from 66 million to 43 million, or 34 per cent. In a similar way that adjusting the poverty line (or its calculation) can lead to very large shifts in the number of poor, so too with changes in household expenditure, on which measures of poverty are often calculated.[13] Small changes in expenditure, whether up or down, can markedly alter the numbers calculated as living in poverty without, of course, leading to any significant change in actual well-being (see Davis and Baulch 2011).

What the data in Figures 5.2a and 5.2b show is that there are large numbers of people in South-East Asia living very close to the $1-a-day poverty line. These individuals and households are particularly vulnerable to the shocks discussed in this chapter, and they often lack the physical resources, economic assets and social capital[14] – and therefore lack the resilience – to respond to negative events. It is also true that the effects of national economic expansion and contraction are far from uniformly experienced. Therefore it is not just that in poor countries there are characteristically many individuals crowding

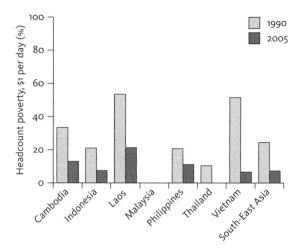

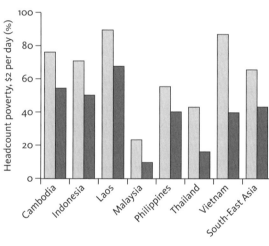

Figures 5.2a and 5.2b The margins of poverty in South-East Asia (1990 and 2005)

close to the poverty line, but also that a change in national economic fortunes will impact on these individuals in varied ways.

The near-poor are much less able to respond creatively to the sorts of shocks that are characteristic of slides into poverty – vehicle accidents, serious illness, dowry demands and wedding and funeral expenses, for example. Such shocks can lead, in turn, to the selling of assets and the withdrawal of children from school, thus transforming a time-specific shock into an inter-generational sequence of effects, as noted above. The non-poor are in a much better position to smooth consumption, to cut discretionary spending, protect assets (including future assets in the form of children's schooling) and trade off different aspects of well-being than the poor and near-poor. For those with assets, even when they descend into poverty, this is far more likely to be short-term than for those who are asset-deficient, particularly if they are in a position to protect their core asset base.[15] It is for this reason that Carter and Barrett (2006; and see Barrett and McPeak 2003) propose that if we are to distinguish between structural and stochastic (non-deterministic) poverty transitions we need to develop asset-based poverty lines that can reveal the structural foundations of poverty, and therefore the longer-term prospects of those who happen to be poor at a particular point in time. For those who are poor but have protected their asset base, time is on their side and their condition of poverty is likely to be short lived; for those who are poor and without assets are caught in a poverty trap with the likely outcome of chronic poverty (Barrett and McPeak 2003: 3). (This important distinction was discussed in connection with the PSID data – see p. 112). It is also the case that descents into poverty (see Box 5.1) are often not limited to single events but sequences of events, or 'event histories', as Krishna terms them (2011: 25). These may be connected or unconnected.

While the poor may be less resilient and more vulnerable than the non-poor, it is important to emphasize that even the 'rich' are susceptible to shocks that can make them vulnerable and then drive them into poverty. As Bird and Shinyekwa write in the case of their study in rural Uganda:

> Membership of a non-poor family provides an individual with a number of positive and mutually reinforcing advantages: good diet; access to education; access to health care; higher status; a network of friends and patrons in and outside the village; the ability to travel outside the village, and therefore exposure to ideas; more land or livestock to inherit; and more likelihood of marrying well. *However, these advantages cannot necessarily be used to predict that an individual and their household will be able to avoid either short or extended periods of poverty.* (2005: 64, emphasis added)

On the basis of their study, Bird and Shinyekwa argue that targeting only vulnerable groups (female-headed households, the disabled, families living with AIDS, the elderly) may mean that richer households which are pulled into poverty owing to a sequence of untoward events are overlooked.

POVERTY DURING THE INDONESIAN *KRISMON* While this chapter makes a case for the central position of ordinary, idiosyncratic events in shaping livelihood pathways, this is far from suggesting that higher-scale events and conditions do not reverberate through communities and households. This was all too clear during the Asian economic crisis of 1997–99, introduced in Chapter 3. In Indonesia, the country of Asia most seriously affected economically, the poverty rate more than doubled from 15 per cent at the start of the crisis in mid-1997 to 33 per cent by the end of 1998, during which the economy shrunk by almost 14 per cent (Suryahadi et al. 2003a). Given the severity of Indonesia's economic contraction, and bearing in mind how many people were living close to the poverty line even before the crisis (see Figures 5.2a and 5.2b), it is not surprising or remarkable that poverty should have increased. Two issues are worth noting, however. First of all, statements such as '36 million additional people were pushed into absolute poverty [in Indonesia] due to the crisis' (ibid.: 240), give the impression that 36 million *new poor* were added to an existing, and comparatively stable, poverty stock. As the earlier discussion emphasized, it is highly likely that the actual numbers moving across the poverty line over this period were substantially greater than 35 million, including not a few moving upwards, and out of poverty. It is just that there were many more still moving downwards, giving us the net figure of 35 million.

Table 5.3 seeks to show how personal, idiosyncratic events or event histories intersect with regional, national, even global, co-variate events. During *krismon*, the balance between co-variate events causing people to fall into or rise out of poverty shifted towards the former as the economic crisis led to cuts in government spending, a reduction in employment, layoffs and bankruptcies. At the same time, however, there were still people rising out of poverty owing to the increasing prices of export crops, inheritance, strategic marriages, and the securing of employment in a buoyant export manufacturing sector.

The point that the stock of poor is not simply being 'added to' during a period of economic contraction, such as that which occurred during *krismon* in Indonesia (or, alternatively, being denuded during a period of economic expansion), is evident from longitudinal surveys that tracked individuals over the course of the crisis. One such survey is the Indonesia Family Life Survey (IFLS1), first undertaken in 1993/94 among 7,224 households and around 22,000 individuals by the RAND Corporation and the Demographic Institute of the University of Indonesia. The survey was repeated in 1997 (IFLS2), 1998 (IFLS2+) and 2000 (IFLS3), thus covering the period of Indonesia's economic crisis and its aftermath. The fourth wave of the IFLS was undertaken in 2007/2008.[16]

Using the IFLS data from 1993, 1997 and 2000, the poverty headcount

TABLE 5.3 Contextual scales in the shaping of livelihood and poverty pathways

Scale	Falling (into poverty)	Rising (out of poverty)
Personal and local (idio-syncratic)	Serious illness or injury Death Major crop failure Dowry and wedding expenses Family disputes Divorce Funeral costs Theft or fire Significant medical outlays Redundancy	New job Inheritance Increasing returns Higher salary Acquired skills/education Positive marriage
Regional (co-variate)	Floods Droughts Storms Civil disturbance Insecurity Reduction in job opportunities	Educational opportunities Non-farm employment opportunities Roads Electrification Clean water Urban development
National (co-variate)	Economic contraction Political instability Corruption and inefficiency	Economic expansion Political stability Good governance

among the surveyed population increased slightly from 14.6 per cent in 1997 to 15.0 per cent in 2000 (Widyanti et al. 2009: 11).[17] Over the three periods, however, while only around 4 per cent of the sample were always poor and some two-thirds never poor, 30 per cent were sometimes poor, divided in Table 5.4 into the chronic poor (twice poor) and the occasionally poor (once poor). These data from Indonesia are supported by studies in other parts of the poorer world.[18] Some of the best studies come from Bangladesh, where research consistently shows the livelihood turbulence of the poor and the near-poor.[19]

The second point to highlight is the way in which the crisis revealed the very large number of people at risk of falling below the poverty line. Just increasing the poverty line from 28,516 to 35,645 rupiah per person per month more than doubled the headcount of poor at the time of the crisis from 10.0 per cent to 22.1 per cent (Suryahadi et al. 2003a: 227–88). Where the poverty line is drawn can have a large effect on the number of people designated poor, especially in developing countries, where a significant proportion of the population are concentrated close to the poverty line (see Figures 5.2a and 5.2b).

TABLE 5.4 Poverty dynamics in Indonesia, 1993, 1997 and 2000

Category of poor	1993	1997	2000	Incidence (%)	
Always poor	poor	poor	poor	4.23	
Chronic poor	poor	poor	not poor	4.33	
(twice poor)	poor	not poor	poor	3.56	9.89
	not poor	poor	poor	2.00	
Occasionally poor	poor	not poor	not poor	10.93	
(once poor)	not poor	poor	not poor	4.00	20.16
	not poor	not poor	poor	5.23	
Never poor	not poor	not poor	not poor	65.72	

Source: Adapted from Widyanti et al. (2009: 11) and based on IFLS data (6,403 observations)

The discussion so far has focused on intra-generational turbulence and unpredictability in livelihood trajectories and therefore poverty dynamics over the life course. These features are often hidden from view when understandings of poverty, prosperity and livelihoods are based on cross-sectional data. This has sometimes led to assumptions that there is a relatively unchanging stock of poor people. Rather, the poor are being continually reconstituted as events – from life-course processes to car accidents and fortuitous inheritances – lift people and households out of poverty or, alternatively, force them to sink into such a state. Using panel data for 240 households in six villages in rural South India regularly collected between 1975 and 1984, Gaiha and Deolalikar (1993: 418) show the churning in the 'stock' of poor over this nine-year period. At the two extremes, 12 per cent of households were never poor and 22 per cent were always (chronically) poor. Between these two extremes, however, was a broad spread of households that were poor for between one and eight years. The turbulence revealed in this study is characteristic of conditions in much of the global South, where poverty, far from having been 'tackled' as the Asian discourse often has it, lies disconcertingly close to the surface. In addition, the events that produce such trajectories of poverty (and prosperity) are not infrequently idiosyncratic and hard to second-guess. As the work discussed above reveals, even the relatively rich can become poor. Finally, the processes and event histories that generate downward momentum are different from those that propel people upwards. What has only been touched on, however, and to which the chapter now turns, is how livelihood conditions are transmitted inter-generationally.

Between the generations: the sins of the father

Inter-generational mobility The inter-generational transmission (IGT) of poverty (and, by implication, prosperity) focuses on the degree to which poverty is passed from one generation to the next. This is not a simple transmission of a poverty 'package', so that one generation's poverty experience is simply handed to and then repeated for the next. It often involves a reproduction of poverty in new ways (Bird 2007: 1). This, then, injects a further element of contingency to those discussed above with regard to intra-generational issues.

The best data on IGT poverty come from the countries of the global North and, especially, the United States. These data reveal that the children of the poor have significantly fewer life chances than the non-poor. Five, not mutually exclusive, conceptual approaches have been developed to explain IGT poverty in the USA, and these overlap to some extent with those developed to explain the intra-generational transmission of poverty outlined towards the start of this chapter. Drawing on and summarizing the work of Bird (ibid.: 4–7) and Corcoran (1995), we can see these explanatory frameworks rippling outwards from the poor subject to the neighbourhood and thence to embrace the prevailing political economy:

- The *economic resources (ER) model* focuses attention on the limited resources that parents have to invest in their children. Poor households focus on immediate survival, rather than investing in (for example) the education of their children to build the human capital that might permit their children to build better lives as adults. Such families are also forced to live in areas with high levels of crime, poor schools and so forth, thus linking the ER model with the social isolation (SI) model (see below).
- The *correlated disadvantages (CD) model* widens the area of concern from income to include other measures of human capital, such as the education level of parents and their health profiles. This explanatory model suggests that it is not economic resources alone which explain IGT poverty but this in conjunction with other parental disadvantages. These other disadvantages can impede a child's development just as much as lack of income in a household.
- The *family structure (FS) model* pays particular attention to the make-up of the family or household; female-headed households and single-parent families more generally, and the children of teenage or unmarried mothers, are more likely to be poor than children of 'intact' families.

- The *social isolation (SI) model* posits that there is a neighbourhood effect where a social underclass exists alongside high levels of unemployment, poor schools, negative role models and long-term poverty.
- Finally, the *welfare culture (WC) model* suggests that welfare systems can lead to cycles of dependency, creating perverse incentives that militate against seeking employment or getting married; a culture of welfare is created and an underclass exhibiting deviant values, behaviours and attitudes with it. This 'underclass' model (Murray 1993) has generally replaced the 'culture of poverty' model.

The inter-generational transmission of livelihood shocks Livelihood shocks such as those discussed in the first half of this chapter not only impact on current generations; they can sometimes also be transmitted inter-generationally. Usually this is seen in terms of transmission from parents to children, although the process can operate the other way, from children to parents (see below).

Using the Indonesian Family Life Survey (IFLS) introduced above, Suryadarma et al. (2009) explore the impacts of orphanhood on young children's health and education.[20] Regarding health outcomes, the data reveal no statistically significant effects. But as to education, maternal orphanhood resulted in young children receiving between 0.6 and 1.7 years less schooling in the short term, and as much as 3.2 years less schooling in the long term. Such is the impact of maternal orphanhood on educational outcomes that 'the effects [of] being a maternal orphan [are], *ceteris paribus*, worse than living in a chronically poor household' (ibid.: 14).

Studies from Africa, where the effects of AIDS have led to particular attention being paid to the issue of orphanhood, provide a richer and still more nuanced view of the effects of the loss of parents on children. Using a panel data set of 1,422 rural households in Kenya collected in 1997, 2000 and 2002, Yamano and Jayne (2005) investigate the effects of orphanhood from AIDS on children's school attendance. While for the poorer half (in terms of initial assets in 1997) of the sample, orphanhood led to a real decline in educational outcomes, for the richer half of families there were no significant detectable effects (ibid.: 621). The effects of orphanhood were, in addition, felt even before the death of the working-age adults, and were experienced particularly acutely among girls. Children, and particularly girls, leave school to care for ailing adults and/or school fees are reallocated to meet escalating medical costs. The data suggest that less poor households are in a position to cope with illness and death by cutting discretionary spending, rather than by withdrawing children from school. Given the effects of education on future life chances, this then helps to protect such families from inter-generational decline.

The role of schooling in shaping the inter-generational transmission of poverty and prosperity has been revealed in various studies, for example in the Philippines (Ghuman et al. 2005) and Vietnam (Behrman and Knowles 1999). There are complex sets of interactions at work. Ghuman et al. (2005) show how the father's schooling impacts on early childhood development in the Philippines, reflected in language skills and various anthropometric indicators. In their study of Vietnam, Behrman and Knowles (1999) show that socio-economic status has a significant bearing on educational attainment, leading them to suggest that this might perpetuate social immobility.[21] It is not only that raw years of schooling are less for the poor than for the non-poor; sometimes of even greater significance is the quality of that schooling. One of the reasons why rural migrants to Vietnam's capital, Hanoi, leave their rural homes and establish a base in the city is so that their children can attend the better schools in the capital. This, in turn, raises the chances of their passing the highly competitive university examinations, gaining access to a high-demand course at one of the country's more prestigious universities and, thus, achieving the qualifications and establishing the social networks that might lead to gainful and remunerative employment (Nguyen et al. 2012). If this is the outcome, then the parent–child bargain (or implicit social contract) should ensure that the child provides for his/her parents in their old age. Conversely, the failure of a child to secure employ-

TABLE 5.5 Transmission of poverty through the life course, Indonesia (1993–2000)

Poverty status of original household in 1993	Poverty status after marriage (%)*		N
	Not poor	Poor	
Not chronically poor	90.4	9.6	782
Chronically poor	51.9	48.1	163
Total	84.6	15.4	945

Note: The study from which this table is drawn focuses on those children who were chronically poor in 1993 (i.e. they were as least twice poor over the three waves of the study in 1993, 1997 and 2000 – see Table 5.4), and were married between 1997 and 2000

Source: Pakpahan et al. (2009: 8)

ment commensurate with that investment may compromise support for parents in their old age. The child–parent bargain, in such an instance, fails and ageing parents are at risk of becoming vulnerable and poor – transmitting poverty from the child (back) to the parent.

Using the Indonesia Family Life Survey (IFLS) data set introduced above, Pakpahan et al. (2009) assess the transmission of poverty through the life course, tracking children in poor and non-poor families as they become adults and then get married. It is evident (Table 5.5) that those children living in chronically poor households in 1993 had a significantly greater chance of remaining poor as adults than those in non-chronically poor households. Nonetheless, even among the original chronically poor they were marginally more likely to become non-poor than to remain poor. The reasons why the children of the chronically poor are more likely to be poor themselves are partly because of their generally poorer education and health profiles. Also significant – and this links back to the earlier discussion – is that such households lack the social (positive networks of association), economic (savings) and physical (land) assets that might protect investment in children during periods of livelihood stress. Nonetheless, just as there are a range of factors that influence upward and downward intra-generational livelihood trajectories (see Table 5.3), so there are a range of influences that shape the inter-generational transmission of poverty (Table 5.6). These are divided in Table 5.6 into the structural and the idiosyncratic, the former of which are predictable and the latter irregular, erratic and unpredictable. These unpredictable events are far more influential than usually assumed, a point that is germane for understanding both the intra- and inter-generational transmission of poverty and prosperity.

TABLE 5.6 Intra- and extra-household factors shaping IGT poverty

	Structural	Idiosyncratic
Intra-household	Culture of poverty Household structure and composition (e.g. female headship) Dependency ratios Under-nutrition Curtailed or poor education	Illness and health shocks Accidents Orphanhood
Extra-household	Conflict Discrimination Caste	Natural disaster – earthquake, tsunami

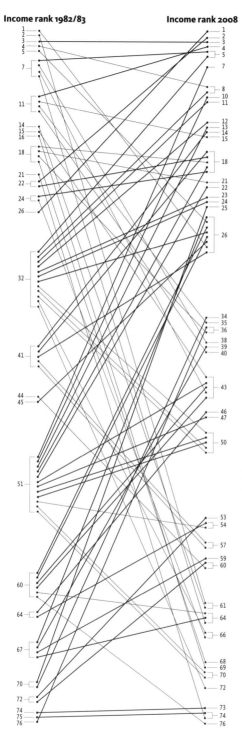

Income rank 1982/83

Income rank 2008

Figure 5.3 Wealth and poverty transitions in north-east Thailand, 1982–83 and 2008

From 35,000 households to 77: tracking the life course and inter-generational transmission of wealth and poverty

Over six years between 2001 and 2007, Anirudh Krishna and his colleagues interviewed 35,000 households in 400 communities of India, Kenya, Uganda, Peru and North Carolina, USA (Krishna 2010; and see Krishna 2011, Krishna and Shariff 2011). The outcome of this massive effort was to highlight three central points regarding the intra- (life course) and inter-generational transmission of poverty. First, that many of the poor were not born into poverty; they became poor over their lifetimes. Secondly, that the reasons *why* they became poor were not because of high-level, country-wide processes (e.g. economic decline) and events (e.g. earthquakes); rather, it was because of low-level, highly personal, discrete and often idiosyncratic events. And thirdly, there was an important geographical dimension to the routes into and out of poverty; country and local context mattered, whether that was bio-environmental, sociocultural or politico-economic (see below).

On a much smaller scale, in 2008 Albert Salamanca and I undertook a longitudinal panel study of two villages in north-eastern Thailand, where I had worked as a PhD student some quarter of a century earlier (in 1982/83). We tracked down 77 of the original 81 households I had surveyed, or their descendants.[22] Of these 77, we then interviewed 15 in detail. Among the larger sample of 77 households, we collected information on 'wealth', as I had done in 1982/83. There are two notable features of this much smaller longitudinal data set. First of all, between 1982 and 2008 *every* household surveyed had become wealthier in (real) income terms, most of them markedly so. Adjusting the data to 2006 prices, while the poorest household in 1982/83 had an income of just 1,180 baht, the poorest household in 2008 had an annual income of 7,380 baht.

The second notable feature – and here the data resonate with Krishna's – is the turbulence in the trajectories of poverty and prosperity over the twenty-five years that divide the surveys (Figure 5.3). Distilling the information presented graphically in Figure 5.3, thirteen households belonged to the poorest 20 per cent in 1982/83. Of these, only three remained in the same quintile in 2008. Of the fifteen households in the richest 20 per cent in 1982/83, five households retained this position based on the 2008 survey. The remainder had slipped down in the rankings, with two of the 'original rich' households becoming 'new poor' households. Although some households in each category had stayed in the same quintile over the twenty-five years, most had shifted their position.

TABLE 5.7 The power of the ordinary – inauspicious events and livelihood effects in north-east Thailand (1982–2009)

Household identifier	Inauspicious events	Livelihood effects
2-225 – Mot	Mot's husband was laid off from his job at a government agricultural research station in 1985. In 1995 he had a stroke, leaving him paralysed. In the same year Mot's son-in-law was involved in a car accident which also left him paralysed. After three years, Mot's husband developed asthma which got worse, leading to his early death in 2006.	Medical costs forced Mot to sell eight head of buffalo, eating into her asset base. As a female head she struggled to improve her standard of living.
2-210 – Ning	Ning's husband was frequently sick prior to his premature death in 1998. A fire gutted her former dwelling around 2005.	Ning's life and livelihood declined leading up to and following her husband's death. He was so sickly that she needed to find money to pay for his medical care.
2-185 – Ob	Ob had a serious car accident in 1997. One of Ob's three sons died, leaving a widow and two children.	The costs of medical care following her accident did not force the sale of this household's 10 rai of land, and the family were able to protect their assets.
2-182 – Somboon	All three of Somboon's sons left the village, leaving Somboon to take care of his grandchildren.	Somboon's livelihood is now shaped by the need to raise his grandchildren, and his sons do not remit sufficient funds to meet the necessary costs.
2-116 – Ann	Ann was divorced at the age of twenty, before having any children.	Ann lives in the household of her younger sister but owns land under her own name.

1-137 – Kai	Kai and his wife had seven children, one of whom died. Kai's wife passed away in 2003, and shortly thereafter one of his daughters died from a kidney ailment in Bangkok. Kai's eyesight began to fail in 2006. He is now frail and depends on his children.	Kai's wife brought in more income than he did, from her job selling food in the local school. After her death, the household ran into financial difficulties and this prevented him from funding his children's higher education, compromising both his and their prospects.
1-111 – Chayan	Chayan had two sons and two daughters. One of Chayan's two sons, who was married with a young child, died in 1995 in a car crash at the age of twenty-one.	–
1-083 – Oy	Oy's husband died in 2001, and of her six children one died in infancy (the only son) and her fourth daughter died in 2002.	The early loss of her husband led to a sharp fall-off in household income, making the running of the small rice mill they owned impossible for Oy alone. Five rai of land were mortgaged to the Bank for Agriculture and Agricultural Cooperatives to meet escalating costs.
1-027 – Kamol	Failure of livestock trading business led to indebtedness.	Kamol was forced to sell 9 rai of land in 1987 to pay off a loan, but despite this distress sale of assets managed to largely absorb the shock of business failure.
1-006 – Achara (see also Box 5.1)	Achara's husband was killed in a lightning strike in 1983. In 1986 she was forced to sell a large portion of her land to pay medical bills after she was hospitalized owing to a liver ailment. Her son subsequently died in a car accident in Pattaya. Achara suffers from heart problems and hypertension.	The death of Achara's husband led to the failure of the family's livestock trading business and a chronic decline in income and well-being. In 1986, Achara was forced to sell a large part of her land to pay medical bills.

Source: Surveys and interviews, 2008/09 (Rigg and Salamanca 2009)

While there are important methodological challenges connected with measuring wealth, it was striking how far the rich and poor households in 1982/83 were not those of 2008. To reiterate a point made earlier in the chapter, while there is always a population of poor people, such is the turbulence in this population that the individuals who comprise the poor and non-poor 'stocks' change from year to year, from generation to generation and from era to era. This dynamism mirrors the findings of Edmundson (1994: 140), who noted on the basis of a village study in Java, Indonesia, that 'the rich and the poor may be "with us always" but the individuals who comprise these groups appear to be always changing'. This emphasizes the tenuousness of a household's wealth ranking. While structural interpretations may stress the degree to which households and individuals are 'trapped' in poverty (and, by implication, others are 'embedded' in a condition of wealth), these data reveal something far more fluid. We may be in a position to identify 'rich' and 'poor' categories but the households that populate these categories change markedly over time.

What surprised us in seeking to understand the patterns revealed in Figure 5.3 was the degree to which household livelihood pathways had been shaped, and sometimes profoundly reoriented, by idiosyncratic shocks. To be sure, the bigger picture was important: the emergence of Thailand as a miracle economy in the mid-1980s and the Thai economic crisis of 1997, for example, were both significant and important events (see Figure 3.1). Nonetheless, looking across the life histories of the fifteen households we investigated in detail, it is hard not to come to the conclusion that serendipitous moments and, more particularly, inauspicious events were critically important in shaping livelihood pathways and outcomes, as summarized in Table 5.7. A particular theme in this table is the role of illness and accident, often leading to the need to meet substantial medical costs, in compromising livelihoods in the long term by impeding educational investment, forcing asset disposal, or leading to business failure. Krishna also found that poor health and the need to meet consequent health-related expenses were principal reasons for descents into poverty in his much larger sample. They are a major reason for descent for 60 per cent of the sample in Rajasthan (India), 88 per cent in Gujarat (India), 74 per cent in Andhra Pradesh (India), 74 per cent in western Kenya, 71 per cent in central and western Uganda, and 67 per cent in Peru (Krishna 2010: 79).

The straightforward implication of Krishna's large-scale, multi-country study and Albert Salamanca and my rather more modest effort in Thailand is to highlight that many of the world's poor are not born into poverty. They become poor. And they become poor for the sorts of reasons that large-scale, cross-sectional, statistical surveys often overlook and which a focus on high-profile co-variate events obscures. One of the fullest studies of inter-generational poverty in the global South comes from a panel survey of 4,198 households across eighteen villages in Rajasthan, India, undertaken at four points between 1977 and 2010 (Krishna 2011). In the study, the inter-generational poor (IGP) were defined as those who were poor at all four points in time – in 1977, 1994, 2002 and 2010.[23] This group amounted to 819 households or 19.5 per cent of the sample. Over the period in question, 61 per cent of households had the *possibility* of being poor, but just one third of this number were always poor. Baulch and Davis's (2008) study of rural Bangladesh shows a similar high level of movement of people in and out of poverty over the survey period.[24]

The role of context in shaping transitions A general conclusion to be drawn from the discussion in this chapter is that there is more turbulence, contingency and complexity in both the character of poverty (and prosperity) at any one point in time and – which is more germane – in the trajectories or transition paths that lift people out of poverty or propel them into a livelihood decline. This, however, should not lead one to overlook the place of context, both national and geographical, in shaping transition paths and experiences. One indication of the importance of context is provided by the monthly exit rates from poverty in different countries.[25] Using published panel study data, Barrett and McPeak (2003: 1–2) provide the following indicative monthly exit rates:

- United States: 6.9 per cent
- Côte d'Ivoire: 1.3 per cent
- KwaZulu-Natal: 0.7 per cent
- Madagascar (rural): 0.6 per cent
- Kenya (rural): 0.4 per cent.

The nature of economic expansion and the policies that accompany expansion, the types and extent of social safety nets that protect the poor and near-poor and their assets, the location and form of government investment in social and physical infrastructure, and the existence of discriminatory tendencies that exclude groups from full participation in social and economic life, all play a role in influencing the transmission of poverty. Using the US PSID dataset and examining poverty dynamics between 1970 and 1982, Bane and Ellwood (1986) show that of the non-elderly poor, 44.5 per cent had exited from poverty within a year, and 60.3 per cent within two years. Only 12 per cent remained poor over the full period.

Context also matters sub-nationally, in terms of *type* of household and livelihood and the often quite specific geographical characteristics of areas in terms of culture, environment and economy (Table 5.8). Even when income or consumption are equivalent, households will exhibit varying levels of resilience, they will be unequally vulnerable, and their chances of descending into poverty or rising from it will also be different. These variations in settlement and household context profiles play an important role in influencing the patterns of vulnerability and resilience that surveys reveal.

TABLE 5.8 Context matters

Context	Example
Geographical characteristics	Proximity to a town or other urban centre
	Availability and access to transport infrastructure
	Customary norms (dowries, funeral feasts, etc.)
	Community support structures (social capital)
Household characteristics	Asset profile
	Age structure (life course moment) of household
	Balance between farm and non-farm income
	Headship (female-headed plus age of household head)
	Household size and ratio of dependants
	Education level of adult household members
Event character	Serious illness/injury
	Production fall (crop failure) due to flood, drought or pest attack
	Economic crises/failure, either general leading to redundancy or inflation or specific (for example, steep fall in commodity prices)

Conclusion

This chapter has highlighted how an apparently simple, indeed almost intuitive, question is far more complex than it appears at first sight. The straightforward question is: who is poor? This appears a simple question because the data are so readily available, and presented with such apparent clarity and precision. The poor population are tabulated by region and occupation, often to one or two decimal points, and their decline or increase neatly graphed. The trend lines are often reassuringly smooth. Macroscopic events and processes, and in particular aggregate economic considerations, are then used to account for the poverty trends that the data appear to reveal.

As the chapter has outlined, however, answering the questions 'who is poor?' and 'why are they poor?' is more complicated than it appears. Furthermore, in answering these two questions a string of even less well-understood questions are shunted into view. Many of these coalesce around the theme of poverty dynamics and transitions. How is poverty transmitted over time and across the generations? What makes some households more vulnerable than others, even when incomes are the same? What are the life chances of those born into poverty relative to the non-poor? Under what circumstances do the non-poor become poor? And what policies might protect the non-poor, support the near-poor and assist the poor? In considering these questions we are encouraged to move from the macroscopic to the microscopic, from structure to agency, and from focusing on momentous and co-variate events such as earthquakes and economic crises to idiosyncratic and ordinary ones, from car accidents to ill-nesses. The knowledge gap lies not so much in the sphere of poverty profiles, about which we know a good deal, but in understanding the conditions and processes that create the profiles that the data outline. Writing of poverty in the USA (and the point that she makes is even more germane for the global South), Sawhill says: 'We are swamped with facts about people's incomes and about the number and composition of people who inhabit the lower [poverty] tail, but we don't know very much about the process that generates these results' (Sawhill 1988: 1085). Sawhill's point is well taken, but even with this knowledge we must still accept – and again, particularly for the global South, where the proportion of the non-poor population who face the *possibility* of being poor is significant – that we are not in a position to predict the future poor.

What does this mean for policy? To pick up on a point made right at the start of this book, 'targeting' policy interventions in such a context is extremely difficult. As Krishna and Shariff write in the con-text of their study of rural poverty dynamics in India between 1993 and 2005: 'No variable is consistently significant (or not significant) across all states. *Thus, no standardized policy can be uniformly effective*' (Krishna and Shariff 2011: 541, emphasis added). For these scholars, simply claiming that growth of aggregate consumption or income will inevitably lift people out of poverty 'does not amount to an adequate policy prescription' (ibid.: 543). We also need to acknowledge that the conditions and therefore policies that might help lift people out of poverty, and the events and processes that cause a decline into poverty, are characteristically differently shaped, the former being gradual and incremental, and the latter sharp and sudden. Furthermore, and as the next chapter will address, how people respond to events and opportunities is also not as clear as some policy prescriptions seem to suggest.

6 | Fertility decline and its consequences in Asia

> The problem is that it is impossible to develop a reasonable popula-
> tion policy without understanding why some people have so many
> children. (Banerjee and Duflo 2011: 106)

Introduction

The notion that we can anticipate and predict – and therefore
plan through targeted interventions – how people will respond to
events and opportunities, and perhaps even shape those responses
in a carefully calibrated way, is a deceit. Chapter 5 focused on the
importance of ordinary, everyday events in people's lives, and how
these can turn prospects upside down. This chapter pays attention
to the ways in which the structures of living and the grammars of
life alter, but in often surprising ways, under the influence of social
and economic transformations. And the way that, in turn, social and
economic transformations are shaped by such grammars. It is, therefore, about the interplay of structure and agency, and the place of the
state and the policies of the state in this relationship. In addition,
however, the chapter concerns itself with the challenge of anticipating
how populations (individuals and groups) will respond to 'stimuli'
and the power of governments, through policy interventions, to alter
behaviours. The question that lies at the core of this chapter is: why
do people do what they do?

This question could, clearly, be considered in the context of a very
wide array of concerns. The focus here, however, is demographic and,
more particularly, on fertility, family planning, marriage, household
and family structure, migration and mobility, and gender and generational relations. The empirical material that will be used to sub-
stantiate the arguments rehearsed will be drawn from the East and
South-East Asian regions, with the experiences of Indonesia, Thailand
and Vietnam foremost.

These demographic concerns are all big topics, and scholars have
built careers on their individual study, producing book-length treat-
ments in the process. This chapter cannot, clearly, provide a comprehensive insight into the empirical minutiae of these important

demographic themes. Instead, the intention is to highlight the complex combinations of factors at work, the different ways that populations have responded to such factors, and the intersection of the processes identified. Falling fertility across Asia is a momentous event in itself; but it has also contributed to changing marriage patterns, altered sexualities, new mobilities, and reworked gender and generational relations. These, like the fall in fertility itself, were not planned for, rarely anticipated, and therefore mostly unintended. Moreover, their importance in understanding the development past and development future in Asia is unquestionable, even though the latter remains uncertain. As will become evident as the chapter unfolds, the words that keep repeating themselves are 'unexpected', 'uncertain', 'unprecedented' and 'unanticipated'.

Framing the demographic picture Because this chapter covers so many interlinked processes that are all too often analysed separately by scholars and analysts working in different subject areas, it is helpful to begin – rather than to end – by framing the themes in terms of their associations. This is not to gloss over the other actors and intervening processes; there are many. Rather it is to provide an explanatory context that will help mutually to situate the different themes of the chapter.

Fertility decline lies at the core of the account that follows. Why fertility declined in such a precipitous manner is the source of considerable debate; it has not fallen equally across the region and the differences between and within countries reveal the shaping influence of cultural and historical context, not infrequently over that of state family planning programmes and levels of economic development. The decline in fertility has meant smaller families, and an associated emphasis on the 'quality' over 'quantity' of children. The rise in educational levels, linked (but not deterministically) with declining fertility, has contributed to men's but especially women's growing mobility and thus to the postponement of marriage as women further their careers, particularly when patriarchal traditions might impede a woman's independence and professional progress. Many men, especially in rural areas of the richer countries of East Asia, face a marriage squeeze and have turned to poorer countries to find marriage partners. At the same time, a growing proportion of unmarried women in their thirties and forties are, it seems, opting for singlehood in a region where marriage was recently generally universal (again, with some important exceptions). Mobility, and the gendered and generational character of mobility, has altered the structure and functioning of households, while delocalizing livelihoods have created new (multi-sited) livelihood footprints. This has impacted on farming as labour shortages have led, *in extremis*, to land standing idle. The position and status of women, and especially young women, have also altered, reconfiguring gender roles and relations.

While we can go some way to generalizing about the presence of these changes across the East and South-East Asian regions, their depth, pattern and interrelationships vary in such a manner as to warn against blanket statements. As this chapter will show, scholars did not anticipate rapid fertility decline, or the complex array of associated changes in economy and society that have, we can see with hindsight, flowed from (and contributed to) this decline in fertility.

Fertility and fertility decline

> Undoubtedly, Asia's reproductive revolution has been one of the most significant and far-reaching changes in human behaviour of the second half of the twentieth century. (Jones and Leete 2002: 122)

The countries of East and South-East Asia have experienced a striking and dramatic decline in fertility over the last half-century – historically unprecedented in terms of its speed and extent (Table 6.1). By 2009, the fertility rates of China, Hong Kong, Japan, South Korea, Singapore, Thailand and Vietnam were all below replacement levels of 2.1 children per woman, and several other countries of the region were well on the way to reaching this figure. Most attention, understandably, has been paid to China, because of both that country's size and its unique and draconian 'one child' policy. However, other countries in the wider Asian region have also seen steep falls in fertility in the absence of coercive policies, and strikingly in the context of populations that were largely rural, often poor and not infrequently illiterate. As Freeman observed in the mid-1990s: 'When I first began studying Asia's fertility and family planning efforts 33 years ago, neither I nor other serious observers expected such rapid fertility declines to occur on that continent ...' (Freeman 1995: 3).[1] To understand the significance of this momentous decline in fertility we need to track back to the 1960s and the conceptual models that framed – and often continue to frame – our understanding of fertility decline.

Explaining fertility decline In the 1960s the reasons for fertility decline were not generally disputed, and were interpreted through the lens of the classical demographic transition model, one of the most cited

145

TABLE 6.1 Fertility decline in East and South-East Asia, 1960–2009 (fertility rate, total – births per woman)

	1960	1965	1970	1975	1980	1985	1990	1995	2000	2005	2009
East Asia											
China	5.47	5.52	5.87	5.51	3.78	2.63	2.64	2.34	1.87	1.74	1.67
Hong Kong	5.16	5.21	4.55	3.42	2.67	2.05	1.49	1.27	1.30	1.04	0.97
Korea, Dem. Rep.	3.64	3.59	3.76	4.04	3.10	2.71	2.72	2.41	2.31	2.11	2.04
South-East Asia											
Brunei Darussalam	6.49	6.49	6.07	5.75	5.37	4.25	3.79	3.53	2.93	2.40	2.18
Cambodia	6.30	6.30	6.31	5.92	4.90	5.86	6.71	5.74	4.90	3.82	3.06
Indonesia	5.67	5.66	5.61	5.47	5.04	4.43	3.75	3.12	2.70	2.45	2.28
Lao PDR	5.96	5.96	5.97	5.97	6.06	6.28	6.36	6.15	5.40	4.23	3.31
Malaysia	6.31	6.28	5.77	4.86	4.21	3.79	3.66	3.51	3.30	3.07	2.83
Myanmar	6.05	6.07	6.13	6.08	5.43	4.57	4.06	3.45	2.85	2.43	2.14
Philippines	7.15	7.09	6.78	6.26	5.72	5.18	4.71	4.32	4.01	3.81	3.49
Singapore	5.45	5.26	4.70	3.09	2.08	1.74	1.61	1.87	1.71	1.25	1.20
Thailand	6.15	6.15	6.13	5.60	4.49	3.39	2.57	2.11	1.86	1.71	1.65
Timor-Leste	6.37	6.38	6.31	5.92	4.79	4.77	5.34	5.34	6.38	7.11	6.33
Vietnam	7.09	7.19	7.42	7.36	6.57	5.39	4.43	3.60	2.67	1.98	1.90

Source: Data extracted from ADB's *Key Indicators for Asia and the Pacific* (beta.adb.org/key-indicators/2011/main)

and influential generalizations in the social sciences: fertility decline
follows both mortality decline and socio-economic transformation,
or modernization. As the benefits of having large families decline
and the costs increase (not least, the costs of education), so families
increasingly value having fewer children and smaller families (Freedman 1979: 2; Kirk 1996).

From the 1960s, however, it became clear that this explanatory
model did not unproblematically apply even for Europe, let alone for
the non-Western world. Fertility decline was occurring (or was not)
in a wide range of developmental contexts, and the link between key
development indicators – including income – and fertility decline, as
the demographic transition model posits, was, at best, weak (ibid.).
Even the link between mortality and fertility has been challenged,
with Galor concluding that such a contention is 'inconsistent with
[the] historical evidence' (Galor 2005: 497). As, year by year, contrary
data accumulated, so demographers came increasingly to accept that
the causes of fertility decline were highly complex, and included cultural as well as economic and institutional factors. In his influential
paper 'Toward a restatement of demographic transition theory' (1976),
Caldwell provocatively concluded that demographic transition theory
had got the relationship between modernization and fertility decline
the wrong way around:

> The major implication of this analysis is that fertility decline in the
> Third World is not dependent on the spread of industrialization or
> even on the rate of economic development. It will of course be affected
> by such development in that modernization produces more money for
> schools, for newspapers, and so on; indeed, the whole question of fam-
> ily nucleation cannot arise in the non-monetized economy. *But fertility
> decline is more likely to precede industrialization and to help bring it about
> than to follow it*. (Ibid.: 358, emphasis added)

For Caldwell, to understand fertility decline we need to distinguish
between 'modernization' (economic transformation) and 'Westernization' (social and cultural transformation). It is the latter, he argued in
his seminal intervention, which primarily influences fertility, and it
can occur independently of – and therefore can precede – economic
development. For him, demographic transition theory fails because it
does not consider the causality of different variables within the catch-
all 'socio-economic transformation'. Caldwell's approach permits us to
begin to understand why fertility declined so rapidly among populations that were still largely agrarian as well as often poor in countries

like Indonesia, Thailand and former North Vietnam. The key features of socio-economic transformation do not lie in the realm of economics, but in the sphere of 'ideational' change and, more particularly, in the processes of secularization and individuation (Lesthaeghe and Surkyn 1988). To assume away 'culture', as many economic approaches do, is to assume away aspects of decision-making that lie at the heart of why people choose to have children. Mason, in her integrative paper 'Explaining fertility transitions', concludes:

> By recognizing that a rich variety of family and social systems existed throughout the world long before any population began widespread fertility limitation, that different family and social systems accommodate or make valuable different numbers of surviving children, and that traditional values make alternatives to fertility limitation more morally acceptable in some populations than in others, we enable ourselves to understand not only fertility transitions, but pre-transitional and post-transitional variation in fertility as well. (Mason 1997: 452)

The expected relationship between socio-economic development and fertility fails to materialize when examined against actual fertility decline. For many countries in East and South-East Asia, fertility levels have been very significantly lower than expected on the basis of their development indicators (Bryant 2007: 108). Demographic transition theory still has some explanatory traction, but only in general: rich, industrial economies have low fertility and poor, agrarian ones have high fertility. 'But what happens in between – the sequence of changes in educational systems, mortality, family structures, and the initiation of fertility change – is not well explained by theory or defined by empirical generalization' (Hirschman and Guest 1990: 148). And the countries that lie in between are just the ones that we are interested in because it is these countries which are undergoing transition. What route do countries take in making the journey from A (high fertility) to B (low fertility)? The key question of the interplay between culture, the mélange of micro-processes that comprise socio-economic change and government policy comes into clearer view when examined country by country.

Fertility decline in South-East Asia: Indonesia, Thailand and Vietnam Fertility decline in Asia occurred for a mosaic of reasons which defy easy generalization – and the relative roles of government intervention, mortality decline, socio-economic transformation (and elements thereof) and cultural context continue to be vigorously debated both across the region and with regard to specific country experiences (Jones and Leete 2002). Three South-East Asian countries that have done much to encourage demographers to reconsider their assumptions about the causalities of fertility decline are Indonesia, Thailand and Vietnam, each of which experienced sharp falls in fertility in contexts where incomes were low, poverty widespread, education limited, and populations mainly agrarian (Figure 6.1).

Indonesia's steep fertility decline is among the most surprising and striking in Asia, and not just because it is the world's fourth most populous country (Gertler and Molyneaux 1994: 36). The large majority of the population are Muslim, a religion which has been said to be resistant to some aspects of family planning, including abortion, IUDs and sterilization (see Lerman et al. 1989; Ong 1990), as well as to the wider issue of the reproductive rights of women (Sciortino et al. 1996);[2] the country was mainly rural and largely poor at the moment when fertility decline began; and its vast size, cultural complexity and archipelagic nature made – and makes – effective government action a considerable challenge. As Hull writes, at the end of the 1960s Indonesia 'was extremely poor, pro-natalist and apparently unconcerned about the interaction of population growth and economic development' (Hull 1987: 90; and see Hull 2007). And yet, notwithstanding these initial conditions and contexts, the total fertility rate halved over the next three decades, from 5.5 children per woman in 1970 to 2.5 in 2000. In 2009 the rate stood at 2.1 children per woman (Figure 6.1). Of the proximate determinants that are associated with fertility decline in Indonesia, two stand out: the increase in contraceptive prevalence and the rise in age of marriage. Regarding the former, the proportion of eligible couples utilizing family planning rose from 2.8 per cent in 1971/72 to 62.6 per cent in 1984/85 (Warwick 1986: 463). The question remains, however, of how and why these changes occurred.

Rather than seeking to highlight one factor in explaining Indonesia's fertility revolution, Hull (1987) prefers to take a 'holistic' view, combining institutional, economic, social and cultural variables. There is no doubt that the Indonesian government's family planning programme, implemented by the National Family Planning Coordinating Board or BKKBN, and the wider role of the New Order's developmental state, did much to mobilize people at the grassroots (Illustration 6.1). Lines of authority from the centre to rural villages, even in the most remote regions, were strong and effective and contraception became very widely available, and very quickly. At the same time, the oil boom provided the means to extend universal education to almost every

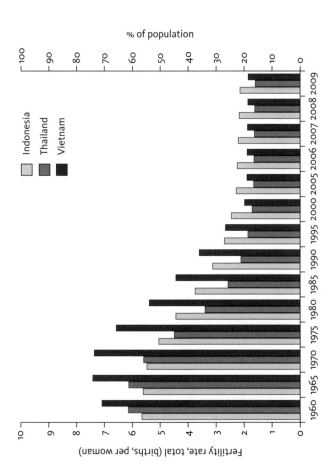

Figure 6.1 Fertility decline in Indonesia, Thailand and Vietnam, 1960–2009 (Fertility rate, total – births per woman)

Illustration 6.1 'Two children are enough': Indonesia's ubiquitous family planning programme

corner of the country, instilling new attitudes about childbearing and family size, helping to rework gender relations and the status of women, and assisting in unpicking prevailing sensibilities about the acceptability of contraception:

> The institutional changes that have made fertility decline possible in Indonesia were not inevitable, nor was any single change unique. However, the pattern of changes, and the fact that these changes occurred in a remarkably heterogeneous society with a history of empires, invasions, colonialism and national struggle, mean that the total change is unique. (Ibid.: 95)

Given the wide prevalence of contraceptive use in Indonesia by the 1980s it is easy to forget the resistance to family planning in some quarters that existed just a decade earlier, in the 1970s. Warwick reminds us that Muslim leaders in many villages were initially hostile, questioning the moral acceptability of family planning 'promoting sterilization and abortion, talking about subjects that should not be discussed, using male doctors to examine female patients, and otherwise violating Islamic traditions' (1986: 467; and see Hull 2007: 241–2). It is all the more remarkable, then, that the programme generally and contraception in particular came to be accepted so widely and so quickly. This transformation was achieved through a combination, Warwick suggests, of individual persuasion[3] and community pressure (Warwick 1986: 469), made possible by Indonesia's developmental state. A surprising outcome was that contraceptive use, in the 1970s, showed a curvilinear relationship with standard of living: those most likely to use contraceptives were the poor(er) and the rich(er) (Freeman 1995: 10).

Thailand reveals an even steeper decline in fertility, but achieved in a context where the development machine and state ideology were less pervasive and powerful than they were in Suharto's New Order Indonesia, but where the culture was more conducive to fertility management. The first study of fertility rates and views of family planning in Thailand was undertaken by Chulalongkorn University's Institute of Population Studies in 1969/70.[4] At the time, Thailand had no population policy, and if anything the country's approach to population matters was gently pro-natalist. In 1970, however, with the encouragement of the National Economic Development Board, the government adopted a National Family Planning Programme (NFPP) aiming to reduce population growth from a rate that was then around 3.0 per cent per year to 2.5 per cent by 1975, and to achieve this through voluntary family planning (Knodel and Pitaktepsombati 1973, 1975). The Chulalongkorn University study was initiated because so little was known about fertility in the country.

What the research revealed was that there existed considerable unmet demand for contraceptive use in rural as well as urban Thailand (Knodel and Pitaktepsombati 1973). In 1969/70, at the onset of the programme, 14 per cent of currently married women aged between fifteen and forty-four were using contraception; nine years later, in 1978/79, the figure was 53 per cent (Rosenfield et al. 1982: 44). To be sure, the family planning programme was innovative in the way that Buddhism, Buddhist values and Buddhist monks were actively used to support contraception. It is also possible to highlight a cultural context where women have considerable reproductive autonomy, where Buddhism emphasizes personal responsibility (ibid.), and where cultural pragmatism ensures that people are open to new ideas (Rosenfield and Min 2007: 230–1). It also seems, however, that there was considerable unmet demand for contraception, even among poor, rural villagers. Thailand, therefore, saw a remarkably broadly based reproductive revolution that was not differentiated by geography (rural/urban), class (rich/poor) or education.

Even more remarkable still than the experiences of Indonesia and Thailand was the fertility decline achieved in North Vietnam in the 1960s and 1970s, when the country was at war, just 10 per cent of the population were classified as urban, incomes were among the lowest in Asia, and life expectancy was little more than fifty years (Bryant 2007: 103).[5] Unlike in Indonesia and Thailand, the fall in fertility cannot be attributed to a well-funded family planning programme. Certainly one existed (from 1963), but Bryant claims that that there was no large-scale distribution of contraceptives until 1973 (1998: 251) and the fertility targets set in the Second Five Year Plan (1976–81) were largely rhetorical. While North Vietnam had some of the means to emulate China's population policies, not least the organizational networks and efficacy of the governing apparatus of the Communist Party, and some incentive to do so bearing in mind the very high rural population densities in the Red River Delta, there is little evidence of coercion by local officials. What, then, explains fertility decline in Vietnam in the 1960 and 1970s?

It is possible to highlight a menu of possible reasons, some particular to Vietnam at this juncture in its history, and some more general. Starting with the latter, rapid mortality decline preceded fertility decline, particularly in urban areas, while the value of education was growing given the desire for children to gain access to cherished state sector jobs. There is a case that the logic for investing in quality rather than quantity of children applied as much in communist Vietnam as it did in the capitalist countries of Asia. Along with these general conditions that contributed to fertility decline were also some specific conditions and characteristics. Most important, the communist system provided a degree of security to the elderly independent of family size, making available subsidized rice, allocating work, even meeting funeral expenses. There may be growing doubts about the efficacy of the commune system in Vietnam (see Kerkvliet 1995, 2005), but even if the 'iron rice bowl' and 'cradle-to-grave' welfare were a flourish rather than a fact, it is still true that communism brought a degree of security that was formerly absent. Finally, there is the role of the war, and America's bombing campaign, in separating couples and disrupting life. Bryant concludes his study of fertility decline in Vietnam by highlighting the surprising intersection of declining fertility and a moribund economy: 'The argument, in a nutshell, is that North Vietnam's communist-era institutions created the conditions for declining mortality, declining fertility, and stagnant incomes' (1998: 264).

FERTILITY AMONG MALAYS AND IN SINGAPORE So far the discussion has focused on country-specific cases of fertility decline to tease out the mosaics of causal factors at work. Jones (1990) takes a different approach and looks at one ethnic group – the Malay – situated across three countries: Indonesia, Malaysia and Singapore. There are important differences between Malays ranged across insular South-East Asia;

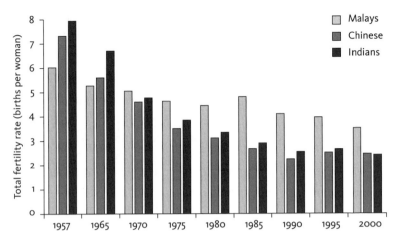

Figure 6.2 Total fertility rates by ethnic group in peninsular Malaysia, 1957–2000

even so, Jones contends that 'there are sufficient cultural, linguistic, and religious commonalities between the Malay populations of the three countries to justify a hypothesis that differences in their fertility trends may be due more to differences in the economic, social, and political setting in which they find themselves than to cultural differences between them' (ibid.: 509).

The greatest puzzle to emerge from Jones's comparison of Malays in Indonesia, Malaysia and Singapore is why fertility rates among the Malays of peninsular Malaysia remained so high compared to those of Indonesia, given sustained economic growth and much higher education levels and standards of living in Malaysia – particularly when compared to the fertility rates of other ethnic groups in Malaysia (Figure 6.2). Part of the explanation lies in the efficacy of Indonesia's family planning programme compared to Malaysia's, and the power and influence of the state in the context of Indonesian president Suharto's New Order. Jones also highlights, however, the way in which Malaysia's New Economic Policy (NEP) bestowed advantages on Malays relative to the Chinese population of the country, and the way that these policies shifted the cost burden of having children to the state and preferentially allocated educational and employment opportunities to Malays. In other words, the quality/quantity trade-off that operated in Indonesia (and Vietnam) and among parents of other ethnic groups in Malaysia did not have the same purchase among Malays (ibid.: 531).[6] The outcome was that while, in peninsular Malaysia, fertility rates between the three main ethnic groups of the country in 1957 showed

Malays having the lowest, by the mid-1970s this had been reversed and by the late 1980s and early 1990s had diverged to such an extent that Malay women, on average, were having almost twice the number of children of Indian and Chinese Malaysians (Figure 6.2).

The example of these countries shows that carefully constructed family planning programmes, particularly when they are allied to an effective state apparatus, *can* play an important role in influencing fertility. What the country experiences show even more starkly, however, is the role of context, across the board – geographical, economic, governmental and cultural – in shaping, even determining, fertility transitions. What is also evident is that governments have not infrequently been kept off balance by their populations. Even the Singapore government, so often lauded for its ability to micro-manage affairs, shape decision-making and see over the planning horizon, has been caught off guard by the fertility decisions of its citizens, and surprisingly ineffectual in getting people to have more children. The Singapore Family Planning and Population Board, which was charged with implementing an anti-natalist policy from January 1966, was wound up in 1986, and a pro-natalist New Population Policy announced the following year (Jones and Leete 2002: 120; Yap 2007). Since then, an ever more imaginative raft of tax incentives, education vouchers, love boats and online dating schemes[7] have failed significantly to change the downward slide in fertility, especially among educated Chinese (see Table 6.1). The slogan 'have three, or more [children] if you can afford it' has been studiously ignored by most Singaporeans, and the total fertility rate has continued to decline, reaching just 1.20 in 2009 (Sun 2012: 21), and 1.15 in 2010.[8] Chinese reproductive behaviour was thought to be significantly shaped by pro-natalist Confucian values; the evidence from Singapore as well as Malaysia is that when this Confucian value has conflicted with another traditional value, namely the value attached to education, the latter has won out.

Fertility decline's effects

Fertility decline, in itself, is an important and interesting field of study with many rich avenues of investigation. As noted above, the steep decline in fertility across wider East Asia was both unprecedented and unexpected. Partly this was because the data on which to make projections and forecasts were either lacking or erroneous; partly because the conceptual models that sought to 'explain' decline were inadequate, based as they were on the European experience (itself probably wrongly diagnosed), with the assumption that the rest of the world would unproblematically follow the path set by Europe; and partly because scholars and practitioners did not fully understand the complex interactions of the components in the process – and in particular the cultural components – making forecasting difficult. These issues have not gone away, and they highlight once more the barriers to 'planning' the population dimension of development (see Chapter 2). As Hull writes, 'even when we do have reasonable estimates of current or past behaviour, there are often reasons to be uncertain about where those trends might lead in the future' (Hull 2009: 8). Improvements in data acquisition, then, do not get around the challenge of anticipating (future) human responses to (past) demographic trends. For example, the estimates of current and recent total fertility rates in Table 6.1 and Figure 6.1 are based on assumptions about the future fertility of currently fecund women.

The discussion now, however, seeks to use fertility decline in Asia as an entry point to think about a mosaic of other, associated, transformations. These are, *inter alia*, late marriage and singlehood, household and family structure, gender and generational relations, and mobility and migration. There is, in each of these pockets of scholarship and investigation, a diversity of surprises which, *in toto*, highlight the complex and often unforeseen ways that people respond to events at any one moment in time and, more difficult still, how responses reverberate through time.

Marriage and singlehood: when, whether, who and why?

The Asian avoidance of marriage is new, and striking. (Economist 2011a: 20)

One of the contributing factors to the fertility decline discussed above – and also a product of it – is delayed or late marriage or, increasingly, singlehood: 'The retreat from universal marriage in Pacific Asia is an important phenomenon in its own right, signifying major changes in family relationships and roles of women and posing serious challenges to official and social attitudes to sexuality in the region' (Jones 2007: 455; and see Leete 1994). The proportion of never-married women aged 35–39 in East and South-East Asia has trebled from around 5 per cent in 1970 to 15 per cent or more in 2005 (Table 6.2). Unlike the situation in Europe, this decline or postponement of marriage has not significantly been countered by a rise in cohabitation, which remains unusual in Asia.[9] Childbearing outside marriage is also very rare in Asia.[10] The data in Table 6.2 are remarkable enough; when the general absence of cohabitation is factored in, they become more striking still. Thus, it is not so much that marriage, as an institution, is breaking down in Asia, to be replaced by cohabitation (as in many Western countries); rather, it is that women are rejecting marriage and alternatives to it as well. Like so much else in matters of demography, however, the reasons for late marriage, which Quah prefers to term 'marriage postponement' (Quah 2003: 8), and the growth of singlehood have been far from predictable.

TABLE 6.2 Proportion of women never married at ages 35–39, 1970–2005 (%)

	1970	1980	1990	2000	2005
Japan	5.8	5.5	7.5	13.8	18.4
South Korea	0.4	1	2.4	4.3	7.6
Taiwan	1.2	2.1	6	11.1	15.9
Singapore	5.1	8.5	14.8	15.1	15
Hong Kong	3	4.5	10.2	17.5	20.3
China		0.3	0.3	0.5	0.7
Thailand	5.2	7.3	9.6	11.6	
Philippines	8	8	8.7	9.5	
Indonesia	1.4	1.9	2.7	3.5	4.3
Myanmar	7	8.9	13.8	18.6	
Simple country average	4.1	4.8	7.6	10.6	11.7

Source: Jones (2010: 20)

The general picture, it is often assumed, is that as countries become wealthier and societies more 'modern', so singlehood (and cohabitation) becomes increasingly prevalent. But Figures 6.3a and 6.3b show that it is more complex than this. One of the poorest countries in Asia, Myanmar (Burma), shows high levels of singlehood that are of long standing. Jones (2007) notes that, historically, remaining single was culturally acceptable in Myanmar, to a degree that was not the case in other countries in the region. In addition, long years of economic stagnation and the uncertain prospects of so many men have made women reluctant to embark on marriage (and men averse as well) (ibid.: 463).[11] Finally, strong disapproval of divorce in Myanmar has probably also played a role in raising the perceived risks of marriage, thus postponing marriage and/or encouraging singlehood.

There is a strong positive correlation between education and female singlehood, evident in Singapore (Figure 6.4), South Korea, Japan and Taiwan; and a negative correlation between education and male

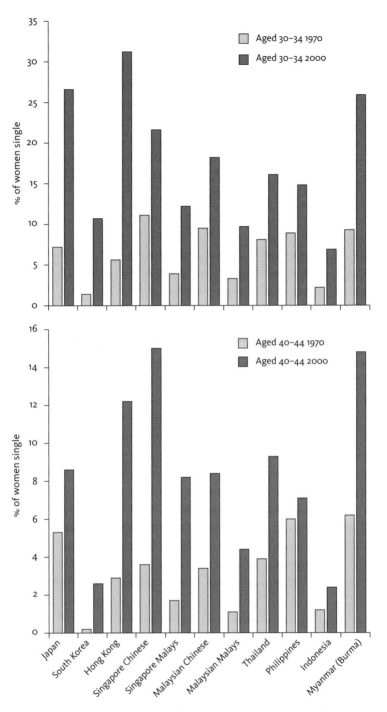

Figures 6.3a and 6.3b Proportion of women single at ages 30–34 and 40–44, 1970 and 2000

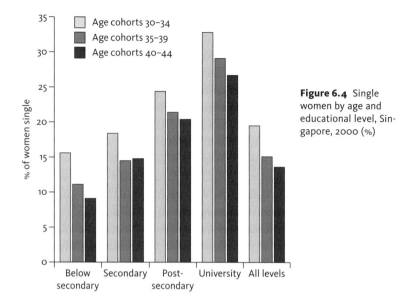

Figure 6.4 Single women by age and educational level, Singapore, 2000 (%)

singlehood. This has been explained partly by a surfeit of women given fertility decline and the traditional age gap between men and women on marriage. The 'marriage squeeze', as Jones terms it (ibid.: 464), is accentuated, however, by the tendency for women to 'marry up' (hypergamy) in educational terms. The rise in education levels among women across Asia, sometimes such that levels of female education are higher than those of male education, has led to a drying up of the pool of potential spouses for high-achieving women, a fact made even more germane when one considers the widening values gap between men and women as the latter embrace feminist values and the former hold fast to Asian gender values. Women are not inclined to marry men who are less educated than they are, particularly when they do not hold to the same values, and many men feel intimidated by the prospect of marrying a woman who is more highly educated than they are. As Figure 6.4 shows, over a quarter of female graduates aged 40–44 in Singapore have never been married.

The marriage squeeze brought about by the tendency in some countries for women to marry up, exacerbated by a situation where many men have been left behind in the education race, has led to different 'responses' by women and men. Women are increasingly, it seems, opting for singlehood rather than lose their hard-won freedoms and autonomy. In a few countries this has led, in turn, to changes in sexual practices, if not in sexual norms (ibid.: 461–2). Sexual relations

Box 6.1 Foreign brides in East Asia

It is usually thought that it is women in transnational and trans-regional marriages, such as those discussed in this chapter, who are in the most problematic position (see Davin 2007). Such unions are depicted as commercial transactions where the woman is a commodity – an exchange good – and behind which are a set of power relations reflecting global disparities in wealth and development. Such women leave their countries of birth, distance themselves from family support networks, often do not speak the language of their new home, and are drawn into and are expected to comply with a set of cultural norms with which they are unfamiliar. The scope for such women to be trafficked and become victims of abuse and domestic violence is high (Bélanger et al. 2010: 1115). But Wang's (2007) study of Vietnamese foreign wives in Taiwan shows that such women are not helpless and without power, and in some respects have *more* agency to challenge patriarchal traditions than their Taiwanese counterparts. As outsiders, they are disembedded from the host society and, Wang argues, therefore do not come under the same social obligations. Their own families cannot exert social pressure to conform, and the *absence* of a kinship network engenders a modicum of freedom, rather than control. They can also levy the ultimate threat – to divorce, and leave – which is made easier because the union is commodified. This is not to suggest that Vietnamese transnational wives are autonomous actors; there are significant pressures to conform to the role models that Taiwanese society ascribes to women. The point is that there is also a hidden space of agency.

outside marriage have become less exceptional among a growing group of well-educated women who will never marry, but who do not desire also to remain celibate.

Men, for their part, often remain keen to marry but are increasingly unable to find a partner from among their compatriots. This is particularly acute among the lower socio-economic classes with low levels of education, and especially those living in the countryside, where farmers find it difficult to entice women to embrace an agricultural life, an occupation seen as low status, low return and characterized by drudgery.[12] With men seeking to marry 'down', the shortage of potential domestic brides has thus been transferred down the social scale, creating particular problems for men of low social status. The response of these men has been to turn to marrying women from other, poorer countries or regions. Men in Japan, South Korea, Taiwan, Hong Kong and Singapore are turning to China, Thailand, the Philippines and Vietnam to secure their life partners, while those living in richer provinces of China, such as Hebei, Anhui and Jiangsu, are seeking their partners in poorer provinces, including Yunnan, Guizhou and Sichuan (Davin 2007: 85) (see Box 6.1). This has, as a result, transferred the shortage of brides regionally and internationally. It is China's poorest provinces, for example, where the proportion of women among the unmarried population is lowest. Demand for brides has created a vibrant matchmaking industry that policy-makers have only belatedly attempted to regulate, largely because its emergence was so unexpected (Jones 2010: 14).[13] Social norms concerning marriage in these countries are increasingly out of step with social practices, which are being renegotiated owing to unprecedented changes in the socio-demographics of marriage.

While in South Korea and Taiwan such marriages may lead to the separation of wives from their natal origins, socially and economically as well as spatially, in Thailand *mia farang* (Thai women married to *'farang'* – foreign – men) maintain and extend transnational relations and networked existences. In their study of two villages in north-east Thailand's Udon Thani province, Angeles and Sunanta (2009) argue that the *phua farang* (foreign husband) phenomenon has led to the emergence of a particular set of obligations which do not stop at the immediate or even extended family, but draw in the wider community as well. This 'diasporic philanthropy', as they term it, implicates 'entire villages, rural populations, and host metropolitan cities ... that participate in imagining alternative worlds and possibilities beyond the local' (ibid.: 558).

The rise in delayed marriage and singlehood seems to be mainly concentrated in urban areas (and, especially, major cities), and linked to higher levels of education and economic development, and to rising female labour force participation rates. But there are evident wrinkles in the empirical picture which makes cross-country generalizations problematic. Some countries, such as Myanmar noted above, show high levels of delayed marriage and singlehood notwithstanding low levels of economic development. This can be partly explained by the persistence of cultural norms which make celibacy socially acceptable.

Although this cultural norm may remain persistent in Myanmar, the seemingly equally strong norm militating against non-marriage in the Sinicized cultures has been quickly challenged with very high levels of late or non-marriage among the Chinese population of Singapore, for example.

Social and cultural norms become remoulded under modernization processes in differential ways. Some aspects of Confucianism have become more malleable, such as the institution of marriage. Others retain their power, and may even have become strengthened. For example, on marriage in many Confucian cultures, it is still assumed that a wife

---

Box 6.2 Migration and the changing family in Vietnam

The majority Kinh (Viet) ethnic group comprise around 90 per cent of the population of Vietnam. This group is traditionally patrilineal and patrilocal. In addition, it is usual for elderly parents to reside (co-residence) with a married son and his family, and to be supported by them (Bryant 2002: 112). However, as Friedman et al. (2003) note, there are considerable regional variations in this pattern, with patrilocality being more pronounced in the north than the south of the country. This 'norm' has also become frayed, broadly speaking, for three sets of reasons: first, because of the long years of war (first against the French and then the Americans) and the instability that this created; secondly, because of attempts, ideologically driven, to create a new Vietnamese society based on socialist and communist principles; and thirdly, because of the 'modernization' effects associated with the reform process (*doi moi*) and Vietnam's continuing integration into the world economy. In brief, the war served to divide, disrupt and displace the population, often making it difficult and in some instances impossible to maintain traditional family relationships and systems. Men and women joined the army and were posted away, people were killed in large numbers and villages destroyed, and populations were divided and relocated. The institution of social/communist principles was aimed at dismantling old 'feudal' systems which were viewed as archaic and exploitative and sustaining gender and other inequalities, and putting in their place a system of social welfare based on the state, rather than the family. This was part of a process of social modernization which dated from 1954 in the north, and from 1976 (with reunification) in the south. The economic reforms introduced progressively since 1986 have once again placed the family at the centre of economic and social decision-making, even though this has not entailed a complete 'return' to the pre-revolutionary era. *Doi moi* has, studies have argued, increased vulnerability as social protection has been removed from the ambit of the state and handed 'back' to family and kin (Rydstrom et al. 2008: 12).

The importance of 'home', emotionally important for many, is made more important in the Vietnamese context (or, at least, among the Kinh) because a patriline (a line for descent from father to son) is recorded, confirmed and celebrated in genealogies inscribed in ancestral altars (Bryant 2002). The eldest son has ritual obligations, and connects dead members of a patriline with those who are yet to come. Migration, clearly, can disrupt these familial connections and obligations, particularly when migrants are male and especially if they are eldest sons. It creates a social and cultural context where 'return', periodic though it may be, becomes important.

The trend towards smaller families in Vietnam, as in much of Asia, has, inevitably, placed strains on the ability of many families to sustain the traditional patrilineal system, and this has led scholars to question whether the patrilineal/patrilocal model is quite as robust as commonly assumed (see ibid.: 121). Eldest sons are building lives away from their natal villages; daughters are taking on roles and responsibilities previously reserved for sons; and the maintenance of the patriline is being achieved in new ways, and often from afar. There is no question that the obligations of sons and the power of the patriline remain strong but, as Bryant writes, 'fertility decline in Viet Nam appears to have entailed couples making difficult trade-offs between conformance with the patrilineal model and other objectives' (ibid.: 123). This, as numerous scholars have pointed out in a range of situations and contexts – Mills (1997, 1999), for example, in the context of gender relations in modernizing Thailand – not infrequently creates tensions as individuals and families carefully negotiate the interface between modernity and tradition.

will give up work, quickly have children,[14] and assume the burdens and responsibilities of child-raising and caregiving. Without a state support network this creates a considerable disincentive to marry for high-achieving, career-focused women. In Vietnam, the economic reforms (*doi moi*) dating from the mid-1980s have modernized the country in many respects, but have also led to the re-emergence and revitalization of some traditional practices relating to patrilineal principles, such as life-cycle ceremonies, while also redirecting responsibilities for social protection from the state back to the family (see Box 6.2).

One of the contributory factors to fertility decline and late marriage is the growing prevalence of female labour force participation in the modern economy. Women (and men), particularly from rural areas, are leaving home to work in the service and industrial sectors of the economy, often for long periods. This has been a contributory factor to late marriage; it also explains some of the pressures that have been placed on the moral envelope of accepted practice, noted in passing in the previous section and returned to later in this chapter. Mobility becomes the process fulcrum that links a number of the social and economic transformations discussed here.

Migration and mobility: reframing living and livelihoods

> While parents are alive, one must not travel far. If one must, one's where-abouts should always be made known. (*Analects*, Book 2: Li Ren 19)

> Migrant workers used a simple term for the move that defines their lives: *chuqu*, to go out. *There was nothing to do at home, so I went out.* This is how a migrant story [in China] begins. (Chang 2008: 11, emphasis in original)

There has always been more mobility in rural Asia than the seden-tary peasant paradigm permits. Nonetheless, until relatively recently, travel beyond the local context remained limited. Very approximately, until the 1960s in Malaysia, the 1970s in Thailand and the Philippines, the 1980s in Indonesia, and the 1990s in Cambodia, the Lao PDR and Vietnam, travel remained sometimes risky, frequently troublesome, usually slow, and more often than not expensive. The risks of leaving home were high and the rewards uncertain.

Asia has experienced a mobility revolution over the four decades since the early 1970s. The numbers involved are huge, and the impli-cations for society and economy also very great indeed. While move-ments of people between countries receive the greatest attention, not least because such movements are politically the most sensitive and often also the most visible, they are far outnumbered – possibly by a factor of six – by intranational migration flows. The UNDP (2009) estimated that there were 740 million internal (domestic) migrants across the globe at the beginning of the millennium, many of these unrecorded, 'irregular' migrants. In Asia there is also a cascade of cross-border movements, reflecting the development contours of the region as South-East Asia becomes a semi-integrated human resource economy: hundreds of thousands of Burmese, Cambodian and Lao work in Thailand; Vietnamese in Taiwan and South Korea; Filipinos in Hong Kong and Singapore; and Indonesians and Bangladeshis in Malaysia (Table 6.3).

We may appreciate the broad shape of population movements in the Asian region, but 'what we know is dwarfed by what we don't know' (ibid.: 28). Migrants slip over borders, ghost past censuses, are overlooked by the authorities, and looked down upon by established populations. 'For the most part', as the UNDP concluded in its major review, 'migration data remain patchy, non-comparable and difficult to access' (ibid.).[15] This is even more so the case when it comes to circular migration, for which no global data exist (Newland 2009: 10). Kundu writes (2009: 14) that 'studies on internal migration are seriously constrained by the fact that no international organisation systematically collects or tabulates even the basic demographic information on this in a cross-sectionally and temporally comparable manner', a situation which he regards as 'tragic'. Asia's 'floating' population, numbering well over 100 million in China (see Ploeg and Jingzhong 2010: 515), as many as 16 million in Vietnam (UNDP 2010) and millions more in the other countries of the region, comprises what has sometimes been depicted as 'phantom' farmers (Rawski and Mead 1998) who have left rural areas but not completely departed their villages. In the absence of accurate baseline data, scholars and officials are left to extrapolate from case studies, many of which take a qualitative rather than quantitative approach.

Unlike the nineteenth-century urbanization process in western Europe and North America and currently in much of Africa and Latin America (Ploeg and Jingzhong 2010), many rural–urban migrants in Asia do not relinquish their attachments – material, emotional and symbolic – to 'home' in the countryside. Each year there are short-lived reverse flows as hundreds of millions of rural migrants return to their natal villages for the lunar New Year celebrations in China (Chang 2008),[16] for Tet in Vietnam, Songkran in Thailand, Christmas in the Philippines, and to celebrate Idul Fitri in Indonesia. These migrants are usually seen as sojourners from the countryside, temporary and

TABLE 6.3 Migrant workers in Asia

Country	Migrant worker numbers	Notes and sources
Net labour-importing countries		
Malaysia	2.1 million (2007)	Official, legal migrant workers mainly from Indonesia and Bangladesh comprising 17.5 per cent of the workforce
Singapore	0.8 million (2010)	Concentrated in domestic service, the construction sector and shipbuilding and repair. Most migrants are from Malaysia, Thailand, the Philippines and Bangladesh and they comprise one third of the workforce
Thailand	1.8 million (2006)	Estimate of legal and irregular migrants living in Thailand, the latter comprising around three-quarters of the total. Most migrants are from Myanmar, the Lao PDR and Cambodia. Since the mid-1990s Thailand has turned from being a significant net labour exporter to a net importer. In 2005 around 130,000 Thais travelled abroad to work
Net labour-exporting countries		
Indonesia	2.5 million (2010)	The large majority of Indonesian migrant workers depart for Malaysia (an estimated 1.4 million) and Saudi Arabia (some 300,000), many of these being female domestic workers. Remittances in 2006 were around US$7 billion
Philippines	8 million (2007)	The Philippines sends more workers abroad than any other Asian country, remitting over US$14 billion each year, representing 10 per cent of GDP
Vietnam	400,000 (2006)	The most popular destinations for Vietnamese overseas workers are Malaysia, Taiwan and South Korea
Domestic migrant worker flows		
China	136.5 million (2007)	Comprising 46.5 per cent of total urban employment
Vietnam	12–16 million (2009)	'Floating population' of Vietnam representing between 12 and 18 per cent of the total

Sources: Martin (2009); UNDP (2009, 2010); Fang et al. (2009); Kelly (2011)

sometimes uncomfortable denizens of the city, a floating and detached population. Their presence is part of a household livelihood 'strategy' whereby rural and urban living are interlocked across space, and where return is inevitable.[17] They are sustaining the living standards of families back home, and perhaps enhancing their own prospects as well. These migrants are also an important component of the Asian economic miracle (see below).

The fact of migration is noteworthy in itself: the growing mobility of Asia's population constitutes one of the great social transformations of the last half-century. But the sheer scale of Asia's migration can seduce us into focusing only on the numbers involved or on the nature of the streams – their directionality, periodization and constitution. More significant in terms of this chapter is what this *means* for livelihoods, identities and relations and the way in which mobility reflects changes 'on the ground' and also contributes to those changes.

In terms of livelihoods, we see the emergence of rural livelihoods that are becoming separated from the immediate locale (i.e. they have become delocalized), and stretched across space and between sectors. In some cases this has been construed as contributing to a 'deagrarianization' of rural living (see Rigg 2001, 2006; Rigg and Nattapoolwat 2001); in other instances the emphasis has been placed rather more on diversification than on deagrarianization. The implications for the sustainability of rural living and the constitution of agrarian livelihoods, though, are manifold. Research in Cambodia has shown how migration interlocks with farming, reshaping the latter in the process, leading to both a feminization and a nascent geriatrification of farming: 'farming has become a refuge for highly mobile, migrant rural labour, and being such has acquired a feminine face' (Resurreccion et al. 2008: 6).[18] The ageing of the farm labour force, significantly beyond that which would be expected purely on the basis of declining fertility, has also been noted in Thailand (Rigg and Salamanca 2011; Molle and Srijantr 2003) and is well established in East Asia (Illustration 6.2). A large part of the explanation for this change in the agricultural labour force is because, not infrequently, villages have become 'hollowed out' (UNDP 2007) by migration as the young leave for work elsewhere. The rural village as an 'intimate universe' (Amyot 1976), where economy, society and livelihoods are interleaved, has been punctured by the frequency with which people leave home (migration) or, alternatively, engage with work outside the immediate locale (mobility).

In light of this, one of the more remarkable aspects of agrarian change in Asia is that rural settlements continue to be fairly resilient,

Illustration 6.2 Ageing farmers in north-east Thailand. This transplanting gang are all in their fifties and sixties (2008)

even in the face of intensifying levels of mobility and growing indus-trialization and structural change (Rigg et al. 2012). There is a paradox here: arguably, it is because so many villagers leave the countryside that rural settlements remain resilient, even with their idle fields, quiet lanes and sometimes empty homes (Illustration 6.3).[19] It is because people have left that others can remain. This increase in mobility is partly an outcome of development processes. Rural livelihoods for many across the Asian region can no longer adequately be sustained through farming. Landholdings have shrunk with fragmentation, terms of trade have turned against agriculture, inequalities have widened, luxuries have become necessities, and opportunities in rural areas have declined relative to those available in urban areas.

Along with migration, education has engendered new views, priori-ties and preferences, leading to situations where the young are either no longer *willing* to farm or, in some instances, no longer *able* to farm – the knowledge bridge that used to link parent and child has been cut. As Chang writes with reference to China, 'most of today's young migrants don't come from the farm: They come from school. Farming is something they have watched their parents do' (Chang 2008: 12; and see Nguyen et al. 2012 on Vietnam). Migration, then, can be seen inscribed in the material and non-material landscapes of Asia, termed 'remittance landscapes' by McKay (2003, 2005) based on her work among the Ifugao of the Philippines:[20] in the crops people grow, in the houses they build, in the technologies they use, and in the things they hold dear. This has engendered a strong, and new, cultural imperative to rural–urban migration flows as young people seek to 'escape' the drudgery of farming and the boredom of village life.[21] In 1980, Cramb's Iban shifting cultivators in Batu Lintang, Sarawak, East Malaysia, told him, with certainty, 'We must always plant hill rice … hill rice cultivation is our way of life.' Thirty years later in 2009, they declared: 'We are no longer hill rice farmers' (Cramb 2012: 74). No hill rice whatsoever was planted on Batu Lintang's lands in 2009. There is very little, it seems, that is not open to negotiation should circumstances require it.

In light of this, whether these so-called sojourning peasants *will* return 'home' is yet another question to which some scholars and many policy-makers and commentators have assumed an answer – namely, 'yes' – but for reasons that should be questioned. The terms used imply where these people truly belong. They are 'phantom farmers' (Rawski and Mead 1998), who, after their sojourn away, will return to their natal homes and inherited livelihoods on the land. But while the migrants of the 1990s may have been sojourning farmers, peasants on the make, so to speak, by the 2000s – as Chang notes for China (above)

Illustration 6.3 An abandoned migrant house in Thanh Hoa, north Vietnam (2010)

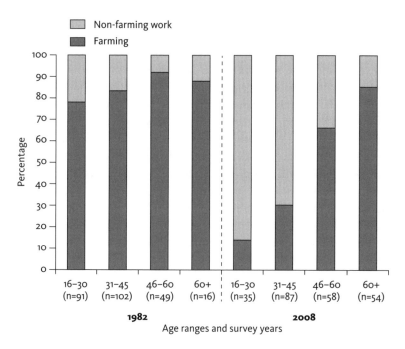

Figure 6.5 Generation and occupation in two villages in Mahasarakham, northeast Thailand, 1982/83 and 2008 (*source*: Surveys, 1982–83 and 2008; 1982, n=275; 2008, n=235)

– they had become aspirational school leavers. Why should we expect that they will return to the village, let alone to farming (see Knodel and Saengtienchai 2007: 198)? As longitudinal studies indicate, what might have been a life course 'moment' for the rural migrants of the 1970s and 1980s as they left home and sojourned as factory employees, domestic servants and building-site workers had, by the 1990s, in many areas been transformed into what appears to be a more profound era-defining change in the nature and location of work (Figure 6.5; and see Rigg et al. 2012). Furthermore, the experience of migration changes the migrant. The act of leaving and all that it entails remakes the migrant, alters their aspirations and world views, and may make return difficult. As one young man said to Moser when he returned to Guayaquil in Ecuador after seven years of absence, 'he could not stand the lack of order – the chaos – and the fact that everything was a mess' (Moser 2009: 227).[22] In Thailand, policy-makers are increasingly concerned about how the elderly will survive in their rural redoubts when so many of the youth are absent.[23] The rural Thai elderly may be much better off in material terms owing to the remittances of absent daughters and sons, and the multi-local household may mean that spatial disaggregation has not (yet) been accompanied by social disintegration (Knodel and Saengtienchai 2007), but whether this is sustainable in the longer term as a mode of social support is questionable. Currently across South-East Asia the role of the public sector in providing support for the elderly is limited; the elderly instead fall back on assets accumulated over their working lives and on familial transfers (see Mason and Lee 2011).

There is, therefore, a question – which is often left hanging – of how rural settlements will reproduce themselves into the future; perhaps as retirement villages rather than as farming communities. In the meantime, many have already become, in Thompson's phrase, 'socially urban'. On the basis of his research in rural Malaysia, he suggests that while his field site of Sungai Siputeh may not be a town, 'in practice, it is in many ways a very urban place' (Thompson 2007: 126; and see Thompson 2004b). Not only have social norms changed as migrants and connections with migrants have altered the template of life, but houses reflect urban preferences, and levels of services and amenities in rural areas are often not far removed from those available in urban settings. While far from universal, it is possible in some rural areas of Malaysia, the Philippines and Thailand to be urbane in the rural.[24]

Such new architectural forms and consumption practices may be dismissed as mere froth, reflecting little more than the intrusion of new tastes into the countryside and the spreading of the infrastructure of development to formerly backward rural areas, and beneath this veneer of modernity much remains the same; these are just peasants in jeans, farmers watching television, rural people taking advantage of the convenience of dried noodles and pre-prepared curry paste. We also see, however, some arguably more profound transformations in the structure of households and families, and in gender, generational and class relations. Once again, few people anticipated these changes and, more particularly, the forms they would take and the implications they would have. It is these transformations which the chapter sketches out in a final section.

Reconstituting the household and the family, reshaping gender and generational relations The discussion of delayed marriage and singlehood directs our attention mainly to urban areas and largely to the more developed countries of Asia and, in turn, to these countries' (relatively) more educated and cosmopolitan populations and their changing values, behaviours and norms.[25] A consideration of migrant flows, however, leads us to rural areas and less prosperous regions, raising questions about the effects of mobility on how households and families are structured and function.

Modernization, and the social and economic transformations this comprises, is often assumed to lead to the de-peasantization of agrarian societies, and the emergence of new social forms. This assumption is made on the basis of historical agrarian transitions elsewhere, where rural populations have been displaced from the countryside, and into an urban-industrial context. In Asia, however, modernization has often not been accompanied by this degree of socio-spatial displacement, as the earlier discussion of mobility showed. Instead, it is possible for modernizing rural populations to maintain links and associations with their rural roots. It is for this reason that Chatterjee suggests that 'the forms of capitalist industrial growth in the twenty-first century may ... make room for the preservation of peasant production and peasant cultures, but under completely altered conditions' (2008: 116). Chatterjee concludes by writing that 'As far as I can see, peasant societies will certainly survive in Asian countries in the twenty-first century, but only by accommodating a substantial non-agricultural component within the village' (ibid.: 125–6).

Households are becoming smaller across Asia. This is partly because couples are having fewer children, as discussed earlier. But more significantly, households are also becoming *different* in terms of their structure, function and spatial footprint. Classically, the household was defined as a 'co-residential dwelling unit': those 'living under one roof' (Evans 1991), or 'eating from the same cooking pot' (Annan et al. 1986; Holtz et al. 2004). The emphasis here is on propinquity – spatial proximity. While notions of the household focus on propinquity, those of the family are concerned with kinship. That said, it was not unusual for studies to use these two terms – 'household' and 'family' – as synonyms, with one acting as a proxy for the other (Brandon and Hogan 2008: 250). This was not caprice; often, in practice, the two conveniently mapped on to each other, or at least were thought to do so at first sight, and particularly in Asia.

Such a formulation of the household – as co-residential – was, however, being challenged at quite an early date as scholars grappled with its applicability to societies where circular migration was part and parcel of normal living (see Bender 1967; Ekejiuba 2005). Moreover, as social and economic transformations proceeded and their spatial implications deepened, so it became increasingly evident that

'traditional descriptions and explanations for household transformations [were both] empirically untrue and theoretically unsatisfactory'
(Smith et al. 1984: 8). As the discussion of mobility above highlights,
increasing numbers of people across Asia sleep, work and eat away
from their rural homes, but often remain functionally and emotionally part of these rural-based households. They usually remit money
as well as making other social and political remittances, sometimes
return 'home' during peak periods in the farming calendar, contribute
significantly to decision-making, and leave their children to be cared
for by grandparents. The spatially unequal nature of the development
process in Asia may have led tens of millions of people to leave the
countryside, whether seasonally or for periods of longer duration, but,
so far at least (although see above), this usually has not meant the
total abandonment of rural areas and homes. The outcome has been
the emergence of multi-sited or shadow households, partially mirroring
the delocalized livelihood footprints noted earlier. As I have written
with Albert Salamanca and Mike Parnwell, and drawing on fieldwork
in north-east Thailand:

> Using spatial propinquity as the basis for defining the household has
> become increasingly empirically problematic as the 'household space
> economy' has been reshaped in line with the reshaping of household
> livelihood footprints. ... Sons, daughters, wives and husbands move
> with ever greater frequency across national space, children are left to
> be raised by their grandparents (known as *liang laan*), and remittances
> of all forms (financial, political, social and cultural) create a lattice of
> relationships and dependencies that link people in different places.
> (Rigg et al. 2012)

The household, then, is not an inert social category that remains
untainted, to be studied, measured and counted from one generation
to the next. Households are caught up in the development process, as
well as contributing in important ways to that process. This requires
that we move away from thinking of 'the household' and 'the family'
in fixed categorical terms, but instead see each as regulated, shaped
and reshaped by *what people do*. Across Asia we see evidence of the
ingenious ways in which people rework what are often characterized
as 'established practices': the emergence of remote parenting in Vietnam (Locke et al. 2012), for example, and new forms of caring in
Singapore (Huang et al. 2012). Western scholarship leads not just to
the transmission of concepts and models – such as the demographic
transition – but also to categories, such as household and family.[26] Of

the shaping processes that highlight the need to question the utility of such categories, migration is among the most important.

Government policies do play an important role in migration. As Ong (1990: 263) writes of her *kampung* (village) of Sungai Jawa in Malaysia: 'with the NEP [New Economic Policy], the outmigration of young *kampung* men and, increasingly, women for higher education and wage work became an irreversible process, dramatically changing parent–child and gender relations'. While Malaysian government policies, notably in the form of the NEP, were crafted to build a modern society that was in tune with and supportive of attempts to build a modern economy, the ways in which this fermented new forms of mobility and, in turn, new social forms and relations was not anticipated. Beginning in the 1970s, tens and then hundreds of thousands of young Malays left their rural 'homes' for industrial and service sector work in urban areas. The industrialization strategy that shaped this process was initially intended, however, to create a Malay *male* working class, and yet quickly it was young women, rather than men, who significantly made modern Malaysia. The same trends, with important differences, can be seen in the factories of Cambodia (Derks 2008), Indonesia (Elmhirst 1997, 2002, 2007), Thailand (Mills 1997, 1999, 2012), the Philippines (Chant 1995) and Vietnam (Agergaard and Thao 2011). Elmhirst's work in Sumatra, Indonesia, provides a particularly compelling insight into how migration can lead to profound social changes.

Elmhirst's work illustrates the point that development is not a snapshot, but needs to be connected up into a moving picture in which one image contributes to an understanding of the next. When Elmhirst first undertook fieldwork in Tiuh Baru in the early 1990s, young, unmarried women were virtually secluded in the home (Elmhirst 2007: 226), and were chaperoned to the field under the watchful eye of male relatives. At the time, the 'idea of independent migration (*merantau*) for women [was] unheard of' (ibid.: 231). When the first, heroic woman left for factory work in Jakarta's extended metropolitan region of Tangerang in the early 1990s, following her cousin, who lived elsewhere in Lampung, she shattered this norm and, in so doing, tacitly challenged the basis of gender (and generational) relations in this staunchly Islamic village. At the start of Tiuh Baru's migration era, these young women were 'assumed out' of the household, and the head of the household did not claim control over their income. 'Young women', Elmhirst writes, 'were drawn towards work in the factories for a variety of reasons, few of which were purely economic, and none of which indicated their desire to help their families' (Elmhirst 2002: 154–5). The question of whether their factory daughters might compromise the honour of the family while they were away was dealt with by taking an out-of-sight-out-of-mind position: 'there is no shame in what cannot be seen', as one respondent explained to Elmhirst. The numbers of female migrants grew to such an extent that, by the late 1990s, all but four unmarried women between the ages of fifteen and twenty in the village had left to work in the factories around Jakarta. Fathers, increasingly cognizant of the sums that were being earned by their absent daughters, began to request and then to expect their daughters to contribute to the household budget.[27] With the *krismon* (monetary crisis) at the end of the decade, this channelling of women's wages back to the natal household became, in some instances, essential for family survival. As Hancock shows in his separate study in Banjaran, Java, while in 1996/97 female factory workers were remitting around one third of income to their natal households, in 1999/2000 it was more than one half (Hancock 2001). Not only did women migrants in Tiuh Baru become, over time, increasingly important to household well-being, but the experience of such work – light, modern, requiring of skills and education – became a marker of Lampungese femininity, thus raising the value of daughters in the local marriage market (Elmhirst 2002: 157).

In the space of a generation, the sedentary daughters of Tiuh Baru, to a large extent confined to their houses and controlled by their fathers, had become mobile, aware and cosmopolitan. In the early years of this migration stream these young women were independent wage earners, able to earn for themselves – largely to assemble a dowry (see also Hewage et al. 2010) and be modern. Over time, however, their work became reclaimed as part of the household enterprise, especially so as other opportunities evaporated in the face of Indonesia's economic crisis. Even so, the experience of travel to and work in Java altered village notions of femininity, recast female migrants as modern women, impacted on the men 'left behind', and had other far-reaching effects. While not always as striking as the transformations in Tiuh Baru, these changes can be seen repeated in village after village, and household after household, across Asia. For married women, the left behind are not just husbands, but children as well. In China in 2005, there were some 35 million six- to fourteen-year olds with at least one parent absent, and half of these had both parents absent (Rachel Murphy, personal communication, 29 March 2012; and see Murphy 2002).

The reworking of households and families is, in part, an outcome of changes in the roles and responsibilities of the genders and generations. It is mainly the young who are taking up opportunities in the new economy and, as noted, they are as likely to be young women as young men. The older generations are often ill equipped to leave the village. Numerous studies have illuminated how migration has opened up the moral envelope of accepted practice, especially for women.[28] 'Factory daughters' have disposable income and new-found – and newly won – freedoms. Their status is altered in the process as, in the space of a generation, they have been transformed from family helpers to independent wage earners. Min, a migrant from the Chinese countryside, returned home a new woman: 'Min enjoyed status in the village – because of her wealth. She expresses her views openly, and does what she likes rather than what custom decrees' (Chang 2008: 292).

As Elmhirst shows, and this is echoed in work across East and South-East Asia, the engagement of women in factory work away from home has not only restructured households but also reshaped gender and generational relations. Migration provides a rich field in which either we can see the interplay of structure and agency at work, or the duality of such an approach to understanding social change is seen as problematic (see Bakewell 2010).[29] For men this is sometimes (but not always) depicted as a 'crisis of masculinity' as men's lives become restricted to the village, marginalized in farming, and thrown into sharp relief by the lives of increasingly mobile, wealthy and cosmopolitan young women able to remake themselves as *Melayu Baru* (New Malays), rather than remaining *Orang Kampung* (Village Women, country bumpkins). Men, of course, have not taken this lying down and have often found ways to reassert their masculinity (see Semedi 2012). In some studies, left-behind husbands have managed to maintain their status even as work patterns have changed (Resurreccion and Khanh 2007).[30]

Conclusion: predicting and interpreting behaviour

Tania Murray Li's book *The Will to Improve* (2007) has a section entitled 'Governmentality's limits' in which she notes that: 'The relations and processes with which government is concerned present intrinsic limits to the capacity of experts to improve things. There is inevitably an excess. There are processes and relations that cannot be preconfigured according to plan' (ibid.: 17).

This is partly because the plans are based on limited knowledge; partly because plans have unintended consequences; and partly because people do not behave in the manner that planners expect. This creates a messiness which, in Li's view, is routine, creating conditions that are intractable to government (ibid.: 18–19). The science of development planning is an exercise in rationalizing the development process, subjecting it through modelling to the logic of mathematics and the rationality imbued in *Homo economicus*. Plans are said to be 'plan rational', and there is an assumption that the objects of planning – the planned population – will also respond and act in a rational manner. There are four particular dilemmas with this view of human behaviour which this chapter has illuminated using South-East Asia's multiple and interlocking demographic transformations as a backdrop.

The first dilemma is general: can the actions of human beings be reduced to and understood as outcomes of rational behaviours? When a person is said to be acting or behaving irrationally, it is often simply that we do not appreciate the grounds for a particular behaviour. Our knowledge is partial, and our assumptions about where priorities lie are flawed or simply erroneous. In a society's or individual's own terms, all behaviours are rational; utility is contextually defined. The second dilemma is the reduction of behaviour to a binary: people are either behaving rationally, or irrationally. Rational choice may not be clearly defined and therefore evident; much decision-making is made under conditions of uncertainty. Only after an event or following a decision does the 'right' (rational) decision become clear. As Caldwell writes with reference to the demographic transition model, and which can be extended to virtually all the themes of this chapter – migration, mobility, marriage, singlehood and gender relations – much 'turns on the definition of rational' (1976: 326). A third problem which this chapter highlights is the question of whether we can export interpretive frameworks to other cultural contexts and, in particular, from the Western to the non-Western world. Is 'rationality' malleable? There is, as Pollak and Watkins (1993: 484) highlight, a danger of simply using culture as the explanatory residual – to account for that part of behaviour which cannot be explained using other means or criteria. Culture is highlighted as an explanation, but *how* it operates is left unsatisfactorily explored. Traditionally economics has taken these cultural questions over, for example, wants and values as givens and left their investigation to other disciplines. Culturally shaped endogenous preferences rarely make much of an appearance in economic explanations of fertility decline. And yet when it comes to understanding, for example, fertility, marriage preferences and singlehood, as this chapter has outlined, the roles of (changing) societal values and norms are key.

What is the value attached to children? What norms militate against singlehood? Why is it that women were more sedentary than men? Unpicking these questions is important enough, but even more so is

177

understanding how and why such norms and values change. This is the fourth dilemma: how to account for change. It may be simpler and neater to assume fixed preferences but, as this chapter has shown, the really interesting – and important – questions are about how preferences change, why they change, and how this impacts on behaviour, ricocheting through society, reshaping gender relations, restructuring households and families, changing patterns of livelihood and, in turn, impacting on national development. Cramb's (2012) study of change among the Iban of Batu Lintang in Sarawak provides a telling vignette of this interleaving of structure, state, process and agency, highlighting the messiness with which governments have to contend. His study is worth quoting at some length:

> Thirty years ago [in 1980], most people lived and worked within the longhouse territory and derived their livelihoods from a combination of subsistence and commercial agriculture, supplemented and buffered by periodic off-farm employment. Now most households derive their livelihoods mainly or exclusively from non-agricultural, urban-based employment, and the population resident in the longhouse has declined and aged. The longhouse is quiet and largely empty for much of the time; the surrounding territory is barely utilized and is reverting to old secondary forest. Yet, surprisingly, traditional forms of social organization have been maintained and adapted to this major economic transformation. The household or *bilek*-family has become a multi-sited extended family but with close social and economic ties, particularly back to the longhouse, providing a diversified and relatively secure livelihood system. The community is now widely dispersed and largely 'de-agrarianized', yet the longhouse and its territorial resources are still highly valued ... *The reasons are complex to articulate, even for the actors concerned* ... (Ibid.: 86, emphasis added)

7 | Contingent development

Learning the lessons of South-East Asian development

There has been a long tradition of trying to tease out the lessons and underlying principles of the South-East Asian (and the broader East Asian) region's economic success for other developing countries and regions. The *East Asian Miracle* (EAM) report (World Bank 1993) is perhaps the best-known such example, and this was discussed in Chapter 3 (p. 49). It is also possible to point to Campos and Root's *The Key to the Asian Miracle* (1996) and the more recent report of the Commission on Growth and Development (CGD 2008), which sought to identify 'strategies for sustained growth and inclusive development', based on thirteen 'success stories', of which nine are East Asian.[1] Like the EAM report fifteen years earlier, the Commission on Growth and Development proceeds to identify the 'right mix of ingredients' for growth, of which taking advantage of opportunities in the global economy (integration) and creating the incentives and investments for private investment are seen to be key. More recent still is the Tracking Development project (2006–12), which, by pairing four South-East Asian and four African countries, 'explain[s] why the former region has developed rapidly in the past half century, and the latter has not' (Donge et al. n.d.; and see Henley n.d.).[2] The conclusions of this most recent study are that three sets of policies are crucial: policies that ensure macroeconomic stability; policies that improve life in the countryside through pro-poor, pro-rural public spending; and policies that liberalize the economy. These conclusions in many respects echo those of the EAM report of 1993, the Campos and Root book of 1996, and the CGD study of 2008 (Table 7.1).

Is it really this straightforward, such that it is possible by looking back over the last half-century of Asian growth to arrive at clear sets of policy prescriptions from which a generalized template of development can be drawn up? Writing of patterns and explanations for economic growth across the world, Durlauf et al. (2005) find few of the rhymes that the studies summarized in Table 7.1 identify:

> There exist a host of factors that appear to affect growth beyond the
> factor accumulation and exogenous technical change that drive the

TABLE 7.1 Recipes for economic success?

Recipe ingredients	East Asian Miracle Report, 1993	The Key to the Asian Miracle, 1996	Commission on Growth and Development, 2008*	Tracking Development, 2011
Outward orientation	–	Export orientation	Full exploitation of the world economy	Industrialization on the basis of foreign direct investment
Economic stability	'Getting the basics right', 'fundamentally sound development policy', 'good macroeconomic management'	–	Macroeconomic stability	Macroeconomic stability (low inflation, little currency overvaluation)
Investment and savings	High levels of domestic financial savings	High levels of private investment	High rates of saving and investment	–
Market rationality	Limited price distortions	Growth-promoting policies	Market allocation of resources	Economic freedom for peasant farmers and small entrepreneurs
Policy stability	Careful policy interventions	Regime legitimacy and stability with predictable policy environment	Committed, credible, and capable governments	–
Shared growth	Equitable sharing of the fruits of growth	Shared growth and wealth sharing	–	Pro-poor, pro-rural public spending on agriculture, and rural infrastructure

Notes: * 'A close look at the 13 cases reveals five striking points of resemblance' (CDG 2008: 21)

Sources: World Bank (1993); Campos and Root (1996); CGD (2008); www.trackingdevelopment.net/

Solow model. These determinants include a range of economic, political, geographic, and social factors. There also appears to be significant evidence of nonlinearity and parameter heterogeneity in the way these factors enter into growth regressions. (Ibid.: 1)

The number of possible determinants of growth just keeps growing, and it is none too clear which are fundamental and which are merely proximate. To put it another way, the nature and direction of causality are far from clear, and when we think they become clear, this is usually after the fact and with the benefit of hindsight.

Across the board, there are four sets of explanatory literatures which are underpinned by four very different hypothetical positions. First, there are those positions which stress the role of geographical factors from location to climate and accessibility in determining economic progress. This is exemplified in the new environmental determinism of scholars such as Jeffrey Sachs, which can be traced back to the work of the environmental determinists over a century ago (Sachs 2001, 2003; Diamond 1997; and see World Bank 2009 and Rigg et al. 2009).[3] Secondly, there are those scholars – most famously Douglas North – who emphasize the primacy of institutions in determining development outcomes (North 1994; Acemoglu et al. 2002; Rodrik et al. 2004; and see Sachs 2003).[4] As North says: 'Institutions form the incentive structure of a society, and the political and economic institutions, in consequence, are the underlying determinants of economic performance' (North 1994: 359). The third hypothetical position is that market integration, in the form of trade, is the key determining factor in explaining relative economic performance (Frankel and Romer 1999; Dufrenot et al. 2010; Buch and Monti 2010). Fourthly and finally, there is the primacy of policy, or what might be termed the policy determinist position (see Carmignani and Chowdhury 2011; Henley n.d.).[5]

Identifying a relationship, however, is not the same as demonstrating causality, and given the difficulties in arriving at variables that capture adequately the essence of the position to be tested, we should expect, first, heterogeneity in effects and, secondly, the likelihood that these positions are not alternatives, but work in tandem (see Alonso 2011). The policy implications are similarly not straightforward but conditional on historical circumstances, geographical context and institutional mix – or, more broadly, on political economy. Making the case, for example, that institutions matter does not tell us *how* institutions matter and therefore what element(s) in the institutional

TABLE 7.2 The axes of development contingency

Axes	Manifestations
Country conditions	The development capacities, capabilities and competencies that characterize a country
	The proximate political, institutional, social and economic conditions
Historical contexts	The prevailing historical context, as it pertains to the domestic situation
	The wider, time-dependent regional and global context
	The role of historical turning points in reshaping opportunities
Personal circumstances	The complex assemblages of assets and capitals that individuals and households bring to bear in their lives and living
	The role of personal (idiosyncratic) unforeseen events, opportune and untoward, in creating turning points in the prospects of individuals and families
Human character(istics)	The choices and behaviours of individuals and collectives
	The role of 'culture' and societal norms

mix is causal. Is it the rule of law, the quality of governance, lack of corruption, presence of clear property rights, or absence of violence, for instance (see Haggard and Tiede 2011)?

Situating development

Many of the issues discussed in the core chapters of the book have emphasized the spatial, social and temporal contingencies that accompany development: very little can be read off – or assumed – that does not first require some reflection concerning where development is situated, in time and space.[6] It is not just, however, that development is shaped by conditions, contexts and circumstances (see below), but also that policies need to be realistic. By realistic, I mean that they must be cognizant of and sensitive to the social and institutional contexts in which they are to be implemented. So, 'good' policies are those that work. And just because they work in one context does not necessarily mean that they will work somewhere else. This may seem obvious but it is commonly overlooked because it is not infrequently assumed that contexts should change to accommodate policies, rather than policies be adjusted for a given context.

The important spatial, social and temporal contingencies with which this book has been concerned can be seen operating across four axes, as set out in summary form in the opening chapter. To reiterate, these axes comprise the *country conditions* of the development milieu within which change is embedded; the prevailing (time-sensitive) national and international *historical contexts* that exist at any given point; the often idiosyncratic local and *personal circumstances* in which communities, households and individuals make choices and experience change; and the *human characteristics* of the people whose choices and actions we are seeking to understand (Table 7.2).

Country conditions 'Country conditions' are the prevailing capacities, competencies and capabilities that characterize a development milieu which emerge from the political, institutional, social and economic conditions that exist. It was this broad issue which informed the discussion in Chapter 2, where it was suggested that planning disappointments were often linked to a failure, first, to be realistic about the capacity of states to plan and, secondly, the tendency to develop plans that are out of step with prevailing conditions and capacities. Rodrik's work (2001, 2007) has arguably been most influential in raising concerns about the dangers of arriving at 'orthodoxies' from country experiences which then become enshrined in rule books and policy packages of best practice. 'China', he writes, has 'followed a highly unorthodox two-track strategy, violating practically every rule in the guidebook (including, most notably, the requirement of private property rights)' (Rodrik 2001: 59).[7] Vietnam is another country which does not tick the boxes of orthodoxy, as Chapter 3 showed, and the same is true in small ways and large of every country in the region. As Datta-Chaudhuri (1990: 28) writes, the statement that an initiative was a 'good plan implemented badly' reflects a failure to shape policies and plans in the light of prevailing conditions. This highlights the need to avoid 'models' that are assumed to have traction across different countries; the experience of Asia is that they usually don't. Alexander (2003) makes this point but in wider terms when he asserts that there can be no 'planning', by which he means that there can be no generic approach to planning. All 'theories, paradigms and models [are] irrelevant for practice ... unless they are deployed in a contingent framework that relates them to the conditions experienced in a planning practitioner's life worlds' (ibid.: 180).

When countries have been encouraged – or forced – to embrace off-the-shelf policies and reforms they have sometimes made things worse rather than better. The response of the international institutions to the Asian financial crisis, as described in Chapter 3, is a case in point. The causes of the crisis were misdiagnosed and the generic cures did not help, and in all likelihood made things worse. There are no cure-alls when it comes to development and grand theorizations and generic approaches characteristically fail. As Joseph Stiglitz (2000) wrote in the aftermath of the crisis, 'critics accuse the [IMF] of taking a cookie-cutter approach to economics, and they're right'. At the same time, when things go right institutions (and sometimes individuals) have been all too quick to take the credit and all too willing to see their own recipes and policy prescriptions reflected in that success. The growth of the East Asian economies during the 'miracle' years is a case in point, with Amsden writing that 'Like Narcissus, the World Bank sees its own reflection in East Asia's success' (1994: 627; and see Baer et al. 1999). As the discussion in Chapter 3 showed, the reasons for the economic growth of the countries of East Asia remain contentious and, therefore, the lessons none too easy to discern. But it is certainly not the case that the Asian miracle was a product of embracing the orthodoxies of the moment.

Historical contexts Recognizing that country conditions, broadly defined, are important is part of the challenge. On top of this, however, is the need to be sensitive to the development moment and the vicissitudes of history, termed here 'historical context'. The role of the former was explored in Chapter 3 and the importance of the latter in Chapter 4.

Regarding the role of the historical moment, the fact that the early industrializers of East Asia – the developmental states of Asia – were able to develop in the way that they did was historically contingent, and predicated on a set of conditions. The fact that these were conditions (possibly even preconditions), however, only became clear *ex post facto*. The passage of history is not predetermined such that the past is deterministic of the future, and the present is just a way station connecting the two. The past is 'constitutive of the present, not determinative of it' (Woolcock et al. 2011: 86). Furthermore, with reference to the growth and development of East Asia, it is conjecture which of the historical conditions were essential (non-negotiable) and which were proximate but non-essential. To requote Chalmers Johnson, 'it would be to reason in an ahistorical and ill-informed manner to fail to note that Japan's high growth system was the product of one of the most painful passages to modernity any nation has ever had to endure' (1982: 306–7). Taiwan, Hong Kong, South Korea and Singapore all also had their own mélange of historical conditions which were important in shaping the circumstances that enabled development to proceed as it did. As argued in Chapter 3, these historical circumstances become not just the backdrop *of* change, but the context *for* change. Historical factors and conditions need to be moved to the foreground rather than seen as mere contextual wallpaper. Moreover, the economic success of East Asia's developmental states was not preordained. At the time that leaders in South Korea, Singapore and Taiwan were putting in place what we now regard, with hindsight, as the key elements of their countries' successful development programmes, so too were equally visionary leaders in Tanzania (Julius Nyerere) and Ghana (Kwame Nkrumah) (Fritz and Menocal 2007: 534–5). The outcomes, however, were markedly different.

Context is also important in a rather different guise: in the manner that 'lumpy' historical turning points play in disturbing notions that the passage of history is smooth. In their grandest form, these have the potential to turn one era into the next. Chapter 4 considers this in the context of the way in which a series of developments in the international economy led to South-East Asia becoming the preferred destination for Japanese foreign direct investment during the 1980s. There are also many more changes with a lower profile which, again with hindsight, we can see were locally and regionally important in shifting development patterns and trajectories.

Work on path dependency in different disciplines has encouraged (some) scholars to recognize the limits of generalization, and our inability to build models of social and economic change with great predictive power. While Pierson (2000: 266) finds the continuing failure of attempts to do just this in political science something of a 'puzzle', the preceding chapters have attempted to outline a set of interlocking reasons why it so often turns out to be futile. Small causes, themselves contingent, can have very large effects indeed (Mahoney 2000; Abbott 1988).

Personal circumstances Country conditions and historical contexts provide an important high-level set of shaping factors. At the local level, however, when it comes to the situation of individuals and families, it is their personal circumstances which will often determine outcomes. As the discussion of poverty in Chapter 5 explored, writing of 'the poor' overlooks the complex and varied ways that poverty is produced and experienced. Livelihoods research has attempted to get at the complexity of circumstances through mapping out the 'capitals' (financial, human, natural, physical and social) or assets that households bring to bear as they try to 'get by' in life, creating a bricolage of activities. While there have been critiques of the sustainable livelihoods framework (see Rigg 2007; Scoones 2009), it does usefully highlight the complexities of living and therefore militates against simple readings and interpretations of individual experiences and their upscaling to problematic generalizations which are seen to have traction at a broader scale.

Writing of 'the poor' is also reductionist in a second sense: it glosses over the role of often idiosyncratic events – both serendipitous and inopportune – in lifting people out of poverty or, alternatively, consigning them to such a condition. While the poor may be always with us, the individuals who comprise the poor population at any one moment in time are continually shifting. Notwithstanding the amount of academic and applied effort that has been put into bringing greater understanding to poverty, standardized policies fail because no single variable can account for the complex contexts and the unforeseen events that determine individual circumstances.

Human character(istics) Finally, there is what is termed here 'human character(istics)', the theme of the final core chapter of the book. This requires us to permit people, through their choices, decisions and actions, to have their say in the explanatory framings that we arrive at. As Chapter 6 made clear through the analysis of fertility decline in Asia and all that has flowed from this, not only was the initial decline unexpected but so too have been the raft of other resulting social and economic changes. To seek to understand what happened, we need to move away from the big questions and overarching conceptual models (such as the demographic transition model) to look at the choices that people have made (Banerjee and Duflo 2011: 107). This permits us at least to begin the process of understanding why fertility declined as it did in Asia, and the ramifications of this decline for human development. It also highlights the point that where current trends will lead still remains far from clear.

Three lessons: induction, empiricism and micro-theorizing

Reflecting on this section – and indeed the book as a whole – emphasizes three closely linked points, which I take to be wider lessons. First, it emphasizes the importance of taking an inductive rather than a deductive approach to understanding, interpreting and explaining development, through the use of case-study-informed theorizing. We need to start with people's actions and choices, not with large questions which encourage large and simplified answers. In reflecting on why so many economists and international institutions were wrong about the economies of East Asia leading up to the Asian financial crisis, Baer et al. (1999: 1746) contend that it was because of an 'excessive reliance on the neoclassical paradigm that led many economists to neglect an examination of the true institutional framework within which economic activity in East Asia was carried out', coupled with 'the current state of the economics profession [in which] deductivism has been dominant'. While deductive theorizing is essential, this needs to be measured and tested against the real-world experience. At the same time, inductive – applied – work has an important role and its denigration as somehow inferior needs to be challenged.

This raises a second theme and lesson: the importance and value of empiricism. It is not unusual for empiricism or positivism to be disparagingly talked of and written off as 'mere description', sometimes also labelled 'atheoretical'. For Raymond Williams, positivism has become a silent swear word (1988: 239), and reports are rejected as 'crudely empirical', by which it is meant indifferent to theory (ibid.: 116–17). But facts, experiences, policies and conditions all matter a great deal when it comes to development and, moreover, they often get in the way of theory. It is surprising how often broad statements are made in the absence of much data or many facts.[8]

The third lesson is to be cautious of generalization and even more vigilant when it comes to grand theorizing. We need to ensure that policy and academic space are opened up to accommodate heterodoxy. Towards the end of his highly influential book *The End of Poverty*, Jeffrey Sachs writes with confidence: 'I have identified the specific investments that are needed [to end poverty]; found ways to plan and implement them; [and] shown that they can be affordable ...' (2005: 328). The experience of South-East Asian growth, whether writ large in the performance of countries or small in the progress of individuals, is one which cautions against such claims. As Wade writes in *Governing the Market* with reference to industrial planning in East Asia, there should be 'more scope for different forms of national capitalism to flourish' (2004 [1990]: li) and '... scholars can help by nurturing a development economics that is more eclectic than the current monoculture and more focused on how to create dynamic capitalisms' (ibid.: liii).

Scholars make their names by grand theorizing, not by arriving, as Booth puts it, at 'parsimonious truths' or 'extended discourses on method' (2012: 2; and see Grindle 2011: 416). At the same time, advisers in international agencies tend to prefer cross-country generalizations to detailed contextual nit-picking. To be told, whether by academics or policy-makers, that 'context matters' is not going to set the world alight. And yet this is the key message of a wide range of studies (e.g. Grindle 2004, 2007, 2011; Rodrik 2007; Banerjee and Duflo 2011; Wade 2004 [1990]). There is a tendency to overlook or gloss over empirical differences and ambiguities in the interests of drawing out what is usually termed the wider point. What, however, if the ambiguities *are* the wider point?[9]

There is a question of whether there is useful space between grand theorizing and cross-country generalization on the one hand, and micro-assertions on the other. Booth suggests that there is, in the form of so-called middle-range propositions that highlight the contextual dimensions that are of greatest importance in shaping development.[10] What form such propositions might take is, however, in large part unresolved (see the next section) and, as this book has shown, the what (development policies to pursue), where (policies are likely to work), when (policies will have traction) and how (these policies impact on people and economies) of development all play a part in challenging the delineation of any recipes. That list of questions, moreover, leaves out the key cross-cutting question of why things work out in the way that they do. This is brought into sharper focus through a consideration of the ongoing debate about whether good policies or good institutions (see above) matter more when it comes to achieving development.

Good policies versus good governance

... appropriate growth policies are almost always context specific. (Rodrik 2007: 4)

... demanding 'good governance' may be asking too much from weak, under-resourced states, [and] may be impossible to translate into pathways that enable developing countries to break out of the 'weak institutions trap' (Fritz and Menocal 2007: 548)

In most recent writings about governance reform and development, recipes are out. So are 'one size fits all' and idealized end states. (Grindle 2011: 415)

One debate that has characterized recent discussions is the respective role and importance of good policies versus good governance in achieving development. Reflecting on the results of the Tracking Development project, Henley (n.d.: 11; and see Booth 2011) asserts that 'getting the policy priorities right is particularly important in countries where the machinery of government is weak, inefficient, or corrupt'. The 'primacy of policy' conclusion of this study was due to the fact that in their comparative analysis of four South-East Asian and four African countries, the research team found that, in fact, institutional quality did not seem to be the critical component explaining the differences in performance between the case-study countries. Instead it was the policies pursued which made the difference (see also Carmignani and Chowdhury 2011).

This is not to say that governance and the institutions of governance are irrelevant to development performance. Rather it is to note that we should not be blind-sided by the primacy of good governance. There are few who would doubt that corruption in Vietnam is currently significant, or that it was also prevalent and substantial during Indonesia and Thailand's period of rapid growth.[11] This has caused some scholars to nuance the good governance debate, and Grindle's (2007: 554) expression 'good enough governance' is emblematic of this, in which she highlights that: (i) not all governance 'deficits' can be addressed at once; (ii) that there is a prioritization or sequencing of institution building; and (iii) that this will likely vary according to country context. By focusing on the essentials, the good enough position moves the debate away from the achievement of a high-level and ideal governance agenda, which is unrealistic for most countries, towards identifying minimum requirements. Vietnam, for example, is a country which does not begin to meet the good governance agenda in the pure sense, but which has nonetheless a climate of governance which to date would seem to have been 'good enough' or conducive to ensure growth.

Stating, however, that we are interested in minimum governance conditions for growth does not tell us what, exactly, those conditions are; aid donors may give the impression that all is clear, but the research (based on empirical evidence drawn from case studies) indicates otherwise (Birdsall 2007). It is not the case that policies matter and governance and institutions do not; or even that policies matter more than governance and institutions. Universal policies for growth and universal means of dealing with governance weakness are both found to be wanting when set against individual country contexts (Booth 2011: S19). To use that popular social science term, policies and governance are co-produced. 'Good' policies are those that are framed with due regard to the country's institutional context; and good institutional contexts play an important role in producing good policies, and ensuring that these are implemented and are therefore more than just nominal (see Banerjee and Duflo 2011: 236).[12] Woolcock et al. (2011: 86–7) liken policy interventions to pouring dye into a stream: 'It joins, diffuses, gets diluted and may or may not change the color of the water in the intended fashion.' Policies' effects are never simply reproduced from one country or moment to another, like a scientific experiment in a Petri dish. An example is the failure to halt the massive illegal trade in wildlife across Vietnam's borders. Since the early 1990s, Vietnam has developed an impressive range of policies that seek to address such trade; there is no 'policy gap', as such (Larsen et al. 2012: 18). Understanding the failure to curtail the trade in wildlife requires an understanding not of policy, but of the operation of state–society relations in contemporary Vietnam.[13]

There are clear overlaps between good policies and good governance. But, importantly, while the former are outcomes and ends focused, the latter is about the conditions (laws, norms, processes, standards, principles) within which states and societies operate (Fritz and Menocal 2007: 537). On top of this, 'good' policies are also historically contingent. So, to return to Grindle's 'good enough governance', good enough needs to be gauged on a case-by-case basis so that even setting out middle-range propositions harbours the risk of arriving at a slate of 'to do's' which prove to be unfeasible, ineffective or inappropriate for a given historical moment and geographical context. 'Good' institutions and interventions in one country context may prove to be 'bad' in another.

Looking back at the experience of development across East Asia, conventional wisdom is either too broadly drawn to be very helpful in policy terms (as in Table 7.1), even when it has rhetorical attractions for policy-makers and international agencies; or so specifying that it is quickly unpicked by looking over the varied conditions that have existed in different growth economies. We can, however, show retrospectively – if also unexpectedly – how these processes might interface with development. We can do this, for example, by looking at the developmental effects of fertility decline in Asia addressed in the last chapter.

From demography to development

The fact that East and South-East Asia's fertility declined so steeply, whatever the causality, has been highlighted as a key contributor to the region's economic miracle (World Bank 1993: 204; and see Chapter 3). The decline in birth rates meant that between 1965 and 1990 the working-age population of East Asia grew at a rate of 2.4 per cent per year, while the population as a whole expanded at 1.6 per cent; the respective figures for South-East Asia were 2.9 and 2.4 per cent (Bloom and Williamson 1998: 442; and see Economist 2011b). These differences, which were even greater among the miracle economies, bestowed a demographic 'gift' or 'dividend' that has been estimated to have accounted for between one third and one half of East Asia's per capita GDP growth during the miracle years (Figure 7.1).[14] Bloom and Williamson conclude (1998: 450) that '... population dynamics may have been the single most important determinant of [East Asia's] growth'.

Although fertility decline has, some scholars have suggested, played a significant part in creating the demographic space for the Asian economic miracle, this would not have helped very much had not millions of (mostly young) people – formerly peasants or the children of peasants – been willing to leave home and find factory work, largely in urban or peri-urban zones. Like so much when it comes to development, this seems obvious only as we look over our shoulder, to gaze back along development's wake. These young men and especially young women were not the usual suspects: formerly stereotyped as *takut dan malu* (fearful and shy), with little education and limited

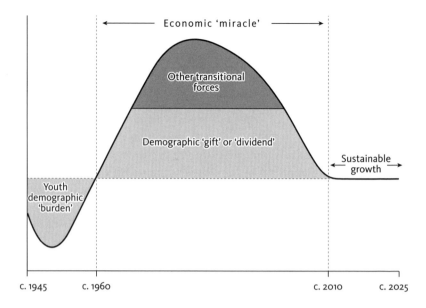

Figure 7.1 From demographic burden to demographic gift: the role of fertility decline in Asia's economic miracle

horizons, they took the heroic step of leaving the familiarity and safety of home, and in so doing individually and cumulatively helped to build the Asian economic miracle. To begin with, ties to the village and farming tended to remain strong, but the first step having been taken much else followed:

> Newer migrants have looser ties to their villages [in China]. Their trips home are no longer dictated by the farming calendar or even by the timing of traditional holidays ... Instead, younger migrants come and go according to their personal schedules ... and these are often tied to the demands of the production cycle. It is the seasons of the factory, rather than the fields, that define migrant life now. (Chang 2008: 105)

Success for different reasons: bringing people back in

This book has sought to question normal interpretations of South-East Asian development through pursuing three avenues of argument: the book has challenged the desire to distil the development 'lessons' of the region; it has problematized attempts at planning and second-guessing the passage of development; and it has privileged the role of small events and ordinary people in trajectories of change. What might have become lost in the discussion, however, is that this book is not one about development failure. Development has, broadly drawn, succeeded in Asia, and done so beyond all expectations. People are better educated and more aware and informed, they are living longer and healthier lives with children far less likely to die during their early years or mothers in childbirth, and they are richer in material terms. What the book has sought to do is provide an account of how this has happened.

There is little doubt in my mind, then, that for the large bulk of the population of South-East Asia – albeit with some notable exceptions (see Chapter 5) – conditions of existence are better today than they have ever been, and that this is linked in important ways to economic expansion. There are very few statements that I feel confident in making when it comes to generalizing across South-East Asia, but this is one and, to my mind, it is not based on conjecture. But my confidence is quickly eroded when I move beyond this lone generalization. And the reason for this, at heart, is because people cannot easily be counted, governed, manipulated or coerced; just as they cannot be developed from above, nor can they be understood from above.

Notes

1 The hidden geometries of development

1 Over the last decade or so, there have been a number of popular books that have dealt with the surprising twists and turns of history and economics. Nassim Taleb's (2008) *The Black Swan: The impact of the highly improbable*; Dan Gardner's (2011) *Future Babble: Why expert predictions fail and why we believe them anyway*; Malcolm Gladwell's two books, *The Tipping Point: How little things can make a big difference* (2001) and *Outliers: The story of success* (2008); and Ed Smith's *Luck: What it means and why it matters* (2012).

2 I am grateful to Holly High for this neat and evocative turn of phrase, which is exemplified best in Scott's book *Seeing Like a State* (1998).

3 See Moser's (2009) book mentioned earlier for an account of such complex interactions in the urban slum of Indio Guayas on the outskirts of Guayaquil, Ecuador; and Bakewell (2010) for an application of the structure/agency binary to migration.

2 From development plans to development planning

1 The Truman 'development doctrine': 'We must embark on a bold new program for making the benefits of our scientific advances and industrial progress available for the improvement and growth of underdeveloped areas. More than half the people of the world are living in conditions approaching misery. Their food is inadequate. They are victims of disease. Their economic life is primitive and stagnant. Their poverty is a handicap and a threat both to them and to more prosperous areas. For the first time in history, humanity possesses the knowledge and skill to relieve suffering of these people. The United States is pre-eminent among nations in the development of industrial and scientific techniques. The material resources which we can afford to use for assistance of other peoples are limited. But our imponderable resources in technical knowledge are constantly growing and are inexhaustible' (accessed at www.saidnews.org/history/United_States_Presidents/PDF_Presidents/President_Speeches/Htruman_1st_inaugural.pdf).

2 Key economists who contributed to this early period of development planning include Simon Kuznets, Gunnar Myrdal, Michael Todaro, Jan Tinbergen, Raul Prebisch and Albert Hirschman.

3 The expert group of nine who wrote the book were from: Brazil, Czechoslovakia, France, India, Japan, the Netherlands, the USA, the USSR and Yugoslavia.

4 Lewis's *Development Planning* (1966) is possibly the best-known planning 'handbook'.

5 The World Bank's 1949–50 Annual Report stated that member

countries 'know, too, that if they formulate a well-balanced development program based on the [Bank] Mission's recommendations, the Bank will stand ready to help them carry out the program by financing appropriate projects' (quoted in Balassa 1990: 562).

6 In his recent review of Pakistan's Planning Commission, Ikram writes: 'It is apparent that the Planning Commission did not adjust its tools, methods, and staffing to deal with the new economic environment ... The five-year plans said virtually nothing about private sector planning. Thus, the Seventh Five-Year Plan (1988–93) devoted a total of six pages to the private sector; the Eighth Plan (1993–98) covered the private sector's contribution in four' (2011: 5).

7 The five-year socio-economic development plan (2006–10) is replete with the words and phrases of twenty-first-century planning philosophy. Its production is said to have involved 'greater community participation in plan development; extensive consultation with research institutions and scientists home and abroad, social organisations, and different social groups, in order to create a wide social consensus in identifying long-term and short-term visions and objectives as well as approaches to implementation which would ensure the realisation of the plan' (MoPI 2009: i).

8 This critique led to a shift from planning as 'event' to planning as 'process', although in most instances this has not overcome the *tendency* for planning to be event focused.

9 This point was most influentially developed in James Ferguson's (1990) *The Anti-Politics Machine:*

'Development', depoliticization and bureaucratic power in Lesotho.

10 With respect to computable general equilibrium (CGE) models, Little writes: '... there is such a wide range of alternative and equally supportable formulations of the general principles [on which CGE models are based], and such a high degree of sensitivity of outcomes to the settings of parameters and exogenous variables, that the predictions of such models must be regarded as speculative' (Little 1995: 267; see also the other contributions to this volume).

11 In her study of irrigation planning in the Gambia, Dey (1982) identifies a gap between farmers' and planners' concerns, experiences and understandings, with the result that irrigations plans have performed poorly. To narrow the gap, she recommends drawing farmers into the planning and implementation processes and underlines the need to 'make a concerted effort to understand the organization of production and consumption' (ibid.: 393).

12 '... despite more than three decades of development planning efforts, most planning exercises appear to be rather isolated from the main concerns of policy- and decision-makers in developing countries' (Sagasti 1988: 431).

13 Numerous scholars have struggled with the issue of Asian exceptionalism. Berger writes: 'It is my contention that these countries [of East and South-East Asia] are sufficiently distinct, as compared with the West, that one is entitled to speak of them as a "second case" of capitalist modernity' (1988: 4).

14 Weber does not dispute that capitalism existed in the Orient,

but rather that it did not achieve its high, rational form which he associated with modern capitalism. To achieve this 'a rational chemistry' had to exist which 'has been absent from all areas of culture except the West' (1930: 14).

15 The National Economic Board (NEB), established in 1950, was the precursor to the NEDB/NESDB.

16 A World Bank advisory mission visited Thailand in 1957 and provided an important impetus to the planning agenda that the NEDB then took forward (Warr and Nidhiprabha 1996: 13).

17 The Third Plan was, significantly, the first National Economic *and Social* Development Plan, reflecting the shift in planning circles towards social as well as economic objectives.

18 To download the current and past plans in English, see www.nesdb.go.th/.

19 Even more dramatic was the fate that was to befall Thailand's Eighth Five-Year Development Plan (1997–2001), which, within months of being released, was effectively redundant. The plan envisaged 'stable and sustainable economic growth' (NESDB 1996: 3); instead the Asian financial crisis meant that the Thai economy contracted more precipitously than at any time since the end of the Second World War. Hill makes a similar point regarding successive national development plans (*Repelitas*) in Indonesia, which 'became dated and virtually irrelevant shortly after their publication', mainly because of the volatility of the price of oil, upon which so much rested (Hill 1996: 95).

20 The NESDB does not have cabinet status and the role of the NESDB in decision-making largely depends on the particular relationship between the secretary-general of the NESDB and the prime minister of the time (Muscat 1994: 178–9).

21 The release of the latter two documents was delayed because the boundaries of Hanoi were substantially revised in 2008. The former province of Ha Tay became part of Hanoi, as well as some areas of Vinh Phuc and Hoa Binh provinces, in so doing expanding the area of the city from 900 km² to 3,300 km² and its population from 3.2 to 6.4 million (Labbé 2010: 10–11).

22 Following the Asian financial crisis, for example, there was a sharp drop-off in FDI to Vietnam in 1998.

23 Leaf writes of Hanoi as 'a quintessential city of the informal sector' (1999: 306).

24 Gillespie comes to a similar conclusion in his review of the legal basis for urban land development in Vietnam, writing that '... [as] bureaucratic rule has failed to control urban development and ... foreign laws are rarely politically or economically appropriate, lawmakers are looking inwards at customary law practice and cultural values as sources of land laws' (Gillespie 1995: 124).

25 See Molle et al. (2009b) for a collection of essays on *Contested Waterscapes in the Mekong Region*.

26 Although water management – in the form of hydraulic systems and hydro-agriculture – dates back many centuries earlier still.

27 Literature on river basin development in South-East Asia is particularly rich and critical. See, for example: Barrow (1998), Molle (2006, 2008, 2009), Hirsch (1988, 2001, 2006), Molle et al. (2009a, 2009b).

28 Hence the notion of the 'multi-purpose' dam that provides

irrigation, controls flooding, generates electricity, boosts tourist revenue, sustains fisheries, and more. Critics view the very notion of the multi-purpose dam as yet further evidence of the over-optimism and overweening ambition of planners who have overlooked the environmental and social impacts of dams while overestimating their returns.

29 These arguments are also echoed in the work of Walker (2001) on the Karen in northern Thailand. See Chapter 4.

30 In their consideration of the anti-politics of Mekong knowledge production, Käkönen and Hirsch, like Li, write about how the mainstreaming of the participatory turn in development runs the risk of causing 'participation … to mirror a type of development-driven participation that can contribute to the de-politicisation of knowledge in support of a particular governance agenda' (2009: 334).

31 'If the quality of plans on paper were the main determinant of success, India would be rated at or near the top among developing countries' (Byrd 1990: 713–14).

3 State and market perfections and imperfections

1 It also worth noting that not only did the crisis afflict Asian economies differently, but there were a number of Asian countries that were not affected, notably India and, to an extent, China. In population terms, more people lived in countries that had no crisis than the number who did, and in that sense the '*Asian* economic crisis' is a misnomer.

2 The term 'East Asia' as used in this chapter includes both the South-East Asian and East Asian

geographical regions, unless otherwise stated.

3 The ADB, in a review of inequality in Asia in 2007, summed up the experience as follows: 'The overall pattern that therefore emerges is one where a majority of developing Asian countries have seen increases in inequality. By and large, however, increases in inequality are not a story of the "rich getting richer and the poor getting poorer". Rather it is the rich getting richer faster than the poor' (ADB 2007: 6). This may be true, but growing inequality nonetheless is politically highly charged when, while everyone is getting absolutely wealthier, some are becoming relatively poorer.

4 The contrast is even starker for the years between 2005 and 2008. Drawing the line at the new cut-off of $1.25 a day, then between 2005 and 2008 150 million people in the Asia Pacific region were 'lifted out' of poverty; if we take a $2-a-day line, then the figure is 18.4 million, little more than one tenth of the former figure (ADB 2011).

5 The term 'Washington Consensus' was coined by John Williamson in 1990. The term encapsulates the policy framework that came to be seen by mainstream, orthodox (or neoliberal) economists and institutions as lying at the heart of an economic framework that would promote economic growth. It was a *Washington* consensus because the three key institutions promoting this economic orthodoxy were based in Washington: the World Bank, the International Monetary Fund and the US Treasury.

6 Jomo states that the EAM report was commissioned by the World Bank only with the funding of Japan and the insistence of the

Japanese executive director on the Bank's board (Jomo 2003: 2; and see Berger and Beeson 1998: 495–6). See Stiglitz (1996) for another 'insider' account that suggests that government interventions were important.

7 This metaphor was first used by Kaname Akamatsu in the mid-1930s, in a Japanese-language publication. He later developed the theme in English-language papers published in the 1960s: 'It is impossible to study the economic growth of the developing countries in modern times without considering the mutual interactions between these economies and those of the advanced countries.' He called such relationships and interactions the 'wild-geese-flying-pattern' (*gankō keitai*) of industrial development (Akamatsu 1962: 3, 11).

8 That said, one of the more provocative conclusions of the tracking development project is that South-East Asia's development success is less about good governance than about good policies (see Donge et al. n.d.).

9 Gainsborough does suggest later in his book that the Vietnamese state's contact with neoliberal agencies has not left it completely unaffected, and sees the emergence of a 'hybrid state', but one where there are important threads of continuity (2010: 172).

10 In the same vein, Wade (2004 [1990]: xv) writes: 'The remarkable thing about the core Washington Consensus is the gulf between the confidence with which it is promulgated and the strength of supporting evidence, historical or contemporary.'

11 Ikram refers to South Korea as the 'most successful example of planning' among developing countries (2011: 10).

12 Beeson (2000: 315) notes, in making his case for a Malaysian developmental state, that such policies were implemented in the absence of an insulated and autonomous bureaucracy.

13 At various times, scholars have suggested that the developmental state debate is settled and over. Weiss (a political scientist), for example, in her book simply accepts that 'active governments pursuing strategic trade and industrial policies have constituted an important component of East Asia's high performance economies', on the basis that the debate has 'more or less run its course' (Weiss 1998: 41–2). Hill and Chu (both economists), some eight years later, find ample reason to question the links between economic policy and economic performance, even in the East Asian developmental states (2006: 46–50).

14 Evans writes of 'embedded autonomy' to describe the manner in which the state and the private sector are fused (Evans 1989: 575).

15 Rodrik approaches this question of picking/making winners slightly differently, suggesting that 'What determines success in industrial policy is not the ability to pick winners, but the capacity to let losers go' (2010).

16 Rent-seeking per se is not necessarily illegal, as Krueger (1974) explores in her highly cited paper. If there are quantitative restrictions on imports, then firms and individuals will devote resources to competing for lucrative import licences. While bribery might be an (illegal) part of this effort, there are many other perfectly legal avenues for competition. Indeed, as Krueger concludes,

'all market economies have some rent-generating restrictions' (ibid.: 302).

17 This is a point that Wade explores in the final chapter of his book.

18 Although note the point above that, for Wade (2004 [1990]: 334), East Asian success was not about 'picking' winners but 'making' them.

19 There are numerous surveys of the Asian economic crisis. Those published in 1998 and 1999 (see Johnson 1998, Krugman 1998, Goldstein 1998, Garnaut 1998, Radelet et al. 1998) are good at showing how there were, to begin with, numerous interpretations of what happened, why and with what imputed policy implications; those published from 2000 onwards (Pasuk Phongpaichit and Baker 2000, Rigg 2002, Hewison 2005, Stiglitz and Yusuf 2001) are generally more reflective.

20 A point that Stiglitz (2002: 90), Radelet and Sachs (1999: 2), Jomo (2005: 16) and King (2001: 442) also make.

21 A background paper for this report written by prominent scholars at the Harvard Institute for International Development stated that 'Asia will continue a remarkable economic transformation' (p. 58), concluding that 'for the fast-growing countries of East Asia, there is a continuing opportunity for rapid growth, though at rates that are likely to be somewhat slower than in the past, precisely because the process of catching up has been so successful to date' (Radelet et al. 1997: 60). This paper was released in July 1997.

22 'Asian countries have glimpsed the future of prosperity and open societies, and have unleashed a positive economic dynamism benefiting the region's grand history. Indeed, the next 30 years have the extraordinary promise to bring durable improvements in the quality of life to many more Asians' (ADB 1997a: 58).

23 'From doing no wrong, the miracle countries overnight became basket cases infested with cronyistic error. It amounted to a gestalt shift, like seeing the famous line drawing as a vase one moment and two faces in profile the next' (Wade 2004 [1990]: xxxii).

24 We can see a parallel debate in the context of the 2011 euro crisis.

25 For discussions of the Post-Washington Consensus, see Stiglitz (2004) and Öniş and Senses (2005).

26 For an insight into the sparring between the World Bank and the IMF and, more particularly, between Stiglitz and Kenneth Rogoff, Economic Counsellor and Director of Research at the IMF, see info.worldbank.org/etools/bspan/PresentationView.asp?EID=145&PID=325. Rogoff ends his open letter to Stiglitz published on 2 July 2002, exactly five years after the onset of the Asian economic crisis, writing: 'Joe, as an academic, you are a towering genius. Like your fellow Nobel Prize winner, John Nash, you have a "beautiful mind." As a policymaker, however, you were just a bit less impressive'; www.imf.org/external/np/vc/2002/070202.htm.

27 In consideration of the EAM report, Stiglitz writes: 'The [East Asian] countries had been successful not only in spite of the fact that they had not followed most of the dictates of the Washington Consensus, but *because* they had not' (2002: 91, emphasis in original).

4 The teleology of development

1 The quotation 'Life is just one damned thing after another' is usually linked to the US author Elbert Hubbard (1856–1915), sometimes to Edna St Vincent Millay (1892–1950), but has become probably more closely associated with Arnold Toynbee, who suggested that those who considered history to be just one damned thing after another were intellectual provincials.

2 Also consider some of the knock-on effects of the Asian crisis in Indonesia: civil unrest in Jakarta; the resignation of Suharto after thirty-two years as president of Indonesia; democratization and decentralization; and the independence of Timor Leste (East Timor) in 2002 after a referendum in 1999. The Asian crisis set in train complex political change in Indonesia, Malaysia, South Korea and Thailand, but nowhere more so than in Indonesia (see Freedman 2005).

3 www.bbc.co.uk/news/business-12294332.

4 In other words, outcomes are tied or linked back to earlier events to different degrees. The importance of sequencing varies. In some instances it may matter a great deal; in others, scarcely at all.

5 A view of societal and economic change at least as teleological as Rostow's (and of which he makes note; Rostow 1960: 148).

6 'These stages are not merely descriptive. They are not merely a way of generalizing certain factual observations about the sequence of development of modern societies. They have an inner logic and continuity. They have an analytic bone structure, rooted in a dynamic theory of production' (Rostow 1960: 12–13).

7 Caldwell, in his revisionist take on the demographic transition model (see Chapter 6) and the role of Westernization in fertility decline, writes: 'Curiously, it is only the well-trained, over-sensitive Western researcher who does not see and hear the obvious. In West Africa, survey respondents (as well as the conversationalist met in the street, the villager in the compound, and the Lagos newspaper) speak continually of adopting European ways – often, in fact, embarrassing the researcher in rural areas by going on to summarize this as "becoming civilized"' (1976: 353).

8 I am grateful to Wasana La-Orngplew for pointing me towards this study and this quote.

9 The title of Forsyth and Walker's book on the politics of environmental knowledge in northern Thailand is *Forest Guardians, Forest Destroyers* (2008).

10 Quoted in Brown (2009: 584).

11 Although most academic historians remain slightly wary of such efforts at 'what if' history, seeing it as a parlour game that has no place in scholarly endeavour (see Ferguson 1997b).

12 This was achieved by the central banks of the G5 economies (France, Japan, the UK, the USA and West Germany) making a coordinated effort to buy dollars and sell yen.

13 Or in full: *Post hoc ergo propter hoc.*

14 The Asean-5 are Indonesia, Malaysia, Philippines, Singapore and Thailand.

15 This concern with everyday technologies is the focus of David Arnold's 'Everyday technology in monsoon Asia, 1880–1960' project at the University of Warwick (see

www2.warwick.ac.uk/fac/arts/history/ghcc/research/globaltechnology/, Arnold 2011 and Arnold and DeWald 2011b and the papers in the special issue of *Modern Asian Studies* [2012] edited by David Arnold).

16 www2.warwick.ac.uk/fac/arts/history/ghcc/research/global technology/.

17 For comparison, the Panama Canal required the extraction of 210 million cubic metres and the Suez Canal 260 million cubic metres (Biggs 2003: 79).

18 In Siam (Thailand), canal digging before the middle of the nineteenth century had little to do with rice growing; canals were dug largely to aid communication and facilitate access or for purposes of defence. The first canal excavated with the express purpose of securing land for rice farming was the *Khlong* (canal) Mahasawat in 1857 (Brummelhuis 2005: 61–2).

19 Mr Van Nam did not patent his invention and other mechanics improved upon the original design.

20 Although one report received by US ambassador Ellsworth Bunker in 1967 lauded the shrimp-tail pump as indicative of how far Vietnamese peasants had embraced modernization, in line with Walt Rostow's and Samuel Huntington's ideas of the nature of progress (Fisher 2006: 48–9).

21 Arabica production is concentrated in the higher-altitude provinces such as Son La.

22 Tan writes: 'In order to sell their coffee, these farmers have to take into account a certain measure of quality control, but almost never in accordance to the dictates of the coffee market's quality discourse' (Tan and Walker 2008: 122).

23 '... the history of Third World development is littered with the debris of huge agricultural schemes and new cities that have failed their residents' (Scott 1998: 3).

24 One of Wasana La-orngplew's key informants in her study of rubber in upland Laos explained: 'It was strange, not like other crops. It [rubber] has come on its own. It was not in the plan. The government promoted corn, cassava, sesame, peanut, chilli and many other crops but not rubber. It has arrived by Chinese and by villagers. The government's awakening to rubber came after villagers who had already started. The government then promoted it but far behind on villagers' (personal communication, 1 March 2012).

5 The power of ordinary events

1 This is similar to the Lancashire proverb 'From clogs to clogs is only three generations'. Clogs were associated with poverty.

2 A panel study is a longitudinal study which follows the *same* group of individuals, families or households over time, and in that sense is distinct from a cross-sectional study.

3 Individuals were interviewed every year over the period, and children were added to the sample and interviewed separately when they had established their own households.

4 Sawhill, in her paper on poverty in the USA, writes: '... we still understand very little about the basic causes of poverty – the extent to which it is a matter of genetic or cultural inheritance, a lack of human capital, a choice variable related to work and family decisions, a result of macroeconomic failures or of social stratification based on race, sex, or family background' (Sawhill 1988: 1113).

5 Although clearly, and as noted earlier, economic growth alone is not enough; the quality of growth is vitally important in creating and transferring opportunities broadly in social terms and widely geographically.

6 See Rigg and Salamanca (2009) for an account of changing risk profiles in the village over the period from 1982 to 2009.

7 The adopted son has also left the village and no longer maintains contact with his adoptive mother.

8 The experiences of Achara can be compared to those of Maymana and Mofizul in Bangladesh, who, 'against the odds', improved their quality of life between 1999 and 2005 (see Hulme 2003 and Hulme and Moore 2010).

9 The so-called 30 baht [= US$1] programme because this is the flat rate for each treatment.

10 Baulch and Davis (2008) describe such sequences of downward lurches as having a 'saw tooth' character.

11 '... then, out of the black beyond, like a hawk on a rat, some nameless catastrophe would swoop into your life and turn everything upside down and inside out forever' (Nicholas Evans, *The Smoke Jumper*, 2001, p. 1).

12 In his analysis of 'primary' poverty in York more than a century ago, Seebohm Rowntree noted the effect that the death of a chief wage earner could have on family living conditions (1901: 119–20).

13 Expenditure-based measures of poverty dominate quantitative poverty assessments.

14 Carter and Maluccio (2003) argue in the case of KwaZulu-Natal, South Africa, that settlements with a greater sense of community and the social capital that goes with the covenant that binds communities are in a better position to weather livelihood shocks.

15 Simply adding up household assets may give a false reading of accumulated wealth; it is not unusual for assets to be purchased on credit. In light of this, it is not just *what* people own in terms of their asset base, but *how* they come to own these things.

16 See www.rand.org/labor/FLS/IFLS.html; for a listing of papers arising from the IFLS study see www.rand.org/labor/FLS/IFLS/papers.html.

17 We can speculate, based on other data sources (see Suryahadi et al. 2003a: 239), that poverty would have peaked in late 1998, and then declined through 1999 and 2000. This peak is not covered by the analysis here of the IFLS data.

18 See, for example, Glauben et al.'s recent (2012) study from China, in which they do not find convincing evidence of a poverty 'trap', but rather of considerable mobility. The transitory nature of poverty, however, is clearest in richer provinces benefiting from high rates of economic expansion; for poorer provinces, poverty is more persistent.

19 See, for example, the working papers of the Chronic Poverty Research Centre (www.chronicpoverty.org/page/publications).

20 They claim that their 2009 study is the first to look at the effects of orphanhood on children's health outside Africa (Suryadarma et al. 2009: 6).

21 Horrell et al. (2001) provide a valuable historical view of IGT poverty in eighteenth- and nineteenth-century England. Under the Old Poor Law (a 'welfare state

in miniature' – Blaug 1964: 229, quoted in ibid.: 353) every parish was expected to support the poor, and at the start of the nineteenth century around one million people were receiving relief, or 11 per cent of the population of England and Wales. This relief was targeted, low cost and effective because parishes knew well the circumstances of recipients; there were scarcely any free-riders. The reform of the Old Poor Law and the introduction of the harsher, more draconian New Poor Law in 1834 increased the incidence of IGT poverty because the law less well protected orphans and the children of the destitute. 'The rewards to this outlay [connected with the Old Poor Law] were manifold; children whose destiny may have been dependence and mendacity could become productive and industrious. They contributed to national income and in many ways were at the vanguard of industrialisation' (ibid.: 363).

22 For a set of fourteen longitudinal studies of agrarian change in South-East Asia covering Cambodia, Indonesia, Malaysia, the Philippines, Thailand and Vietnam, see Rigg and Vandergeest 2012.

23 Although, as Krishna points out, we do not know whether these households became non-poor between those dates and, moreover, whether their parents and grandparents were poor as well. Nonetheless, they do count as a long-term and consistently poor population.

24 For an early panel study from India, using two data points from a village in the 'famine tract' of Maharashtra in 1920 and 1970, see Attwood et al. (1979). Focusing on access to land, the study shows that of the original landed households in 1920, 44 per cent had become land-less by 1970, while of the original landless, 24 per cent had become landed fifty years later (ibid.: 501).

25 In other words, the proportion of the poor population who exit poverty between the beginning and end of the month.

6 Fertility decline

1 This is a common *mea culpa* in the demographic literature: 'The modern demographic transitions in Southeast Asia are proceeding much faster than almost any observer would have predicted 20 years ago' (Hirschman and Guest 1990: 150). 'In the period from 1970 to the present, Asia has experienced a transition from high to low fertility of an unexpected magnitude and at an unprecedented speed' (Jones and Leete 2002: 115).

2 The variation in family planning practices and patterns of adoption across Muslim-majority countries indicates that Islam itself is not a constraint. Responses to family planning and the putative role of religion in the process are instead linked to political strategies and wider cultural conditions (see Obermeyer 1994; Underwood 2000).

3 In some provinces – such as East Java – it seems that 'persuasion' became sufficiently heavy handed to be better termed coercion.

4 The Longitudinal Study of Social, Economic and Demographic Change. For papers on Thailand's fertility decline and its implications, see Knodel and Van de Walle (1979); Knodel and Van Landingham (2003); and Prachuabmoh et al. (1974).

5 Data on fertility for North Vietnam at this time are sketchy and incomplete and therefore calculating a rate of decline, according to Bryant, 'futile' (1998: 239).

6 Jones also notes the role of ethnic nationalism and religious fundamentalism in Malaysia (1990: 531).

7 See www.lovebyte.org.sg/web/ent_p_home.asp – 'A world of possibilities, just a click away'.

8 www.singstat.gov.sg/stats/themes/people/popnindicators.pdf. There is the hope that this might rise somewhat in 2012, the Year of the Dragon in the Chinese calendar and a particularly auspicious year to have a child. This is unlikely, however, to herald a change in the established pattern of low fertility.

9 Data on rates of cohabitation in Asia are not widely available but as it remains socially unacceptable in many Asian societies a reasonable assumption is that cohabitation rates are low, albeit probably not as low as commonly thought.

10 In Japan in 2007, just 2 per cent of births occurred outside wedlock (Economist 2011a: 19).

11 The same point has also been made with regard to the increasing prevalence of childlessness in Japan (Jolivet 1997) and South Korea (Yang and Rosenblatt 2008), both Confucian societies which emphasize the maintenance of the paternal family line.

12 Davin (2007: 89) notes that in China one third of illiterate and semi-literate men and nearly one in ten men with only primary-level education remain unmarried in their late thirties. Given that there are almost no women in this position, she concludes that 'clearly most of these men will never be able to marry' (p. 91).

13 'Taiwanese men pay around US$7,000 to join a one-week match-making tour [to Vietnam] organized by an agency, and they can meet as many girls as they wish until they choose one, then hold the wedding ceremony in that same week. All necessary immigration documents will be applied for later by the commercial agency. After two months, the "Vietnamese bride" can move to Taiwan' (Wang 2007: 707).

14 This is one factor promoting delayed marriage: the assumption that immediately following marriage women will have children, a real disincentive for a woman aiming to build a career.

15 The ILO has estimated that the number of undocumented Indonesians working abroad is two to four times higher than the documented figure of four million (Tirtosudarm 2009: 25).

16 China has some 130 million rural–urban migrant workers: 'Together they represent the largest migration in human history; three times the number of people who emigrated to America from Europe over a century' (Chang 2008: 12). Including rural–rural migrants, the total number on the move at the end of 2008 numbered 225 million (Ploeg and Jingzhong 2010: 515).

17 For various studies and reports that reflect this discourse, see: UNDP (2009: 71–2); GSO (2006: 2); Anh et al. (1997: 313); Martin (2009: 10); Fang et al. (2009: 8–10); Tirtosudarm (2009: 29).

18 Writing of China, Chang says: 'Migration is emptying villages of young people. Across the Chinese countryside, those ploughing and harvesting in the fields are elderly men and women, charged with running the farm and caring for the younger children who are still in school. Money sent home by migrants is already the biggest source of wealth accumulation in

rural China. Yet earning money isn't the only reason people migrate. ... *There was nothing to do at home, so I went out*' (2008: 13, emphasis in original).

19 See Nguyen et al. (2012) on Vietnam; Mustapha and Shaik (1985) and Kato (1994) on peninsular Malaysia; Cramb (2012) on East Malaysia; Preston (1989) on Java, Indonesia; and UNDP (2007) and Bruneau (2012) on Thailand.

20 '... the crops that are planted in Ifugao fields say volumes about how the people planting them envision themselves in relation to both the state and to global labour markets. Bean gardens can be read as remittance landscapes – they both anticipate remittances and produce the capital needed to go overseas – and are thus tied to the translocal nature of apparently local places' (McKay 2003: 306; see also Kelly 2012).

21 See the chapters in Rigg and Vandergeest (2012).

22 Juliette Koning's (2005) paper on female circular migrants in Java is entitled 'The impossible return'.

23 In an editorial, the *Bangkok Post* worried that: 'Many [of the elderly] are being left to fend for themselves as the traditional family unit breaks apart, creating a social crisis that must be dealt with. ... Caring for the elderly has long been one of the great filial obligations of Thai society. But as the times change, so do attitudes towards marriage and family, backed by a growing desire for greater individualism. ... As the extended family disintegrates, many of the aged are being forced to seek help elsewhere and the filial piety that has long been a core value of society throughout Asia melts away, to be replaced by pricy care homes and

support groups' ('Tackling plight of the elderly', *Bangkok Post*, 8 May 2010, www.bangkokpost.com/opinion/opinion/36995/tackling-plight-of-the-elderly).

24 Jeffrey writes, in the context of India's Uttar Pradesh, 'rich Jat farmers' practice of constructing urban-style homes in their villages [which] was contributing to a process wherein rural areas increasingly looked like suburbs of [the city of] Meerut'. Return students educated in Meerut also became 'conduits along which urban goods and ideas flowed into the countryside' (2010: 176–7).

25 We should not imagine that urban populations are necessarily more cosmopolitan and worldly than rural populations. Thai rural north-easterners may be viewed by the urban elite as unsophisticated 'buffalo' – country bumpkins – but yet, as Keyes (2010) notes, more of these parochial peasants have passports than do Bangkok's lower middle classes. They are rural cosmopolitans who have become insinuated into the global labour force and yet to a greater or lesser extent remain partially beholden to their peasant background and rural origins.

26 I have taken this from a point that Philip Kraeger raised at a workshop on population dynamics in East Asia (30 March 2012).

27 By 1998, a 'pattern of particular "remittance behaviours" had begun to emerge, in which daughters' direct and indirect economic contribution was increasingly recognised' in Tiuh Baru (Elmhirst 2002: 158).

28 See, for example: Chang (2008) on China; and Mills (1997, 1999) on Thailand.

29 Bakewell makes a case for a critical realist approach to migration where '"social structure" ... can exert causal power on migration processes and serve to thwart not only the policies of states but potentially the interests of existing migrants' (2010: 1703).

30 For a collection of papers on the 'left behind' in Asia see the special issue of *Population, Space and Place* edited by Toyota et al. (2007).

7 Contingent development

1 The others are: Botswana, Brazil, Malta and Oman.

2 The pairings are: Indonesia and Nigeria; Malaysia and Kenya; Vietnam and Tanzania; and Cambodia and Uganda.

3 In the introduction to a working paper, Sachs writes: 'In a series of papers, my colleagues and I have demonstrated that levels of per capita income, economic growth, and other economic and demographic dimensions are strongly correlated with key geographical and ecological variables, such as climate zone, disease ecology, and distance from the coast' (Sachs 2003: 2).

4 In contrast to Sachs, Acemoglu et al. (2002: 1279) argue that: 'This reversal in relative incomes [across the globe] is inconsistent with the simple geography hypothesis which explains the bulk of the income differences across countries by the direct effect of geographic differences, thus predicting a high degree of persistence in economic outcomes. ... Instead, the reversal in relative incomes over the past 500 years appears to reflect the effect of institutions (and the institutional reversal caused by European colonialism) on income today.'

5 '... good policies help create favourable conditions for development. In this sense, countries are not condemned to be underdeveloped by initial conditions, geography, or historical legacies. By implementing the appropriate set of policies, a country can achieve the scenario of positive growth with declining inequality that provides the most favourable conditions for sustained development' (Carmignani and Chowdhury 2011: 530).

6 A new generation of thinking is required that 'emphasizes the importance of knowing the context in which reformed policies, institutions, and processes are to be introduced, and designing interventions that are appropriate to time, place, historical experience, and local capacity' (Grindle 2011: 415).

7 For Grindle (ibid.: 415), best practice is not far from the 'conceptual dustbin'.

8 See Ghemawat (2011: 33–5) for a critique of discussions of globalization that are situated in a 'data-free zone'.

9 Grindle explains this tendency as follows: '... publications often provide illustrations of how particular countries have resolved specific governance challenges or examples of best practice, even while the research described ... frequently insists that such experiences cannot be isolated from the contextual factors that made particular achievements possible' (2007: 561).

10 Arguably, this is what the Tracking Development research project mentioned earlier in this chapter seeks to do. Booth writes that 'it is possible to arrive at some reasonably parsimonious but empirically grounded and contextualised claims about the way the world of

governance and development works' (2012: 10).

11 Henley (n.d.: 13) writes of an 'acceptable' level of corruption and, moreover, an acceptable level of the right sort of corruption. Corruption that does not prevent developmental ends being achieved – the building of schools and roads, the provision of irrigation, the delivery of health services – is acceptable, it seems. Corruption that prevents the achievement of such developmental ends is when problems really arise. In successful developmental states, 'achieving that goal [of improving material living conditions] may involve tolerating corruption, bending rules, and infringing rights. It is the end that counts, not the means' (ibid.: 16).

12 'If the politics [i.e. governance] are right, good policies will eventually emerge. And conversely, without good politics, it is impossible to design or implement good policies ...' (Banerjee and Duflo 2011: 236).

13 This is also the essence of the argument made in relation to 'everyday' politics in Vietnam and the economic reforms introduced from the 1980s (see p. 103).

14 A similar sharp fall in birth rates occurred in Europe following the end of the Second World War – sometimes referred to as '*les trentes glorieuses*', drawing on French demographer Jean Fourastié's 1979 book of the same name (Economist 2011b: 32).

Bibliography

Abbott, A. (1988) 'Transcending general linear reality', *Sociological Theory*, 6(2): 169–86.

Acemoglu, D., S. Johnson and J. A. Robinson (2002) 'Reversal of fortune: geography and institutions in the making of the modern world income distribution', *Quarterly Journal of Economics*, 117(4): 1231–94.

Adas, M. (1974) *The Burma Delta: Economic development and social change on an Asian rice frontier, 1852–1941*, Madison: University of Wisconsin Press.

— (1989) *Machines as the Measure of Man: Science, technology, and ideologies of Western dominance*, Ithaca, NY, and London: Cornell University Press.

ADB (1997a) *Emerging Asia: Changes and challenges*, Manila: Asian Development Bank.

— (1997b) *Asian Development Outlook 1996 and 1997*, Manila: Asian Development Bank.

— (1998) *Asian Development Outlook 1998*, Manila: Asian Development Bank.

— (2000) *Asian Development Outlook 2000*, Manila: Asian Development Bank.

— (2001) *Participatory Poverty Assessment: Lao People's Democratic Republic*, Manila: Asian Development Bank.

— (2002) *Key Indicators 2002: Population and human resource trends and challenges*, Manila: Asian Development Bank.

— (2007) *Key Indicators 2007: Inequality in Asia*, Manila: Asian Development Bank.

— (2008) *Asian Development Outlook 2008*, Manila: Asian Development Bank.

— (2011) *Key Indicators for Asia and the Pacific 2011*, Manila: Asian Development Bank.

Agergaard, J. and V. T. Thao (2011) 'Mobile, flexible, and adaptable: female migrants in Hanoi's informal sector', *Population, Space and Place*, 17(5): 407–20.

Aghion, P., M. Dewatripont, L. Du, A. Harrison and P. Legros (2011) 'Industrial policy and competition', Grasp Working Paper 17, www.economics.harvard.edu/faculty/aghion/files/Industrial%20Policy.pdf.

Ahuja, V., B. Bidani, F. Ferreira and M. Walton (1997) *Everyone's Miracle? Revisiting poverty and inequality in East Asia*, Washington, DC: World Bank.

Akamatsu, K. (1962) 'A historical pattern of economic growth in developing countries', *Developing Economies*, 1(1): 3–25.

Alexander, E. R. (2003) 'Response to "Why do planning theory?"', *Planning Theory*, 2(3): 179–82.

Ali, I. and J. Zhuang (2007) 'Inclusive growth toward a prosperous Asia: policy implications', ERD Working Paper no. 97, Manila: Asian Development Bank.

Aliber, M. (2003) 'Chronic poverty in South Africa: incidence, causes and policies', *World Development*, 31(3): 473–90.

Alonso, J. A. (2011) 'Colonisation, institutions and development: new evidence', *Journal of Development Studies*, 47(7): 937–58.

Amsden, A. (1989) *Asia's Next Giant: South Korea and late industrialization*, New York: Oxford University Press.

— (1994) 'Why isn't the whole world experimenting with the East Asian model to develop?: review of the East Asian miracle', *World Development*, 22(4): 627–33.

Amyot, J. (1976) *Village Ayutthaya: Social and economic conditions of a rural population in Central Thailand*, Bangkok: Chulalongkorn University Social Research Institute.

Anderson, B. (1998) 'From miracle to crash', *London Review of Books*, 20(8): 3–7.

Anderson, N. B. (1999) 'Solving the puzzle of socioeconomic status and health: the need for integrated, multilevel, interdisciplinary research', *Annals of the New York Academy of Sciences*, 896(1): 302–12.

Angeles, L. C. and S. Sunanta (2009) 'Demanding daughter duty', *Critical Asian Studies*, 41(4): 549–74.

Anh, D., C. Goldstein et al. (1997) 'Internal migration and development in Vietnam', *International Migration Review*, 31(2): 312–37.

Annan, A., D. W. T. Crompton, D. E. Walters and S. E. Arnold (1986) 'An investigation of the prevalence of intestinal parasites in pre-school children in Ghana', *Parasitology*, 92: 209–17.

Antlöv, H. (1995) *Exemplary Centre, Administrative Periphery: Rural leadership and the New Order in Java*, Richmond: Curzon Press.

Aoki, M., K. Murdock and M. Okuno-Fujiwara (1997) 'Beyond *The East Asian Miracle*: introducing the market-enhancing view', in M. Aoki, H.-K. Kim and M. Okuno-Fujiwara, *The Role of Government in East Asian Economic Development: Comparative institutional analysis*, Oxford: Clarendon Press, pp. 1–37.

Arnold, D. (2011) 'Global goods and local usages: the small world of the Indian sewing machine, 1875–1952', *Journal of Global History*, 6: 407–29.

Arnold, D. and E. DeWald (2011a) 'Cycles of empowerment? The bicycle and everyday technology in colonial India and Vietnam', *Comparative Studies in Society and History*, 53(4): 1–26.

— (2011b) 'Everyday technology in South and Southeast Asia: an introduction', *Modern Asian Studies*.

Aron, L. (2011) 'Everything you think you know about the collapse of the Soviet Union is wrong', *Foreign Policy*, July/August.

Attwood, D. W., M. L. Apte et al. (1979) 'Why some of the poor get richer: economic change and mobility in rural western India [and comments]', *Current Anthropology*, 20(3): 495–516.

Baek, S.-W. (2005) 'Does China follow "the East Asian development model"?', *Journal of Contemporary Asia*, 35(4): 485–98.

Baer, W., W. R. Miles and A. B. Moran (1999) 'The end of the Asian myth: why were the experts fooled?', *World Development*, 27(10): 1735–47.

Baig, T. and I. Goldfajn (1999) 'Financial market contagion in the Asian crisis', *IMF Staff Papers*, 46(2): 167–95.

Baird, I. G. (2011) 'Land, rubber and people: rapid agrarian changes and responses in southern Laos', *Journal of Lao Studies*, 1(1): 1–47.

Bakewell, O. (2010) 'Some reflections on structure and agency in migration theory', *Journal of Ethnic and Migration Studies*, 36(10): 1689–708.

Balassa, B. (1990) 'Indicative planning in developing countries', *Journal of Comparative Economics*, 14(4): 560–74.

Bane, M. J. and D. T. Ellwood (1986) 'Slipping into and out of poverty: the dynamics of spells', *Journal of Human Resources*, 21(1): 1–23.

Banerjee, A. V. and E. Duflo (2011) *Poor Economics: A radical rethinking of the way to fight global poverty*, New York: Public Affairs.

Barker, R. and F. Molle (2005) 'Irrigation management in rice-based cropping systems: issues and challenges in Southeast Asia', *Extension Bulletin*, 543, Taipei: Food & Fertilizer Technology Centre.

Barrett, C. B. and J. G. McPeak (2003) 'Poverty traps and safety nets', Working Paper 45, Department of Applied Economics and Management, Cornell University, Ithaca, NY.

Barrow, C. J. (1998) 'River basin development planning and management: a critical review', *World Development*, 26(1): 171–86.

Baulch, B. and P. Davis (2008) 'Poverty dynamics and life trajectories in rural Bangladesh', *International Journal of Multiple Research Approaches*, 2(2): 176–90.

Beeson, M. (2000) 'Mahathir and the markets: globalisation and the pursuit of economic autonomy in Malaysia', *Pacific Affairs*, 73(3): 335–51.

Beeson, M. and P. H. Hung (forthcoming) 'Developmentalism with Vietnamese characteristics: the persistence of state-led development in East Asia', *Journal of Contemporary Asia*.

Behrman, J. R. and J. C. Knowles (1999) 'Household income and child schooling in Vietnam', *World Bank Economic Review*, 13(2): 211–56.

Bélanger, D., H.-K. Lee and H.-Z. Wang (2010) 'Ethnic diversity and statistics in East Asia: "foreign brides" surveys in Taiwan and South Korea', *Ethnic and Racial Studies*, 33(6): 1108–30.

Bender, D. R. (1967) 'A refinement of the concept of household: families, co-residence, and domestic functions', *American Anthropologist*, 69(5): 493–504.

Berger, M. T. (1999) 'Bringing history back in: the making and unmaking of the East Asian miracle', *IPG*, 3: 237–52.

— (2003) 'Decolonisation, modernisation and nation-building: political development theory and the appeal of communism in Southeast Asia, 1945–1975', *Journal of Southeast Asian Studies*, 34(3): 421–48.

Berger, M. T. and M. Beeson (1998) 'Lineages of liberalism and miracles of modernisation: the World Bank, the East Asian trajectory and the international development debate', *Third World Quarterly*, 19(3): 487–504.

Berger, P. L. (1988) 'An East Asian development model?', in P. L. Berger and H.-H. M. Hsiao, *In Search of an East Asian Development Model*, New Brunswick, NJ, and Oxford: Transaction Books, pp. 3–11.

Bering, H. (2005) 'Taking the Great out of Britain', *Policy Review*, 133.

Biggs, D. (2003) 'Problematic progress: reading environmental and social change in the Mekong Delta', *Journal of Southeast Asian Studies*, 34(1): 77–96.

— (2012) 'Small machines in the garden: everyday technology and revolution in the Mekong Delta', *Modern Asian Studies*, 46(Special Issue 01): 47–70.

Bird, K. (2007) 'The inter-generational transmission of poverty: an overview', CPRC Working Paper no. 99, Overseas Development Institute, London.

Bird, K. and I. Shinyekwa (2005) 'Even the "rich" are vulnerable: multiple shocks and downward mobility in rural Uganda', *Development Policy Review*, 23(1): 55–85.

Birdsall, N. (2007) 'Do no harm: aid, weak institutions and the missing middle in Africa', *Development Policy Review*, 25(5): 575–98.

Bloom, D. E. and J. G. Williamson (1998) 'Demographic transitions and economic miracles in emerging Asia', *World Bank Economic Review*, 12(3): 419–55.

Boettke, P. J. (ed.) (1994) *The Collapse of Development Planning*, New York: New York University Press.

Boggess, S., M. Corcoran and S. P. Jenkins (2005) *Cycles of Disadvantage?*, Wellington: Institute of Policy Studies.

Booth, D. (2011) 'Aid, institutions and governance: what have we learned?', *Development Policy Review*, 29: s5–s26.

— (2012) 'Beyond "context matters". The new agenda of applied governance research in Africa', Draft, Overseas Development Institute, London.

Bowles, S. and H. Gintis (2002) 'The inheritance of inequality', *Journal of Economic Perspectives*, 16(3): 3–30.

Bowles, S., H. Gintis and M. O. Groves (eds) (2005) *Unequal Chances: Family background and economic success*, Princeton, NJ: Princeton University Press.

Brandon, P. and D. Hogan (2008) 'New approaches to household diversity and change', *Journal of Population Research*, 25(3): 247–50.

Brooks, D. H. and M. Queisser (eds) (1999) *Financial Liberalisation in Asia: Analysis and prospects*, Development Centre Seminars, Paris: OECD and ADB.

Brown, A. (2009) *The Rise and Fall of Communism*, London: Bodley Head.

Brown, I. (1997) *Economic Change in South-East Asia, c.1830–1980*, Kuala Lumpur: Oxford University Press.

Brummelhuis, H. t. (2005) *King of the Waters: Homan van der Heide and the origin of modern irrigation in Siam*, Singapore and Bangkok: Institute of Southeast Asian Studies and Silkworm Books.

Bruneau, M. (2012) 'Agrarian transitions in northern Thailand: from peri-urban to mountain margins, 1966–2006', in J. Rigg and P. Vandergeest, *Revisiting Rural Places: Pathways to poverty and prosperity in Southeast Asia*, Singapore and Honolulu: National University of Singapore Press and Hawaii University Press, pp. 38–51.

Bryant, J. (1998) 'Communism, poverty, and demographic change in North Vietnam', *Population and Development Review*, 24(2): 235–69.

— (2002) 'Patrilines, patrilocality and fertility decline in Viet Nam', *Asia Pacific Population Journal*, 17(2): 111–28.

— (2007) 'Theories of fertility

decline and the evidence from development indicators', *Population and Development Review*, 33(1): 101–27.

Bryant, R. and M. Parnwell (eds) (1996) *Environmental Change in South East Asia: People, politics and sustainable development*, London: Routledge.

Buch, C. M. and P. Monti (2010) 'Openness and income disparities: does trade explain the "Mezzogiorno effect"?', *Review of World Economics/Weltwirtschaftliches Archiv*, 145(4): 667–88.

Bush, S. R. and M. Duijf (2011) 'Searching for (un)sustainabilty in Pangasius aquaculture: a political economy of quality in European retail', *Geoforum*, 42(2): 185–96.

Bush, S. R., N. T. Khiem and L. X. Sinh (2009) 'Governing the environmental and social dimensions of Pangasius production in Vietnam: a review', *Aquaculture Economics and Management*, 13(4): 271–93.

Byrd, W. A. (1990) 'Planning in India: lessons from four decades of development experience', *Journal of Comparative Economics*, 14(4): 713–35.

Caldwell, J. C. (1976) 'Toward a restatement of demographic transition theory', *Population and Development Review*, 2(3/4): 321–66.

Campos, J. E. and H. L. Root (1996) *The Key to the Asian Miracle: Making shared growth credible*, Washington, DC: Brookings Institution.

Carmignani, F. and A. Chowdhury (2011) 'Four scenarios of development and the role of economic policy', *Journal of Development Studies*, 47(3): 519–32.

Carter, M. R. and C. B. Barrett (2006) 'The economics of poverty traps and persistent poverty: an asset-based approach', *Journal of Development Studies*, 42(2): 178–99.

Carter, M. R. and J. A. Maluccio (2003) 'Social capital and coping with economic shocks: an analysis of stunting of South African children', *World Development*, 31(7): 1147–63.

CGD (2008) *The Growth Report: Strategies for sustained growth and inclusive development*, Washington, DC: World Bank.

Chakravarty, S. (1991) 'Development planning: a reappraisal', *Cambridge Journal of Economics*, 15: 5–20.

Chamberlain, J. R. and P. Phomsombath (2002) *Poverty Alleviation for All: Potentials and options for peoples in the uplands*, Vientiane: SIDA.

Chanda, N. (1998) 'Rebuilding Asia', *Far Eastern Economic Review*, Hong Kong, pp. 46–50.

Chandrasekhar, C. P., J. Ghosh and S. Francis (2004) 'Fluid finance, systemic risk and the IMF's SDRM proposal', in K. S. Jomo, *After the Storm: Crisis, recovery and sustaining development in four Asian economies*, Singapore: Singapore University Press, pp. 75–97.

Chang, L. T. (2008) *Factory Girls: Voices from the heart of modern China*, New York: Spiegel and Grau.

Chant, S. (1995) 'Gender and export manufacturing in the Philippines: continuity or change in female employment? The case of the Mactan Export Processing Zone', *Gender, Place & Culture*, 2(2): 147–76.

Chatterjee, P. (2008) 'Peasant cultures of the twenty-first century',

Inter-Asia Cultural Studies, 9(1): 116–26.

Chen, S. and M. Ravallion (2004) 'How have the world's poorest fared since the early 1980s?', World Bank Policy Research Working Paper 3341, Washington, DC: World Bank.

Chua, S. Y., S. Dibooglu and S. C. Sharma (1999) 'The impact of the US and Japanese economies on Korea and Malaysia after the Plaza Accord', *Asian Economic Journal*, 13(1): 19–37.

Cohen, P. T. (2009) 'The post-opium scenario and rubber in northern Laos: alternative Western and Chinese models of development', *International Journal of Drug Policy*, 20(5): 424–30.

Corcoran, M. (1995) 'Rags to rags: poverty and mobility in the United States', *Annual Review of Sociology*, 21: 237–67.

Cowen, M. and R. Shenton (1995) 'The invention of development', in J. Crush, *Power of Development*, London: Routledge, pp. 27–43.

— (1996) *Doctrines of Development*, London: Routledge.

CPRC (2009) *The Chronic Poverty Report 2008–9: Escaping poverty traps*, London: Chronic Poverty Research Centre.

Cramb, R. A. (2012) 'Beyond the longhouse: Iban shifting cultivators come to town', in J. Rigg and P. Vandergeest, *Revisiting Rural Places: Pathways to poverty and prosperity in Southeast Asia*, Singapore and Honolulu: National University of Singapore Press and Hawaii University Press, pp. 68–87.

Dao, N. (2010) 'Dam development in Vietnam: the evolution of dam-induced resettlement policy', *Water Alternatives*, 3(2): 324–40.

Dasgupta, P. (1997) 'Nutritional status, the capacity for work, and poverty traps', *Journal of Econometrics*, 77(1): 5–37.

Datta-Chaudhuri, M. (1990) 'Market failure and government failure', *Journal of Economic Perspectives*, 4(3): 25–39.

Davin, D. (2007) 'Marriage migration in China and East Asia', *Journal of Contemporary China*, 16(50): 83–95.

Davis, P. (2006) 'Poverty in time: exploring poverty dynamics from life history interviews in Bangladesh', CPRC Working Paper 69, Chronic Poverty Research Centre, Manchester.

— (2007) 'Discussions among the poor: exploring poverty dynamics with focus groups in Bangladesh', CPRC Working Paper 73, Chronic Poverty Research Centre, Manchester.

Davis, P. and B. Baulch (2011) 'Parallel realities: exploring poverty dynamics using mixed methods in rural Bangladesh', *Journal of Development Studies*, 47(1): 118–42.

Deans, P. (2004) 'The People's Republic of China: the post-socialist developmental state', in L. Low, *Developmental States: Relevancy, redundancy or reconfiguration?*, New York: Nova, pp. 133–46.

Demaine, H. (1986) 'Kanpatthana: Thai views of development', in M. Hobart and R. H. Taylor, *Context, Meaning and Power in Southeast Asia*, Ithaca, NY: Southeast Asia Program, Cornell University, pp. 93–114.

Derks, A. (2008) *Khmer Women on the Move: Exploring work and life in urban Cambodia*, Honolulu: University of Hawaii Press.

Dey, J. (1982) 'Development planning in the Gambia: the gap between planners' and farmers' perceptions, expectations and objectives', *World Development*, 10(5): 377–96.

Dhanani, S. and I. Islam (2002) 'Poverty, vulnerability and social protection in a period of crisis: the case of Indonesia', *World Development*, 30(7): 1211–31.

Diamond, J. (1997) *Guns, Germs, and Steel*, New York: W. W. Norton and Co.

Dixon, C. (2001) 'The causes of the Thai economic crisis: the internal perspective', *Geoforum*, 32(1): 47–60.

Donge, J. K. v., D. Henley and P. Lewis (n.d.) *Tracking Development in Southeast Asia and sub-Saharan Africa: The primacy of policy*. Leiden: Tracking Development research project.

Douglass, M. (2002) *The Urban Transition in Vietnam*, Hanoi: United Nations Development Programme.

Doutriaux, S., C. Geisler and G. Shively (2008) 'Competing for coffee space: development-induced displacement in the Central Highlands of Vietnam', *Rural Sociology*, 73(4): 528–54.

Dryden, J. (1745) *Fables antient and modern; translated into verse from Homer, Ovid, Boccace, and Chaucer: with original poems*, London: Printed for J. and R. Tonson and S. Draper in the Strand.

Dufrenot, G., V. Mignon and C. Tsangarides. (2010) 'The trade-growth nexus in the developing countries: a quantile regression approach', *Review of World Economics/Weltwirtschaftliches Archiv*, 146(4): 731–61.

Durlauf, S. N., A. Kourtellos and Chih Ming Tan (2005) 'Empirics of growth and development', www.ssc.wisc.edu/econ/Durlauf/research.html.

Economist, The (2011a) 'The flight from marriage', *The Economist*, 20 August.

— (2011b) 'A tale of three islands', *The Economist*, 22 October, pp. 31–4.

Edmundson, W. C. (1994) 'Do the rich get richer, do the poor get poorer? East Java, two decades, three villages, 46 people', *Bulletin of Indonesian Economic Studies*, 30(2): 133–48.

Ekejiuba, F. (2005) 'Down to fundamentals: women-centred households in rural West Africa', in A. Cornwall, *Readings in Gender in Africa*, Bloomington: Indiana University Press, pp. 41–6.

Elmhirst, R. (1997) 'Gender, environment and culture: a political ecology of transmigration in Indonesia', *Geography*, London University.

— (2002) 'Daughters and displacement: migration dynamics in an Indonesian transmigration area', *Journal of Development Studies*, 38(5): 143–66.

— (2007) 'Tigers and gangsters: masculinities and feminised migration in Indonesia', *Population, Space and Place*, 13(3): 225–38.

Ensor, T. I. M. and P. B. San (1996) 'Access and payment for health care: the poor of northern Vietnam', *International Journal of Health Planning and Management*, 11(1): 69–83.

Evans, A. (1991) 'Gender issues in rural household economics', *IDS Bulletin*, 22(1): 51–9.

Evans, P. (2004) 'Development as institutional change: the pitfalls of monocropping and the potentials of deliberation', *Studies in Comparative International Development*, 38(4): 30–52.

Evans, P. B. (1989) 'Predatory, developmental, and other apparatuses: a comparative political economy perspective on the Third World state', *Sociological Forum*, 4(4): 561–87.

Faber, M. and D. Seers (eds) (1972) *The Crisis in Planning*, London: Chatto and Windus.

Fang, C., D. Yang et al. (2009) 'Migration and labor mobility in China', Human Development Reports Research Paper, New York: United Nations Development Programme.

Ferguson, J. (1990) *The Anti-Politics Machine: 'Development', depoliticization and bureaucratic power in Lesotho*, Cambridge: Cambridge University Press.

— (1994) *The Anti-Politics Machine: 'Development', depoliticization, and bureaucratic power in Lesotho*, Minneapolis: University of Minnesota Press.

— (1999) *Expectations of Modernity: Myths and meanings of urban life on the Zambian copperbelt*, Berkeley: University of California Press.

Ferguson, N. (1997a) 'Introduction: towards a "chaotic" theory of the past', in N. Ferguson, *Virtual History: Alternatives and counterfactuals*, Basingstoke and Oxford: Pan Macmillan, pp. 1–90.

— (1997b) *Virtual History: Alternatives and counterfactuals*, Basingstoke and Oxford: Pan Macmillan.

Fforde, A. and S. de Vylder (1996) *From Plan to Market: The economic transition in Vietnam*, Boulder, CO: Westview Press.

Fisher, C. T. (2006) 'The illusion of progress', *Pacific Historical Review*, 75(1): 25–51.

Foran, T. and K. Manorom (2009)

'Pak Mun Dam: perpetually contested?', in F. Molle, T. Foran and M. Käkönen, *Contested Waterscapes in the Mekong Region: Hydropower, livelihoods and governance*, London: Earthscan, pp. 55–80.

Forsyth, T. and A. Walker (eds) (2008) *Forest Guardians, Forest Destroyers: The politics of environmental knowledge in northern Thailand*, Seattle: University of Washington Press.

Frankel, J. A. and D. Romer (1999) 'Does trade cause growth?', *American Economic Review*, 89(3): 379–99.

Freedman, A. L. (2005) 'Economic crises and political change: Indonesia, South Korea, and Malaysia', *Asian Affairs*, 31(4): 232–49.

Freedman, R. (1979) 'Theories of fertility decline: a reappraisal', *Social Forces*, 58(1): 1–17.

Freeman, R. (1995) 'Asia's recent fertility decline and prospects for future demographic change', Asia-Pacific Population Research Reports, East-West Center, Honolulu.

Friederichsen, R. (2012) 'The mixed blessings of national integration: new perspectives on development in Vietnam's northern uplands', *East Asia*, 29(1): 43–61.

Friedman, J., J. Knodel, B. T. Cuong and T. S. Anh (2003) 'Gender dimensions of support for elderly in Vietnam', *Research on Aging*, 25(6): 587–630.

Friedmann, J. (1998) 'Planning theory revisited', *European Planning Studies*, 6(3): 245.

— (2003) 'Why do planning theory?', *Planning Theory*, 2(1): 7–10.

Fritz, V. and A. R. Menocal (2007) 'Developmental states in the new millennium: concepts and challenges for a new aid agenda', *Development Policy Review*, 25(5): 531–52.

Fukuyama, F. (1992) *The End of History and the Last Man*, London: Hamish Hamilton.

— (1995) 'Reflections on the end of history, five years later', *History and Theory*, 34(2): 27–43.

Fung, K. C., H. Iizaka and A. Siu (2002) 'Japanese direct investment in China and other Asian countries', International Conference on WTO, China and the Asian Economies, University of Hong Kong.

Gaiha, R. and A. B. Deolalikar (1993) 'Persistent, expected and innate poverty: estimates for semi-arid rural South India, 1975–1984', *Cambridge Journal of Economics*, 17(4): 409–21.

Gainsborough, M. (2010) *Vietnam: Rethinking the state*, London: Zed Books.

Galor, O. (2005) 'The demographic transition and the emergence of sustained economic growth', *Journal of the European Economic Association*, 3(2/3): 494–504.

Galor, O. and D. N. Weil (2000) 'Population, technology, and growth: from Malthusian stagnation to the demographic transition and beyond', *American Economic Review*, 90(4): 806–28.

Gardner, D. (2011) *Future Babble: Why expert predictions fail and why we believe them anyway*, London: Virgin Books.

Garnaut, R. (1998) 'The East Asian crisis', in R. H. McLeod and R. Garnaut, *East Asia in Crisis: From being a miracle to needing one?*, London: Routledge, pp. 3–27.

Gertler, P. J. and J. W. Molyneaux (1994) 'How economic development and family planning programs combined to reduce Indonesian fertility', *Demography*, 31(1): 33–63.

Ghemawat, P. (2011) *World 3.0: Global prosperity and how to achieve it*, Boston, MA: Harvard Business Review Press.

Ghuman, S., J. R. Behrman, J. B. Borja, S. Gultiano and E. M. King (2005) 'Family background, service providers, and early childhood development in the Philippines: proxies and interactions', *Economic Development and Cultural Change*, 54(1): 129–64.

Gillespie, J. (1995) 'The role of the bureaucracy in managing urban land in Vietnam', *Pacific Rim Law and Policy Journal*, 5: 59–124.

Gladwell, M. (2001) *The Tipping Point: How little things can make a big difference*, London: Abacus.

— (2008) *Outliers: The story of success*, London: Penguin.

Glauben, T., T. Herzfeld and S. Rozelle (2012) 'Persistent poverty in rural China: where, why, and how to escape?', *World Development*, 40(4): 784–95.

Goldstein, M. (1998) *The Asian Financial Crisis: Causes, cures and systemic implications*, Washington, DC: Institute for International Economics.

GoM (2010) *Tenth Malaysia Plan 2011–2015*, Economic Planning Unit, Prime Minister's Department.

Grant, W. (ed.) (1995) *Industrial Policy*, Aldershot: Edward Elgar.

Gregory, C., G. Brierley and R. Le Heron (2011) 'Governance spaces for sustainable river management', *Geography Compass*, 5(4): 182–99.

Grindle, M. S. (2004) 'Good enough governance: poverty reduction and reform in developing countries', *Governance*, 17(4): 525–48.

— (2007) 'Good enough governance revisited', *Development Policy Review*, 25(5): 533–74.

— (2011) 'Governance reform: the new analytics of next steps', *Governance*, 24(3): 415–18.

GSO (2006) *The 2004 Vietnam Migration Survey: The quality of life of migrants in Vietnam*, Hanoi: General Statistics Office and United Nations Population Fund.

Ha, D. T. and G. Shively (2008) 'Coffee boom, coffee bust and smallholder response in Vietnam's Central Highlands', *Review of Development Economics*, 12(2): 312–26.

Haggard, S. and L. Tiede (2011) 'The rule of law and economic growth: where are we?', *World Development*, 39(5): 673–85.

Hall, D. (2011) 'Land grabs, land control, and Southeast Asian crop booms', *Journal of Peasant Studies*, 38(4): 837–57.

Hancock, P. (2001) 'Rural women earning income in Indonesian factories: the impact on gender relations', *Gender & Development*, 9(1): 18–24.

Hanna, N. and R. Agarwala (2000) *Toward a Comprehensive Development Strategy*, Washington, DC: World Bank.

Harper, C., R. Marcus and K. Moore (2003) 'Enduring poverty and the conditions of childhood: lifecourse and intergenerational poverty transmissions', *World Development*, 31(3): 535–54.

Harris, Lord (2002) 'Adam Smith: revolutionary for the third millennium?', *Economic Affairs*, 22(3): 37–42.

Hart, G. (2001) 'Development critiques in the 1990s: culs de sac

and promising paths', *Progress in Human Geography*, 25(4): 649–58.

Hayashi, S. (2010) 'The developmental state in the era of globalization: beyond the Northeast Asian model of political economy', *Pacific Review*, 23(1): 45–69.

Henley, D. (n.d.) *Three Principles of Successful Development Strategy: Outreach, urgency, expediency*, Leiden: Tracking Development research project.

Hewage, P., C. Kumara and J. Rigg (2010) 'Connecting and disconnecting people and places: migrants, migration, and the household in Sri Lanka', *Annals of the Association of American Geographers*, 101(1): 202–19.

Hewison, K. (2005) 'Neo-liberalism and domestic capital: the political outcomes of the economic crisis in Thailand', *Journal of Development Studies*, 41(2): 310–30.

Hill, H. (1996) *The Indonesian Economy since 1966: Southeast Asia's emerging giant*, Cambridge: Cambridge University Press.

Hill, H. and Y.-P. Chu (2006) 'An overview of the issues', in Y.-P. Chu and H. Hill, *The East Asian High-tech Drive*, Cheltenham: Edward Elgar, pp. 1–56.

Hirsch, P. (1988) 'Dammed or damned? Hydropower versus people's power', *Bulletin of Concerned Asian Scholars*, 20(1): 2–10.

— (2001) 'Globalisation, regionalization and local voices: the Asian Development Bank and rescaled politics of environment in the Mekong region', *Singapore Journal of Tropical Geography*, 22(3): 237–51.

— (2006) 'Water governance reform and catchment management in the Mekong region', *Journal of*

Environment and Development,
15(2): 184–201.

— (2010) 'The changing political
dynamics of dam building on the
Mekong', Water Alternatives, 3(2):
312–23.

Hirschman, A. O. (1958) The Strategy
of Economic Development, New
Haven, CT: Yale University Press.

Hirschman, C. and P. Guest (1990)
'The emerging demographic
transitions of Southeast Asia',
Population and Development
Review, 16(1): 121–52.

Holtz, T. H., S. Patrick Kachur et
al. (2004) 'Use of antenatal care
services and intermittent preven-
tive treatment for malaria among
pregnant women in Blantyre District, Malawi', Tropical Medicine &
International Health, 9: 77–82.

Horrell, S., J. Humphries and
V. Hans-Joachim (2001) 'Destined
for deprivation: human capital
formation and intergenerational
poverty in nineteenth-century
England', Explorations in Economic History, 38(3): 339–65.

Huang, S., B. S. A. Yeoh and
M. Toyota (2012) 'Caring for the
elderly: the embodied labour
of migrant care workers in
Singapore', Global Networks: A
Journal of Transnational Affairs,
12(2): 195–215.

Huff, W. G. (1994) The Economic
Growth of Singapore: Trade and
development in the twentieth
century, Cambridge: Cambridge
University Press.

— (1995a) 'The developmental state,
government, and Singapore's economic development since 1960',
World Development, 23(8): 1421–38.

— (1995b) 'What is the Singapore
model of economic development?', Cambridge Journal of
Economics, 19(6): 735–59.

Hull, T. H. (1987) 'Fertility decline
in Indonesia: an institutionalist
interpretation', International
Family Planning Perspectives, 13(3):
90–5.

— (2007) 'Formative years of family
planning in Indonesia', in W. C.
Robinson and J. A. Ross, The
Global Family Planning Revolution:
Three decades of population poli-
cies and programs, Washington,
DC: World Bank, pp. 235–56.

— (2009) 'Fertility prospects in
South-Eastern Asia', United
Nations Expert Group Meeting
on Recent and Future Trends in
Fertility, Population Division,
United Nations Department of
Social and Economic Affairs, New
York.

Hulme, D. (2003) 'Thinking small
and the understanding of
poverty: Maymana and Mofizul's
story', CPRC Working Paper 22,
Chronic Poverty Research Centre,
IDPM, University of Manchester.

Hulme, D. and K. Moore (2010)
'Thinking small, and thinking
big about poverty: Maymana
and Mofizul's story updated',
Bangladesh Development Studies,
33(3): 69–96.

Hulme, D. and A. Shepherd (2003)
'Conceptualizing chronic
poverty', World Development, 31(3):
403–23.

Ikram, K. (2011) Revitalizing the Planning Commission: Some recommendations, London: International
Growth Centre, London School of
Economics.

Ish-Shalom, P. (2006) 'Theory gets
real, and the case for a normative
ethic: Rostow, modernization
theory, and the Alliance for
Progress', International Studies
Quarterly, 50(2): 287–311.

Ito, T. (2001) 'Growth, crisis and the

future of economic recovery in East Asia', in J. E. Stiglitz and S. Yusuf, *Rethinking the East Asian Miracle*, Washington, DC, and New York: World Bank and Oxford University Press, pp. 55–94.

JDR (2007) 'Vietnam Development Report 2008: social protection', Joint donor report to the Vietnam consultative group meeting, Hanoi.

Jeffrey, C. (2010) *Timepass: Youth, class and the politics of waiting in India*, Stanford, CA: Stanford University Press.

Johnson, C. (1982) *MITI and the Japanese Miracle: The growth of industrial policy, 1925–1975*, Stanford, CA: Stanford University Press.

— (1998) 'Economic crisis in East Asia: the clash of capitalisms', *Cambridge Journal of Economics*, 22(6): 653–61.

Jolivet, M. (1997) *Japan, the Childless Society?: The crisis of motherhood*, London: Routledge.

Jomo, K. S. (1996) 'Explaining the Southeast Asian economic miracle', in *The Empowerment of Asia: Reshaping global society*, Vancouver: Institute of Asian Research, University of British Columbia, pp. 53–78.

— (2003) 'Southeast Asia's ersatz miracle', in K. S. Jomo, *Southeast Asian Paper Tigers? From miracle to debacle and beyond*, London: Routledge Curzon, pp. 1–18.

— (2005) 'The 1997–98 East Asian crises', in S. C. Wong, K. S. Jomo and K. F. Chin, *Malaysian 'Bail Outs'? Capital controls, restructuring and recovery*, Singapore: Singapore University Press, pp. 1–22.

Jones, G. and R. Leete (2002) 'Asia's family planning programs as low fertility is attained', *Studies in Family Planning*, 33(1): 114–26.

Jones, G. W. (1990) 'Fertility transitions among Malay populations of Southeast Asia: puzzles of interpretation', *Population and Development Review*, 16(3): 507–37.

— (2007) 'Delayed marriage and very low fertility in Pacific Asia', *Population and Development Review*, 33(3): 453–78.

— (2010) 'Changing marriage patterns in Asia', Working Paper series no. 131, Asia Research Institute, Singapore.

Käkönen, M. and P. Hirsch (2009) 'The anti-politics of Mekong knowledge production', in F. Molle, T. Foran and M. Käkönen, *Contested Waterscapes in the Mekong Region: Hydropower, livelihoods and governance*, London: Earthscan, pp. 333–55.

Kaminsky, G. L. and S. L. Schmukler (1999) 'What triggers market jitters? A chronicle of the Asian crisis', *Journal of International Money and Finance*, 18: 537–60.

Kato, T. (1994) 'The emergence of abandoned paddy fields in Negeri Sembilan, Malaysia', *Southeast Asian Studies*, 32(2): 145–72.

Kelly, P. F. (2011) 'Migration, agrarian transition, and rural change in Southeast Asia', *Critical Asian Studies*, 43(4): 479–506.

— (2012) 'Class reproduction in a transitional agrarian setting: youth trajectories in a peri-urban Philippine village', in J. Rigg and P. Vandergeest, *Revisiting Rural Places: Pathways to poverty and prosperity in Southeast Asia*, Singapore and Honolulu: National University of Singapore Press and Hawaii University Press, pp. 229–49.

Kerkvliet, B. J. T. (1995) 'Village–state

relations in Vietnam: the effects of everyday politics on decollectivization', *Journal of Asian Studies*, 54(2): 396–418.

— (2005) *The Power of Everyday Politics: How Vietnamese peasants transformed national policy*, Singapore: Institute of Southeast Asian Studies.

— (2009) 'Everyday politics in peasant societies (and ours)', *Journal of Peasant Studies*, 36(1): 227–43.

Keyes, C. (2010) 'Dealing with "the devil", the reds and looking within', *Bangkok Post*, 26 May.

Killick, T. (1976) 'The possibilities of development planning', *Oxford Economic Papers*, 28(2): 161–84.

— (1983) 'Development planning in Africa: experiences, weaknesses and prescriptions', *Development Policy Review*, 1(1): 47–76.

— (1986) 'Twenty-five years in development: the rise and impending decline of market solutions', *Development Policy Review*, 4(2): 99–116.

King, M. R. (2001) 'Who triggered the Asian financial crisis?', *Review of International Political Economy*, 8(3): 438–66.

Kirk, D. (1996) 'Demographic transition theory', *Population Studies*, 50(3): 361–87.

Knodel, J. and P. Pitaktepsombati (1973) 'Thailand: fertility and family planning among rural and urban women', *Studies in Family Planning*, 4(9): 229–55.

— (1975) 'Fertility and family planning in Thailand: results from two rounds of a national study', *Studies in Family Planning*, 6(11): 402–13.

Knodel, J. and C. Saengtienchai (2007) 'Rural parents with urban children: social and economic implications of migration for the rural elderly in Thailand', *Population, Space and Place*, 13(3): 193–210.

Knodel, J. and M. van Landingham (2003) 'Return migration in the context of parental assistance in the AIDS epidemic: the Thai experience', *Social Science & Medicine*, 57(2): 327–42.

Knodel, J. and E. van de Walle (1979) 'Lessons from the past: policy implications of historical fertility studies', *Population and Development Review*, 5(2): 217–45.

Koning, J. (2005) 'The impossible return? The post-migration narratives of young women in rural Java', *Asian Journal of Social Science*, 33(2): 165–85.

Korten, D. C. (1984) 'Rural development programming: the learning process approach', in D. C. Korten and R. Klauss, *People-centred Development: Contributions towards theory and planning frameworks*, West Hartford, CT: Kumarian Press, pp. 176–88.

Krishna, A. (2010) *One Illness Away: Why people become poor and how they escape poverty*, Oxford: Oxford University Press.

— (2011) 'Characteristics and patterns of intergenerational poverty traps and escapes in rural north India', Working Paper no. 189, Chronic Poverty Research Centre, IDPM, University of Manchester.

Krishna, A. and A. Shariff (2011) 'The irrelevance of national strategies? Rural poverty dynamics in states and regions of India, 1993–2005', *World Development*, 39(4): 533–49.

Krueger, A. O. (1974) 'The political economy of the rent-seeking society', *American Economic Review*, 64(3): 291–303.

— (1990) 'Government failures in

development', *Journal of Economic Perspectives*, 4(3): 9–23.

Krugman, P. (1994) 'The myth of Asia's miracle', *Foreign Affairs*, 73(6): 62–78.

— (1998) 'Will Asia bounce back?', Speech to Credit Suisse First Boston, web.mit.edu/krugman/www/suisse.html.

Kundu, A. (2009) 'Urbanisation and migration: an analysis of trend, pattern and policies in Asia', Human Development Reports Research Paper, United Nations Development Programme, New York.

Labbé, D. (2010) *Facing the Urban Transition in Hanoi: Recent urban planning issues and initiatives*, Montreal: Institut national de la recherche scientifique.

Labbé, D. and J.-A. Boudreau (2011) 'Understanding the causes of urban fragmentation in Hanoi: the case of new urban areas', *International Development Planning Review*, 33(3): 273–91.

Lall, S. (1996) *Learning from the Asian Tigers: Studies in technology and industrial policy*, London: Macmillan Press.

Lao PDR (2006) *National Socio-economic Development Plan (2006–2010)*, Vientiane: Committee for Planning and Investment.

Larsen, P. B., Tran Chi Trung, S. Gagnon and M. Hufty (2012) 'Biodiversity, liberalization and wildlife trade in Vietnam: exploring the failure of command and control policies', Paper presented at the Oxford Southeast Asia Symposium, Oxford University, 10/11 March.

Laungaramsri, P. (2000) 'The ambiguity of "watershed": the politics of people and conservation in northern Thailand', *SOJOURN: Journal of Social Issues in Southeast Asia*, 15(1): 52–75.

Law, J. (2004) *After Method: Mess in social science research*, London and New York: Routledge.

Leaf, M. (1998) 'Urban planning and urban reality under Chinese economic reforms', *Journal of Planning Education and Research*, 18(2): 145–53.

— (1999) 'Vietnam's urban edge: the administration of urban development in Hanoi', *Third World Planning Review*, 21(3): 297–315.

— (2002) 'A tale of two villages: globalization and peri-urban change in China and Vietnam', *Cities*, 19(1): 23–31.

Lee, S. A. (1973) *Industrialization in Singapore*, Camberwell, Victoria: Longman Australia.

Leete, R. (1994) 'The continuing flight from marriage and parenthood among the overseas Chinese in East and Southeast Asia: dimensions and implications', *Population and Development Review*, 20(4): 811–29.

Leftwich, A. (1995) 'Bringing politics back in: towards a model of the developmental state', *Journal of Development Studies*, 31(3): 400–27.

Lerman, C., J. W. Molyneaux, S. Moeljodihardjo and S. Pandjaitan (1989) 'The correlation between family planning program inputs and contraceptive use in Indonesia', *Studies in Family Planning*, 20(1): 26–37.

Lesthaeghe, R. and J. Surkyn (1988) 'Cultural dynamics and economic theories of fertility change', *Population and Development Review*, 14(1): 1–45.

Lewis, W. A. (1966) *Development Planning*, Abingdon: Routledge.

Li, T. M. (2002a) 'Engaging simplifications: community-based resource management, market processes and state agendas in upland Southeast Asia', *World Development*, 30(2): 265–83.

— (2002b) 'Local histories, global markets: cocoa and class in upland Sulawesi', *Development and Change*, 33(3): 415–37.

— (2005) 'Beyond "the state" and failed schemes', *American Anthropologist*, 107(3): 383–94.

— (2007) *The Will to Improve: Governmentality, development, and the practice of politics*, Durham, NC, and London: Duke University Press.

— (2012) 'Why so fast? Rapid class differentiation in upland Sulawesi', in J. Rigg and P. Vandergeest, *Revisiting Rural Places: Pathways to poverty and prosperity in Southeast Asia*, Singapore and Honolulu: National University of Singapore Press and University of Hawaii Press, pp. 193–210.

Lim, J. (2004) 'Macroeconomic implications of the Southeast Asian crises', in K. S. Jomo, *After the Storm: Crisis, recovery and sustaining development in four Asian economies*, Singapore: Singapore University Press, pp. 40–74.

Little, D. (1995) 'Economic models in development economics', in D. Little, *On the Reliability of Economic Models: Essays in the philosophy of economics*, Boston, MA: Kluwer Academic, pp. 243–70.

Locke, C., N. T. N. Hoa and N. T. T. Tam (2012) 'Visiting marriages and remote parenting: changing strategies of rural–urban migrants to Hanoi, Vietnam', *Journal of Development Studies*, 48(1): 10–25.

Mahoney, J. (2000) 'Path dependence in historical sociology', *Theory and Society*, 29(4): 507–48.

Martin, P. (2009) 'Migration in the Asia-Pacific region: trends, factors, impacts', Human Development Reports Research Paper, United Nations Development Programme, New York.

Mason, A. and S. H. Lee (2011) 'Population aging and economic progress in Asia: a bumpy road ahead?', *Asia Pacific Issues*, 99, Honolulu: East-West Center.

Mason, K. O. (1997) 'Explaining fertility transitions', *Demography*, 34(4): 443–54.

Maswood, S. J. (2002) 'Developmental states in crisis', in M. Beeson, *Reconfiguring East Asia: Regional institutions and organisations after the crisis*, London: Routledge Curzon, pp. 31–48.

McDonough, P., A. Sacker and R. D. Wiggins (2005) 'Time on my side? Life course trajectories of poverty and health', *Social Science & Medicine*, 61(8): 1795–808.

McGee, T. G. (2009) 'Interrogating the production of urban space in China and Vietnam under market socialism', *Asia Pacific Viewpoint*, 50(2): 228–46.

McKay, D. (2003) 'Cultivating new local futures: remittance economies and land-use patterns in Ifugao, Philippines', *Journal of Southeast Asian Studies*, 34(2): 285–306.

— (2005) 'Reading remittance landscapes: female migration and agricultural transition in the Philippines', *Geografisk Tidsskrift/ Danish Journal of Geography*, 105(1): 89–99.

McLeod, R. H. (1999) 'Indonesia's crisis and future prospects', in K. D. Jackson, *Asian Contagion: The causes and consequences of a financial crisis*, Boulder, CO: Westview Press, pp. 209–40.

Mills, M. B. (1997) 'Contesting the margins of modernity: women, migration, and consumption in Thailand', *American Ethnologist*, 24(1): 37–61.

— (1999) *Thai Women in the Global Labor Force: Consumed desires, contested selves*, New Brunswick, NJ: Rutgers University Press.

— (2012) 'Thai mobilities and cultural citizenship', *Critical Asian Studies*, 44(1): 85–112.

Molle, F. (2006) 'Planning and managing water resources at the river-basin level: emergence and evolution of a concept', Comprehensive Assessment Research Report 16, International Water Management Institute, Colombo.

— (2008) 'Nirvana concepts, narratives and policy models: insights from the water sector', *Water Alternatives*, 1(1): 131–56.

— (2009) 'River-basin planning and management: the social life of a concept', *Geoforum*, 40(3): 484–94.

Molle, F. and C. T. Hoanh (2007) 'Implementing integrated river basin management: lessons from the Red River Basin, Vietnam', IWMI Research Report 131, International Waster Management Institute, Colombo.

Molle, F. and T. Srijantr (eds) (2003) *Thailand's Rice Bowl: Perspectives on agricultural and social change in the Chao Phraya Delta*, Bangkok: White Lotus Press.

Molle, F., T. Foran and P. Floch (2009a) 'Introduction: changing waterscapes in the Mekong region – historical background and context', in F. Molle, T. Foran and P. Floch, *Contested Waterscapes in the Mekong Region: Hydropower, livelihoods and governance*, London: Earthscan, pp. 1–19.

— (eds) (2009b) *Contested Water-scapes in the Mekong Region: Hydropower, livelihoods and governance*, London: Earthscan.

Molle, F., T. Shah and R. Barker (2003) 'The groundswell of pumps: multi-level impacts of a silent revolution', International Water Management Institute (IWMI), publications.iwmi.org/pdf/H033367.pdf.

MoPI (2009) *Results-based mid-term review report: for implementation of the five-year socio-economic development plan, 2006–2010*, Hanoi: Ministry of Planning and Investment.

Moser, C. O. N. (2009) *Ordinary Families, Extraordinary Lives: Assets and poverty reduction in Guayaquil, 1978–2004*, Washington, DC: Brookings Institution Press.

Mosse, D. (2005) *Cultivating Development: An ethnography of aid policy and practice*, London: Pluto Press.

Murphy, R. (2002) *How Migrant Labor is Changing Rural China*, Cambridge: Cambridge University Press.

Murray, C. (1993) 'Welfare and the family: the U.S. experience', *Journal of Labor Economics*, 11(1): S224–S262.

Muscat, R. J. (1994) *The Fifth Tiger: A study of Thai development policy*, New York: United Nations University Press.

Mustapha, Z. H. and M. N. A. Shaik (1985) 'Idle agricultural land in Peninsular Malaysia: problems and opportunities', *Malaysian Journal of Agricultural Economics*, 2(1): 36–53.

Myrdal, G. (1968) *Asian Drama: An inquiry into the poverty of nations*, London: Allen and Unwin.

NESDB (1981) *The Fifth National Economic and Social Development Plan (1982–1986)*, Bangkok:

National Economic and Social Development Board.

— (1996) *The Eighth Five-Year National Development Plan (1997–2001)*, Bangkok: National Economic and Social Development Board.

— (2010) *Summary of the Direction of the Eleventh National Development Plan*, Bangkok: National Economic and Social Development Board.

Newland, K. (2009) 'Circular migration and human development', Human Development Reports Research Paper, United Nations Development Programme, New York.

Nguyen, T. A., J. Rigg, L. T. T. Huong and D. T. Dieu (2012) 'Becoming and being urban in Hanoi: rural–urban migration and relations in Viet Nam', *Journal of Peasant Studies*, DOI: 10.1080/03066150.2011.652618.

North, D. C. (1994) 'Economic performance through time', *American Economic Review*, 84(3): 359–68.

Obermeyer, C. M. (1994) 'Reproductive choice in Islam: gender and state in Iran and Tunisia', *Studies in Family Planning*, 25(1): 41–51.

Ong, A. (1990) 'State versus Islam: Malay families, women's bodies, and the body politic in Malaysia', *American Ethnologist*, 17(2): 258–76.

Öniş, Z. (1991) 'The logic of the developmental state', *Comparative Politics*, 24(1): 109–26.

Öniş, Z. and F. Senses (2005) 'Rethinking the emerging post-Washington consensus', *Development and Change*, 36(2): 263–90.

Ormerod, P. (1998) *Butterfly Economics: A new general theory of social and economic behaviour*, New York: Pantheon Books.

Painter, M. (2003) 'The politics of economic restructuring in Vietnam: the case of state-owned enterprise "reform"', *Contemporary Southeast Asia*, 25(1): 20–43.

— (2005) 'The politics of state sector reforms in Vietnam: contested agendas and uncertain trajectories', *Journal of Development Studies*, 41(2): 261–83.

Pakpahan, Y. M., D. Suryadarma and A. Suryahadi (2009) 'Destined for destitution: intergenerational poverty persistence in Indonesia', CPRC Working Paper 134, Chronic Poverty Research Centre, IDPM, University of Manchester.

Paul, T. C. (2009) 'The post-opium scenario and rubber in northern Laos: alternative Western and Chinese models of development', *International Journal of Drug Policy*, 20(5): 424–30.

Phongpaichit, P. and C. Baker (2000) *Thailand's Crisis*, Chiang Mai: Silkworm Books.

Pierson, P. (2000) 'Increasing returns, path dependence, and the study of politics', *American Political Science Review*, 94(2): 251–67.

Ploeg, J. D. van der and Y. Jingzhong (2010) 'Multiple job holding in rural villages and the Chinese road to development', *Journal of Peasant Studies*, 37(3): 513–30.

Pollak, R. A. and S. C. Watkins (1993) 'Cultural and economic approaches to fertility: proper marriage or mesalliance?', *Population and Development Review*, 19(3): 467–96.

Prachuabmoh, V., J. Knodel and J. O. Alers (1974) 'Preference for sons, desire for additional children, and family planning in Thailand', *Journal of Marriage and Family*, 36(3): 601–14.

Preston, D. A. (1989) 'Too busy to farm: under-utilisation of farm land in central Java', *Journal of Development Studies*, 26(1): 43–57.

Quah, S. R. (2003) *Major Trends Affecting Families in East and Southeast Asia*, New York: Department of Economic and Social Affairs, United Nations.

Quibria, M. G. (2002) 'Growth and poverty: lessons from the East Asian miracle revisited', ADB Institute Research Paper Series no. 33, Asian Development Bank, Manila.

Radelet, S. and J. D. Sachs (1999) 'What have we learned, so far, from the Asian financial crisis?', Harvard University, www.cid.harvard.edu/archive/hiid/papers/aea122.pdf.

Radelet, S., J. D. Sachs and Jong-Wha Lee (1997) *Economic Growth in Asia*, Harvard Institute for International Development.

Radelet, S., J. D. Sachs, R. N. Cooper and B. P. Bosworth (1998) 'The East Asian financial crisis: diagnosis, remedies, prospects', *Brookings Papers on Economic Activity*, 1998(1): 1–90.

Rambo, A. T., R. R. Reed, Le Trong Cuc and M. R. DiGregorio (eds) (1995) *The Challenges of Highland Development in Vietnam*, Honolulu: East-West Center.

Ravallion, M. (2001) 'Growth, inequality and poverty: looking beyond averages', *World Development*, 29(11): 1803–15.

Rawski, T. G. and R. W. Mead (1998) 'On the trail of China's phantom farmers', *World Development*, 26(5): 767–81.

Resurreccion, B. P. and H. T. V. Khanh (2007) 'Able to come and go: reproducing gender in female rural–urban migration in the Red River Delta', *Population, Space and Place*, 13(3): 211–24.

Resurreccion, B. P., E. E. Sajor and H. Sophea (2008) 'Gender dimensions of the adoption of the system of rice intensification (SRI) in Cambodia', Oxfam America, Phnom Penh.

Rigg, J. (2001) *More than the Soil: Rural change in Southeast Asia*, Harlow: Pearson Education.

— (2002) 'Of miracles and crises: (re-)interpretations of growth and decline in East and Southeast Asia', *Asia Pacific Viewpoint*, 43(2): 137–56.

— (2003) *Southeast Asia: The human landscape of modernisation and development*, London: Routledge.

— (2005) 'Poverty and livelihoods after full-time farming: a South-East Asian view', *Asia Pacific Viewpoint*, 46(2): 173–84.

— (2006) 'Land, farming, livelihoods, and poverty: rethinking the links in the rural South', *World Development*, 34(1): 180–202.

— (2007) *An Everyday Geography of the Global South*, London: Routledge.

Rigg, J. and S. Nattapoolwat (2001) 'Embracing the global in Thailand: activism and pragmatism in an era of deagrarianization', *World Development*, 29(6): 945–60.

Rigg, J. and A. Salamanca (2009) 'Managing risk and vulnerability in Asia: a (re)study from Thailand, 1982–83 and 2008', *Asia Pacific Viewpoint*, 50(3): 255–70.

— (2011) 'Connecting lives and places: mobility and spatial signatures in Northeast Thailand, 1982–2009', *Critical Asian Studies*, 43(4): 551–75.

Rigg, J. and P. Vandergeest (eds) (2012) *Revisiting Rural Places: Pathways to poverty and prosperity in Southeast Asia*, Singapore and

Honolulu: National University of Singapore Press and Hawaii University Press.

Rigg, J., A. Salamanca and M. J. G. Parnwell (2012) 'Joining the dots of agrarian change in Asia: a 25 year view from Thailand', *World Development*, 40(7): 1469–81.

Rigg, J., A. Allott, R. Harrison and U. Kratz (1999) 'Understanding languages of modernization: a Southeast Asian view', *Modern Asian Studies*, 33(3): 581–602.

Rigg, J., A. Bebbington, K. V. Gough, D. F. Bryceson, J. Agergaard, N. Fold and C. Tacoli (2009) 'The World Development Report 2009 "reshapes economic geography": geographical reflections', *Transactions of the Institute of British Geographers*, 34(2): 128–36.

Robinson, W. C. and J. A. Ross (eds) (2007) *The Global Family Planning Revolution: Three decades of population policies and programs*, Washington, DC: World Bank.

Rodan, G. (1989) *The Political Economy of Singapore's Industrialization: National state and international capital*, Basingstoke: Macmillan.

Rodrik, D. (2001) 'Trading in illusions', *Foreign Policy*, (123): 55–62.

— (2007) *One Economics, Many Recipes: Globalization, institutions, and economic growth*, Princeton, NJ, and Oxford: Princeton University Press.

— (2010) 'The return of industrial policy', www.project-syndicate. org/commentary/rodrik42/ English, accessed 7 October 2011.

Rodrik, D., A. Subramanian and F. Trebbi (2004) 'Institutions rule: the primacy of institutions over geography and integration in economic development', *Journal of Economic Growth*, 9(2): 131–65, www.nber.org/papers/w9305.

Rose, N. (1999) *Powers of Freedom: Reframing political thought*, Cambridge: Cambridge University Press.

Rosenfield, A., A. Bennett, S. Varakamin and D. Lauro (1982) 'Thailand's family planning program: an Asian success story', *International Family Planning Perspectives*, 8(2): 43–51.

Rosenfield, A. G. and C. J. Min (2007) 'The emergence of Thailand's national family planning program', in W. C. Robinson and J. A. Ross, *The Global Family Planning Revolution: Three decades of population policies and programs*, Washington, DC: World Bank, pp. 221–33.

Rostow, W. W. (1959) 'The stages of economic growth', *Economic History Review*, 12(1): 1–16.

— (1960) *The Stages of Economic Growth: A non-communist manifesto*, Cambridge: Cambridge University Press.

Rowen, H. S. (1998) 'The political and social foundations of the rise of East Asia: an overview', in H. S. Rowen, *Behind East Asian Growth: The political and social foundations of prosperity*, London: Routledge, pp. 1–36.

Rowntree, B. S. (1901) *Poverty: A study of town life*, London: Macmillan and Co.

Rydstrom, H., T. D. Luan and W. Burghoorn (2008) 'Introduction', in T. D. Luan, H. Rydstrom and W. Burghoorn, *Rural Families in Transitional Vietnam*, Hanoi: Social Sciences Publishing House, pp. 7–36.

Sachs, J. D. (2001) 'Tropical underdevelopment', NBER Working Paper no. 8119, National Bureau of Economic Research, Cambridge, MA.

— (2003) 'Institutions don't rule: direct effects of geography on per capita income', NBER Working Paper no. 9490, National Bureau of Economic Research, Cambridge, MA.

— (2005) *The End of Poverty: Economic possibilities for our time*, London: Penguin.

Sachs, J. D. and P. Malaney (2002) 'The economic and social burden of malaria', *Nature*, 415(6872): 680–5.

Sagasti, F. R. (1988) 'National development planning in turbulent times: new approaches and criteria for institutional design', *World Development*, 16(4): 431–48.

Sansom, R. L. (1969) 'The motor pump: a case study of innovation and development', *Oxford Economic Papers*, 21(1): 109–21.

— (1970) *The Economics of Insurgency in the Mekong Delta of Vietnam*, Cambridge, MA: MIT Press.

Santasombat, Y. (2003) *Biodiversity: Local knowledge and sustainable development*, Chiang Mai: Regional Center for Social Science and Sustainable Development (RCSD).

— (2004) 'Karen cultural capital and the political economy of symbolic power', *Asian Ethnicity*, 5(1): 105–20.

Sawhill, I. V. (1988) 'Poverty in the U.S.: why is it so persistent?', *Journal of Economic Literature*, 26(3): 1073–119.

Schein, E. H. (1996) *Strategic Pragmatism: The culture of Singapore's Economic Development Board*, Cambridge, MA: MIT Press.

Sciortino, R., L. M. Natsir and M. F. Mas'udi (1996) 'Learning from Islam: advocacy of reproductive rights in Indonesian Pesantren', *Reproductive Health Matters*, 4(8): 86–96.

Scoones, I. (2009) 'Livelihoods perspectives and rural development', *Journal of Peasant Studies*, 36(1): 171–96.

Scott, J. C. (1998) *Seeing Like a State: How certain schemes to improve the human condition have failed*, New Haven, CT, and London: Yale University Press.

— (2009) *The Art of Not Being Governed: An Anarchist History of Upland Southeast Asia*, New Haven, CT: Yale University Press.

Semedi, P. (2012) 'Masculinization of the Javanese farming community's household economy: Petungkriono, 1984–2009', in J. Rigg and P. Vandergeest, *Revisiting Rural Places: Pathways to poverty and prosperity in Southeast Asia*, Singapore and Honolulu: National University of Singapore Press and Hawaii University Press, pp. 179–92.

Sen, A. (1981) *Poverty and Famines: An essay on entitlement and deprivation*, Oxford: Clarendon Press.

— (1999a) 'The possibility of social choice', *American Economic Review*, 89(3): 349–78.

— (1999b) *Development as Freedom*, New York: Knopf.

— (2003) 'Drivers of escape and descent: changing household fortunes in rural Bangladesh', *World Development*, 31(3): 513–34.

Sewell, W. H., Jr (1996) 'Historical events as transformations of structures: inventing revolution at the Bastille', *Theory and Society*, 25(6): 841–81.

Shi, W. (2008) *Rubber Boom in Luang Namtha: A transnational perspective*, Vientiane: GTZ.

Siddiqi, Q. H. (1964) *An Introduction to Economic Planning*, Karachi: The Book Corporation.

Smith, E. (2012) *Luck: What it means*

and why it matters, London: Bloomsbury.

Smith, J., I. Wallerstein et al. (1984) 'Introduction', in J. Smith, I. Wallerstein and H.-D. Evers, *Households and the World Economy*, Beverly Hills, CA: Sage, pp. 7–13.

Smith, M. K. (2002) 'Gender, poverty, and intergenerational vulnerability to HIV/AIDS', *Gender & Development*, 10(3): 63–70.

Souvanthong, P. (1995) 'Shifting cultivation in the Lao PDR: an overview of land use and policy initiatives', IIED Forestry and Land Use Series no. 5, International Institute for Environment and Development, London.

Sparkes, S. (1998) 'Public consultation and participation on the Nakai Plateau (April–May 1998)', Nam Theun 2 Electricity Consortium, Vientiane.

Standing, G. (2000) 'Brave new worlds? A critique of Stiglitz's World Bank rethink', *Development and Change*, 31: 737–63.

Stern, N. (1991) 'Public policy and the economics of development', *European Economic Review*, 35(2/3): 241–71.

Stiglitz, J. E. (1989) *The Economic Role of the State*, Oxford: Basil Blackwell in association with Bank Insinger de Beaufort NV.

— (1996) 'Some lessons from the East Asian miracle', *World Bank Research Observer*, 11(2): 151–77.

— (1998a) 'Towards a new paradigm for development: strategies, policies, and processes', Prebisch Lecture.

— (1998b) 'More instruments and broader goals: moving toward the post-Washington consensus', WIDER Annual Lecture, United Nations University, Helsinki.

— (2000) 'The insider: what I learned at the world economic crisis', *New Republic*, 56.

— (2001) 'From miracle to crisis to recovery: lessons from four decades of East Asian experience', in J. E. Stiglitz and S. Yusuf, *Rethinking the East Asian Miracle*, Washington, DC, and New York: World Bank and Oxford University Press, pp. 509–26.

— (2002) *Globalization and Its Discontents*, London: Penguin.

— (2004) 'Post Washington Consensus consensus', Initiative for Policy Dialogue Working Paper, Columbia University.

Stiglitz, J. E. and S. Yusuf (eds) (2001) *Rethinking the East Asian Miracle*, Washington, DC, and New York: World Bank and Oxford University Press.

Stubbs, R. (2009) 'What ever happened to the East Asian developmental state? The unfolding debate', *Pacific Review*, 22(1): 1–22.

— (2011) 'The East Asian developmental state and the Great Recession: evolving contesting coalitions', *Contemporary Politics*, 17(2): 151–66.

Sun, S. H.-L. (2012) *Population Policy and Reproduction in Singapore: Making future citizens*, London: Routledge.

Suryadarma, D., Y. M. Pakpahan and A. Suryahadi (2009) 'The effects of parental death and chronic poverty on children's education and health: evidence from Indonesia', CPRC Working Paper 133, Chronic Poverty Research Centre, IDPM, University of Manchester.

Suryahadi, A., S. Sumarto and L. Pritchett (2003a) 'Evolution of poverty during the crisis in Indonesia', *Asian Economic Journal*, 17(3): 221–41.

Suryahadi, A., W. Widyanti and S. Sumarto (2003b) 'Short-term poverty dynamics in rural Indonesia during the economic crisis', *Journal of International Development*, 15(2): 133–44.

Suryahadi, A., D. Suryadarma and S. Sumarto (2009) 'The effects of location and sectoral components of economic growth on poverty: evidence from Indonesia', *Journal of Development Economics*, 89(1): 109–17.

Tai, H.-c. (1989) 'The Oriental alternative: an hypothesis on culture and economy', in H.-c. Tai, *Confucianism and Economic Development: An Oriental alternative*, Washington, DC: Washington Institute Press, pp. 6–37.

Taleb, N. N. (2008) *The Black Swan: The impact of the highly improbable*, New York: Random House.

Tan, S. B.-H. (2000) 'Coffee frontiers in the Central Highlands of Vietnam: networks of connectivity', *Asia Pacific Viewpoint*, 41(1): 51–67.

Tan, S. B.-H. and A. Walker (2008) 'Beyond hills and plains: rethinking ethnic relations in Vietnam and Thailand', *Journal of Vietnamese Studies*, 3(3): 117–57.

TDRI (2000) *Pak Mun Case Study*, Bangkok: Thai Development Research Institute.

Tey, N. P. (2007) 'The family planning program in Peninsular Malaysia', in W. C. Robinson and J. A. Ross, *The Global Family Planning Revolution: Three decades of population policies and programs*, Washington, DC: World Bank, pp. 257–76.

Thompson, E. C. (2004a) 'Pacific Asia after "Asian values": authoritarianism, democracy, and "good governance"', *Third World Quarterly*, 25(6): 1079–95.

Thompson, E. C. (2004b) 'Rural villages as socially urban spaces in Malaysia', *Urban Studies* (Routledge), 41(12): 2357–76.

Thompson, E. C. (2007) *Unsettling Absences: Place, migration, and urbanism in rural Malaysia*, Singapore: NUS Press.

Thomsen, S. (1999) 'Southeast Asia: the role of foreign direct investment policies in development', Working Papers on International Investment, Organisation for Economic Co-operation and Development.

Tirtosudarm, R. (2009) 'Mobility and human development in Indonesia', Human Development Reports Research Paper, United Nations Development Programme, New York.

Todaro, M. P. (1971) *Development Planning: Models and methods*, Nairobi: Oxford University Press.

Toh, M. H. and L. Low (1988) 'Economic planning and policy-making in Singapore', *Economic Bulletin for Asia and the Pacific*, 39(1): 22–32.

Toyota, M., B. S. A. Yeoh and L. Nguyen (2007) 'Bringing the "left behind" back into view in Asia: a framework for understanding the "migration–left behind nexus"', *Population, Space and Place*, 13(3): 157–61.

UN (1963) *Planning for Economic Development*, New York: Department of Economic and Social Affairs, United Nations.

Underwood, C. (2000) 'Islamic precepts and family planning: the perceptions of Jordanian religious leaders and their constituents', *International Family Planning Perspectives*, 26(3): 110–36.

UNDP (1986) *Muong Hom Integrated*

Rural Development Project: Irrigated rice schemes, Vientiane: United Nations Development Programme.

— (2007) *Thailand Human Development Report 2007: Sufficiency economy and human development*, Bangkok: United Nations Development Programme.

— (2009) *Human Development Report 2009: Overcoming barriers – human mobility and development*, New York: United Nations Development Programme.

— (2010) *Internal Migration and Socio-economic Development in Viet Nam: A call to action*, Hanoi: United Nations Development Programme.

Unger, D. (1998) *Building Social Capital in Thailand: Fibers, finance, and infrastructure*, Cambridge: Cambridge University Press.

Urata, S. (2001) 'Emergence of an FDI–trade nexus and economic growth in East Asia', in J. E. Stiglitz and S. Yusuf, *Rethinking the East Asia Miracle*, Oxford: Oxford University Press, pp. 409–59.

Vandergeest, P. (1991) 'Gifts and rights: cautionary notes on community self-help in Thailand', *Development and Change*, 22(3): 421–43.

Vestergaard, J. (2004) 'The Asian crisis and the shaping of "proper" economies', *Cambridge Journal of Economics*, 28(6): 809–27.

Vu, T. (2007) 'State formation and the origins of developmental states in South Korea and Indonesia', *Studies in Comparative International Development*, 41(4): 27–56.

Wade, R. (1988) 'The role of government in overcoming market failure: Tawain, Republic of Korea and Japan', in H. Hughes, *Achieving Industrialization in East Asia*, Cambridge: Cambridge University Press, pp. 129–63.

— (1992) 'East Asia's economic success: conflicting perspectives, partial insights, shaky evidence', *World Politics*, 44(2): 270–320.

— (2004 [1990]) *Governing the Market: Economic theory and the role of government in East Asian industrialization*, Princeton, NJ, and Oxford: Princeton University Press.

Wagstaff, A. and E. van Doorslaer (2003) 'Catastrophe and impoverishment in paying for health care: with applications to Vietnam 1993–1998', *Health Economics*, 12(11): 921–33.

Walker, A. (1999) *The Legend of the Golden Boat: Regulation, trade and traders in the borderlands of Laos, Thailand, China and Burma*, Richmond: Curzon Press.

— (2001) 'The "Karen consensus", ethnic politics and resource-use legitimacy in northern Thailand', *Asian Ethnicity*, 2(2): 145–62.

— (2004) 'Response', *Asian Ethnicity*, 5(2): 259–65.

Wan, G. and I. Sebastian (2011) *Poverty in Asia and the Pacific: An update*, Manila: Asian Development Bank.

Wang, H.-z. (2007) 'Hidden spaces of resistance of the subordinated: case studies from Vietnamese female migrant partners in Taiwan', *International Migration Review*, 41(3): 706–27.

Warr, P. G. (1994) 'Myths about dragons: the case of Thailand', *Agenda*, 1(2): 215–28.

— (1999) 'What happened to Thailand?', *World Economy*, 22(5): 631–50.

Warr, P. G. and B. Nidhiprabha (1996) *Thailand's Macroeconomic Miracle:*

Stable adjustment and sustained growth, Washington, DC, and Kuala Lumpur: World Bank and Oxford University Press.

Warwick, D. P. (1986) 'The Indonesian family planning program: government influence and client choice', *Population and Development Review*, 12(3): 453–90.

WCD (2000) *The Pak Mun Dam in Mekong River Basin, Thailand*, Final draft: Annexes, Cape Town: World Commission on Dams.

Weber, M. (1930) *The Protestant Ethic and the Spirit of Capitalism*, London: George Allen and Unwin.

Weiss, L. (1998) *The Myth of the Powerless State: Governing the economy in a global era*, Cambridge: Polity Press.

— (2000) 'Developmental states in transition: adapting, dismantling, innovating, not "normalizing"', *Pacific Review*, 13(1): 21–55.

Widyanti, W., A. Suryahadi et al. (2009) 'The relationship between chronic poverty and household dynamics: evidence from Indonesia', CPRC Working Paper 132, Chronic Poverty Research Centre, University of Manchester.

Williams, R. (1988) *Keywords: A vocabulary of culture and society*, London: Fontana.

Williamson, J. (1990) 'What Washington means by policy reform', in J. Williamson, *Latin American Adjustment: How much has happened?*, Washington, DC: Institute for International Economics.

— (2000) 'What should the World Bank think about the Washington Consensus?', *World Bank Research Observer*, 15(2): 251–64.

Winichakul, T. (2000) 'The quest for "Siwilai": a geographical discourse of civilizational thinking in the late nineteenth and early twentieth-century Siam', *Journal of Asian Studies*, 59(3): 528–49.

Wittayapak, C. (2008) 'History and geography of identifications related to resource conflicts and ethnic violence in Northern Thailand', *Asia Pacific Viewpoint*, 49(1): 111–27.

Woodside, A. (1996) 'The empowerment of Asia and the weakness of global theory', in *The Empowerment of Asia: Reshaping global society*, Vancouver: Institute of Asian Research, University of British Columbia, pp. 9–31.

Woolcock, M., S. Szreter and V. Rao (2011) 'How and why does history matter for development policy?', *Journal of Development Studies*, 47(1): 70–96.

World Bank (1978) *Thailand: Towards a development strategy of full participation*, Washington, DC: World Bank.

— (1993) *The East Asian Miracle: Economic growth and public policy*, Oxford: Oxford University Press for the World Bank.

— (1998) *East Asia: The road to recovery*, Washington, DC: World Bank.

— (2003) *Urban Poverty in East Asia: A review of Indonesia, the Philippines, and Vietnam*, Washington, DC: World Bank.

— (2009) *World Development Report 2009: Reshaping economic geography*, Washington, DC: World Bank.

— (2011) *World Development Indicators and Global Development Finance*, Washington, DC: World Bank.

Yamano, T. and T. S. Jayne (2005) 'Working-age adult mortality and primary school attendance in rural Kenya', *Economic*

Development and Cultural Change, 53(3): 619–53.

Yamazawa, I. (1992) 'On Pacific economic integration', *Economic Journal*, 102(415): 1519–29.

Yang, S. and P. C. Rosenblatt (2008) 'Confucian family values and childless couples in South Korea', *Journal of Family Issues*, 29(5): 571–91.

Yap, M. T. (2003) 'Fertility and population policy: the Singapore experience', *Journal of Population and Social Security (Population)*, 1(supplement): 643–58.

— (2007) 'Singapore: population policies and programmes', in W. C. Robinson and J. A. Ross, *The Global Family Planning Revolution: Three decades of population policies and programs*, Washington, DC: World Bank, pp. 201–19.

Yusuf, S. (2001) 'The East Asian miracle at the Millennium', in J. E. Stiglitz and S. Yusuf, *Rethinking the East Asian Miracle*, Washington, DC, and New York: World Bank and Oxford University Press, pp. 1–53.

Zakaria, F. (1994) 'Culture is destiny: a conversation with Lee Kuan Yew', *Foreign Affairs*, 73(2): 109–26.

Index

abortion, resistance to, 151

administrative competence, assumption of, 23

agencies: institutional structure of, 23; marginalization of, 33; planning, establishment of, 16

agency: limits of, 5–6; of poor farmers, 101–2, 106; of women, 160

aggregate stories, omissions of, 8

agriculture: abandonment of, 168; agency of poor farmers, 101–2; agrarian transformation, 96, 172; coffee farming in Vietnam, 104–5; de-peasantization of, 172; effects of migration on, 168; geriatrification of, 167; reform of, in China, 61; women resistant to, 160 *see also* rice, cultivation of *and* shifting cultivation

AIDS, relation to orphanhood, 131

Amsden, Alice, *Asia's Next Giant ...*, 63

Anderson, B., 49

Angeles, L. C., 61

Arab Spring, 82

Arnold, D., 107

Asian Development Bank (ADB), 42, 69; *Emerging Asia* report, 69–70

Asian economic crisis, 7, 46–9, 127, 184, 187; epidemiology of, 72–3; lessons of, 69–75

Asian economic miracle, 7, 47, 93–6, 192

assets, rated in poverty assessment, 126

Association of Southeast Asian Nations (Asean), 20, 95

bad luck, 122

baht: devaluation of, 46; speculative attack on, 72

Baker, James, 93

Banerjee, A. V., 1, 143

Bangladesh, rural study of, 139

Bank of Thailand, 46

Barrett, C. B., 139

Batu Litang, Sarawak, farmers in, 169, 178

behaviour, prediction and interpretation of, 177–8, 176

Behrman, J. R., 132

binary reductions of behaviour, 177

Bird, K., 126

black children, and poverty, 113

Boettke, P. J., *The Collapse of Development Planning*, 22

boom crops in South-East Asia, 83, 101–6

'bounce-back-ability', 124

Buddhism, context of family planning, 152

'bumping along the bottom', 124–6

bureaucracy, 29

Burma *see* Myanmar

Burns, Robert, 108

Caldwell, J. C., 147, 177

Cambodia, effects of migration on farming in, 167

Campos, J. E., and H. L. Root, *The Key to the Asian Miracle*, 179

capacity-raising, investment in, 29

Catfish Farmers of America (CFA), 103

celibacy, social acceptability of, 161–2

Central Sulawesi Integrated Development and Conservation project (Indonesia), 42

Chang, L. T., 164, 169

change, accounting for, 178

Chatterjee, P., 172

child–parent bargain, 133

children: black, and poverty, 113; of the poor, restricted life chances of, 130; value attached to, 177

China, 39, 52–3, 65, 72, 169, 183; absent parents in, 175; Cultural Revolution, 67; economic growth

directional, 85; 'end' of, 85; turbulence of, 109

HIV, inter-generational effects of, 122

Hmong people, agricultural practices of, 89–92

home: attachment to, 165; importance of, 163; leaving of, 191 (risks of, 164); return to, 169, 192

Homo economicus, 1, 30, 177

Hong Kong, 63, 67, 185

households, 110; become different, 172–3; become smaller, 172; co-residential definition of, 172; engagement with local authorities, 35; function of, 1; multi-sited, 173, 178; reconstitution of, 171–6; registration system, in Vietnam, 26, 34, 105; resilience of, 141; transformation of, 171; types of, as context, 140

Hull, T. H., 149, 156

human characteristics, as axis of contingency, 2, 183, 186–7

hysteresis, 119

idiosyncratic events, 138, 186; impact of, 135

ill health, as asset risk, 122

implementation of plans, 27

India, 72; as failed developmental state, 68; planning in, 12, 27 (failures of, 43–4)

indicative planning, 15

individualization hypothesis of poverty, 111, 112

Indonesia, 143–78 *passim*; crisis and poverty in, 126–8, 175; development planning in, 15; family planning in, 149, 152, 154; migration in, 174–5; participatory planning in, 41–3

Indonesia Family Life Survey (IFLS), 127–9, 131, 133

induction, 187–9

industrial policy, 44, 62–8; relation to rent-seeking behaviour, 67

industrialization, 17, 39, 53, 147, 174; environmental issues arising from, 50; of Thailand, 119

informal city, 35–6

inheritance of wealth, 111

innovation, technological *see* technological innovation

institution, determining primacy of, 181

institution building, 189

institutional quality, 189

Integrated Water Resources Management (IWRM), 37

inter-generational mobility, 109

inter-generational transmission (IGT): of livelihood shocks, 131–4; of mobility, 144–5; of poverty and prosperity (IGT), 109, 121, 125, 129, 130, 135–40 (influences affecting, 133)

interdependency between planning domains, 23

International Monetary Fund (IMF), 53, 69, 75, 184; failure to understand Asian crisis, 73

International Rice Research Institute (IRRI), 101

interpretative frameworks, export of, 177

interventionist initiatives, 13

intra-generational mobility, 109, 113–29

intra-generational transmission of poverty, 110–13

intra-generational turbulence in livelihood trajectories, 129

Islam, and reproductive rights of women, 149, 151

Japan, 54, 55, 65, 67, 157; as developmental state, 62; economic growth in, 56; overseas shift of production, 94–5; shift of investments abroad, 185

Java, migration study in, 175

Johnson, Chalmers, 185; *MITI and the Japanese Miracle*, 62

Jones, G. W., 153–4

Kaminsky, G. L., 72

Karen people, 91

Kerkvliet, B. J. T., 61, 106

Killick, T., 22, 27–9

Kinh people, 106, 162

Knowles, J. C., 132